MW00988036

# Digital *Woes*

# Digital *Woes*

## Why We Should Not
## Depend on Software

## Lauren Ruth Wiener

Addison-Wesley Publishing Company

Reading, Massachusetts  Menlo Park, California  New York
Don Mills, Ontario  Wokingham, England  Amsterdam  Bonn
Sydney  Singapore  Tokyo  Madrid  San Juan
Paris  Seoul  Milan  Mexico City  Taipei

■

Many of the designations used by manufacturers and sellers to distinguish their products are claimed as trademarks. Where those designations appear in this book and Addison-Wesley was aware of a trademark claim, the designations have been printed in initial capital letters.

**Library of Congress Cataloging-in-Publication Data**
Wiener, Lauren.
 Digital woes : why we should not depend on software / Lauren Ruth Wiener.
  p. cm.
 Includes bibliographical references and index.
 ISBN 0-201-62609-8
 ISBN 0-201-40796-5 (pbk.)
 1. Computer software—Reliability.  I. Title.
QA76.76.R44W53  1993
005.1—dc20
                                                              93-2141
                                                               CIP

Copyright © 1993 by Lauren Ruth Wiener
Epilogue © 1994 by Lauren Ruth Wiener

All rights reserved. No part of this publication may be reproduced, stored in a retrieval system, or transmitted, in any form or by any means, electronic, mechanical, photocopying, recording, or otherwise, without the prior written permission of the publisher. Printed in the United States of America. Published simultaneously in Canada.

Cover design by Lynne Reed
Text design by David Kelley Design
Set in 11-point Minion by DEKR Corporation
Cover and title page art © Mike Cressy/Stockworks

1 2 3 4 5 6 7 8 9 10–MA–9897969594
First printing, September 1993
First paperback printing, September 1994
■

*Dedicated to my mother,*

*with love*

*and gratitude.*

# CONTENTS

# FOREWORD

## by Prof. David L. Parnas

*Communications Research Laboratory*
*Department of Electrical and Computer Engineering*
*MacMaster University, Hamilton, Ontario, Canada*

Many of the important decisions that our society must make in the next few years hinge upon scientific and technological questions. Consider the following public issues:

- Should we invest in space-based defenses against nuclear weapons?
- Should we build more nuclear power generating stations?
- How urgent is the need to reduce the level of greenhouse gases?
- How much climatic warming is acceptable?
- Is it safe to allow computers to control cars and trucks?
- Is it safe to allow the safety systems in a nuclear power plant to be controlled by computers?
- Is it safe to allow robots to perform surgery on humans?
- How much automation is wise in commercial airplane cockpits?
- Is it prudent to keep financial records, medical records, and voting records in digital form that is volatile, easily modified, and easily searched?

Difficult scientific and technological issues lie behind each of these questions, but the decisions will be made by people who are neither scientists nor technologists.

Technology is the black magic of our time. Engineers are seen as wizards; their knowledge of arcane rituals and obscure terminology seems to endow them with an understanding not shared by the laity. The public, dazzled by the many visible achievements of modern technology, often regards engineers as magicians who can solve any problem, given the

funds. Many are so awed by technological advances that they make no attempt to understand how things work. As soon as we see that scientists
disagree on an issue, we conclude that we cannot understand it. Instead,
we often allow ourselves to be swayed by rhetoric, including appeals to
patriotism, fear, and greed. In other cases, we just assume that the issue
is too difficult and switch to another channel. Instead of trying to understand, we rely on public officials to make these decisions for us.

Unfortunately, most public officials, even those charged with the evaluation and funding of scientific work, share this approach. They, too, assume that they will not understand major issues of science and technology. They expect to be mystified and amazed. When forced to decide
between conflicting positions, they base their decisions on the apparent
trustworthiness of the advocates rather than on the merit of the arguments. In recent years I have had the opportunity to observe this situation firsthand, and I have seen the kinds of problems it can cause.

In 1985, I was asked to join a panel convened by the Strategic Defense
Initiative Organization (SDIO) to advise them on computer-related research needed to implement President Reagan's "Star Wars" plans. The
goal, shooting down incoming nuclear ballistic missiles before they could
reach the United States, obviously required extensive support from computers. Software would have to distinguish targets from decoys, aim
weapons at the targets, fire the weapons, and track the results to determine if additional attempts were necessary. A large number of sensors
and weapons had to be coordinated under tight and unforgiving time
constraints. The Strategic Defense Initiative Organization knew that implementing this plan would require a great deal of software research.
They convened a panel on Computing in Support of Battle Management
to guide them in spending their research and development funds.

People familiar with both software engineering and older engineering
disciplines observe that the state of the art in software is significantly behind that in other areas of engineering. When most engineering products have been completed, tested, and sold, it is reasonable to expect
that the product design is correct and that the product will work reliably. With software products, it is usual to find that the software has major "bugs" and does not work reliably. No experienced software
developer expects a product to work well the first time that it is used.
Problems may persist for years and sometimes worsen as the software is
"improved." Where most product labels have an explicit warranty, software products usually carry an explicit disclaimer, a statement denying
that any warranty is made at all.

If you are familiar with only a few incidents of software failure, you
may regard tham as exceptions caused by inept programmers. Software

professionals know better; the most competent programmers in the world cannot avoid such problems. They are endemic to the nature of software itself—complex systems, often poorly structured, that can take on so many possible states that no human mind can grasp them all.

As the work got underway, I observed that neither the Strategic Defense Initiative Organization nor the public fully appreciated the critical problems that computer systems pose. Although SDI was much debated, software problems were rarely discussed; the discussion focused on various hardware issues. Yet, given the goals of the system, the problems presented by the software seemed to me to be ultimately insurmountable. For example:

- No large-scale software system has ever been installed without extensive testing under realistic conditions. In operational software for military aircraft, even minor modifications require extensive ground testing, and then flight testing, in which battle conditions can be closely approximated. Even with these tests, bugs can and do show up in battle. To test a strategic defense system under field conditions would require above-ground nuclear explosions. This is clearly impossible. Without such a test before we actually need the system, no knowledgeable person can have faith in it.

- It is not unusual for software modifications to be made to systems after they are deployed. Programmers are transported by helicopter to Navy ships. I have seen debugging notes written on the walls of trucks carrying battlefield computers and have been told that those programs were debugged by programmers in Vietnam. It is only through such modifications that software becomes reliable. Such opportunities would not be available in the thirty-to-ninety-minute war to be fought by a strategic defense battle management system.

- Battle management software must meet hard real-time deadlines reliably. This is a difficult problem; in practice, efficiency and predictability often require programmers to build schedules for the worst case into the program ahead of time. Unless we can confidently predict the worst case (and we could not do this for "Star Wars"), we cannot be sure that the system will meet its deadlines when its service is required.

- All of our experience indicates that the difficulties in building software increase with the size of the system, with the number of independently modifiable subsystems (such as sensors and weapons), and with the number of interfaces between them. Problems worsen when the interfaces themselves can change. The consequent modifications make the software even more complex and make it even harder to change something without affecting many other things.

I came to the conclusion that the public must be reminded of these facts while the debate about SDI was raging.

Many scientists are proud to serve as advisors to governmental agencies, elected officials, and political parties. They believe that, by working with these people, they maximize their influence. However, my personal involvement in public policy issues led me to realize that public officials often feel that they are not free to make decisions. Instead they feel severely constrained by public opinion.

After serving on the SDIO panel, I had the opportunity to meet many U. S. and Canadian policymakers. One U. S. congressman openly expressed a thought that explained the behavior of many of his colleagues. He told me that he thought SDI was nonsense and that he would love to vote against it. But he felt he could not because, in the next election, he would be opposed by someone on his right. Because SDI was so popular, he would lose if he opposed it; opponents of SDI would be accused of being uninterested in protecting Americans against nuclear destruction, and the electorate would believe the accusations. He ended by saying that, if I could convince his electorate that SDI was bad defense, he would be happy to vote against it.

I resigned from the SDIO panel in 1985 with a renewed appreciation of the need for public understanding of technological issues. As Churchill pointed out: "democracy is the worst form of Government except all those other forms that have been tried from time to time." If a politician has the courage to take an unpopular stand, another politician will attempt to use that position against him. Few politicians respond by trying to educate their electorate. Politicians who try to change voters' views on contentious issues do not usually stay in office very long. Even appointed officials are aware that their bosses are elected, and everything they do must be explained to the electorate. Ultimately, the voters make the policies. That's how a democracy is supposed to function: voters make the decisions. It follows that an educated and informed electorate is essential to the proper functioning of democracy, and scientists and engineers who care about democracy must devote some of their time to educating the public.

There are no shortcuts to education: scientists cannot simply state their conclusions and expect the public to accept them. They must explain the models that they are based on, so that others can understand how those conclusions were reached.

Public misunderstandings about technology abound, in part because technologists are seldom willing to talk about the limitations of their technologies. For example, the misunderstandings about my own field, computers, are immense. People have learned to think of computers as "giant brains" rather than finite state machines that work by mechanically interpreting many simple rules. Purveyors of software and scientists trying for research grants have sometimes made extreme claims. One Canadian provincial government, for instance, actually believed that they could invest a few million dollars and produce a system to translate laws from English into French automatically. Scientists were willing to promise such technology twenty years ago, but the truth is that such a system is far from feasible even today. But such exaggerated claims have been made, almost as a matter of course, by many developers of computer-based systems, and for obvious reasons. In a world where science is treated as a branch of magic, the rewards often go to those who behave as illusionists, using sleight of hand and distraction to create the impression that difficult problems have easy answers.

Wise choices cannot be made unless those who make decisions understand the relevant scientific and technical facts. One of those relevant facts is that science is uncertain and technology is unreliable. Science is a search for truth that is never complete. Decisions that are made on the belief that we have found *absolute truth* will be bad decisions.

The dependence of our society upon computers and software is great and will increase. Every day, decisions are made about new applications. There are often economic advantages to using computers, but there are also risks to us all. The decision-makers, and that means all of us, must understand about computers so that the decisions can be made wisely. The book you are now holding is a good place to start. It presents, in clear and often entertaining language, a basic background useful for understanding software. It explains why we should be cautious about introducing software into systems, and it suggests criteria we might use to evaluate proposals to do so.

It is easy to ignore social responsibility. It is easy to believe that what we do about social issues will not make any difference. And if we all think so, it certainly won't. But if all of us live as if our actions can make a difference, we can improve things. If we all understand a little more about the new technologies available to us, perhaps we can use them more wisely.

# PREFACE

Software can make a machine do almost anything. That is its great strength, and that is why we are putting it into cars and trains and subways and airplanes and ferry boats, hospitals and laboratories and clinics, banks and automatic teller machines, telephone switching systems and telephone answering machines, fax machines, traffic lights, power plants, dishwashers, air conditioners, television sets, video cassette recorders, compact disc players, toasters, microwave ovens, and cruise missiles. Not to mention spreadsheets and word processors and video games.

We rely on software, and sometimes it fails us. Some of those failures are nuisances; some are disasters. It is not news that technology presents risks and dangers, but software is unique and presents unique risks. Adding software to a system may make the service it provides cheaper, more generally available, or more adaptable to change, but it will not make it more reliable. The growing use of software for such critical missions as flying commercial airplanes, monitoring hospital patients, or controlling automobile engines therefore represents a social experiment.

But it is a social experiment that has been carried out with little public debate. Such issues of digital technology are discussed in professional journals and on-line bulletin boards, but public participation is negligible. Many of us feel that this stuff is incomprehensible, so we give up. It isn't and we mustn't. We cannot afford to take for granted the assurances of those who build these systems and who stand to profit from them. All of us need to participate in these decisions; a lot is at stake. Our lives are changing drastically. It would be wise to guide this change for the better.

The argument put forward in this book can be summarized as follows:

*Chapter 1 • Attack of the Killer Software.*
As abundantly demonstrated by history, software has bugs.

*Chapter 2 • Why Does Software Have Bugs?*
Software is a structure of logic embedded in a physical machine that is connected to the rest of the world. It is in the nature of such a structure to have bugs.

*Chapter 3 • The Resource Sink*
Developing software is an expensive and time-consuming enterprise
whose result is likely to be unreliable, as well as less functional than the
product originally specified.

*Chapter 4 • Extraordinary Measures*
Developing software for critical systems—if it is done right—is even
more expensive, time-consuming, and painstaking. The gain in reliability
will be modest.

*Chapter 5 • Big Plans*
Enormous numbers of software systems have been proposed, designed,
and even started. Some of these systems are unrealistically ambitious and
inordinately risky. Few people are even discussing these risks.

*Chapter 6 • The Wise Use of Smart Stuff*
Software is not the answer to every problem. We cannot afford to build
everything that's been proposed, nor should we allow ourselves to be
placed at such risk. We must choose *how* we want to use software, computers, and digital technology.

## ABOUT THE NOTES

As far as was practicable, references are given at the end of each chapter for points discussed in the chapter. If you wish, you can ignore
them; the book stands without them. I have provided them for two reasons: to help those wishing to discover the original sources that led to
my conclusions, and also to encourage what some have called *systems
thinking.*

This book, like most things, is a system unto itself and at the same
time part of a larger system. Books and libraries and periodicals and reference works and now CD-ROM and Internet newsgroups make up an
enormous, rich, complex, and wonderful system to which this book adds
its mite. Making something new always means changing an existing system.

# ACKNOWLEDGMENTS

Books are always teamwork. A lot of people have helped me in this endeavor, and I'd like to thank them.

For fruitful discussions over lunch or long walks—Philip Goward, Don Harvey, Verna Knapp, Ralph London, Mike Miller, Larry Morandi, Richelle Riedl, Jacob Stein, Roberta Taussig, Marlin Wilson. For all sorts of useful materials—Dave Akers, Mark Barnett, Philip and Louise Goward, Roger Hart, John Helm, Verna Knapp, Larry Morandi, Bruce Riedl, Marlin Wilson. For being peppered with all those questions all the time—Dave Akers, Philip Goward, Roger Hart, Yuriko and Yataro Kudo, Dave Lowry, Larry Morandi, Bruce Riedl, Marlin Wilson. For time and insights reviewing chapters—Philip Goward, Roger Hart, Mike Miller, Brian Phillips, Carolyn Strong. For reviewing *all* the chapters (and with that schedule!), and for her refreshing viewpoint—Lise Storc. Thank you all for your support and your friendship.

Thanks to all who gave so freely of their expertise—Gray Haertig, Haertig & Associates; Jim Harris, Portland International Airport Tower Traffic Control; Jonathan Jacky, Research Scientist, Department of Radiology Oncology, University of Washington; William C. Kloos, Bureau of Traffic Management, City of Portland Office of Transportation; Glen Martin, Bell Northern Research; and Steve MacIntyre, Intel Automotive Division. And my deep gratitude to Dr. David Parnas of the Communications Research Laboratory, Department of Electrical and Computer Engineering, McMaster University.

The hardcover edition of this book has received many gratifyingly favorable reviews. One reviewer, however, has gone beyond the usual charter, thoroughly combing the book for errors as well. Thank you, Dr. Peter Mellor of the Centre for Software Reliability, City University, London, for generously donating your expertise to help me improve this book.

Peter G. Neumann, moderator of that most educational periodical, *Forum on Risks to the Public in Computers and Related Systems,* known on Internet as the *comp.risks* newsgroup, is doing the world a service that it does not sufficiently appreciate. We can learn a lot from our failures, but not if they are buried. This dilemma is felt in most technical fields, but in software engineering it is particularly pertinent. The *comp.risks* newsgroup is a unique marvel brought to you through the miracle of computer networks. It is an ongoing frank, intelligent, and concerned discussion of failures, near-failures, and problems encountered all over the world, in systems of all kinds, analyzed with insight, experience, and blazing honesty by some of the most talented people in their fields. Listening in on this discussion has been a real education. Thanks to all those who have contributed to the newsgroup, and thank you, Peter G. Neumann, for creating, shaping, and sustaining this remarkable channel.

To my dear Uncle Lou, my beta site, who was so generous with his time, his support, and his insightful comments—thank you.

My sincere gratitude to Sey Chassler for his support and guidance, and to Robert Lescher for his advice, and to Jack Repcheck of Addison-Wesley for his helpful and intelligent editing.

My final thanks go to the good folks of the Portland high-tech community, from whom I have learned so much.

# Digital *Woes*

# CHAPTER 1

# ATTACK
## of
# THE KILLER SOFTWARE

I'm sitting in
an airplane, looking out
the window at the tops of fluffy white clouds. Once upon
a time, this sight
was not vouchsafed
to humans. It comes to me courtesy of the commercial airline industry, one of the twentieth century's impressive achievements. Computers and software have contributed a lot toward this experience:

In the cockpit, the pilot is using more software right now than I use in a year. Software helps determine our position, speed, route, and altitude; keeps the plane in balance as fuel is consumed; interprets sensor readings and displays their values for the pilot; manages certain aspects of the pilot's communications; translates some of the pilot's gestures on the controls into movements of the wing and tail surfaces; raises or lowers the landing gear.

The pilot is following a route, a path through the three-dimensional air space that blankets North America eight miles thick. A lot of other airplanes are buzzing around up here with us, and a collision would be calamitous; this airplane alone has four hundred passengers. The air traffic controllers depend on software to assign our path through airspace. The transponder on our airplane broadcasts its identification, and near an airport its signal is translated into a little tag on a radar screen that includes our ID and altitude. Altitude appears as a number because the screen is two-dimensional and cannot reflect altitude directly. The software has to move the tag around on the screen in ways that reflect the airplane's movements through the air in two dimensions, but the air traffic controllers have to reconstruct three-dimensional reality in their heads, quickly and coolly, using the altitude numbers. The system involves a lot of pieces—transponders, radar, radar screens, air traffic controllers, a computer—separated widely in space. Some of them are moving all the time. The action on the radar screen must keep up with the action in the air. This is a complex problem. Knowing this, I am grateful for our safe progress through the sky today, as I enjoy the sunny cloud tops.

The airplane is holding up pretty well, too. Computers and software were used extensively to design it and to design the process by which it was manufactured. Figuring out how to make something like a jet is an underappreciated problem. You have to design a machine that can fly, and also one that can be manufactured and maintained. Sky and runway, the world is a rough place, and hundreds of thousands of parts may need replacing. You also have to design the process that produces those parts, and that will get them where they are needed. An enterprise such as Boeing's is an enormous consumer of software, computers, and programmers.

Then we have amenities. Meals, including the kosher one for seat 3B and the vegetarian ones for 12A and 22E and F, just like it said in the database. For each of us, our own personal copy of *Wings & Things*, the in-flight magazine. Bland and predictable it may be, but it took quite a system to get it there, and software again played an extensive role. Articles had to be commissioned and written; the faxes flew. It was laid out nicely on a Macintosh screen, using an expensive page-layout software product. The underpaid talent who performed this task is now listening to a compact disc through wireless headphones while making the daily backup diskette.

None of us passengers would even be here, of course, without the airline reservation system. The network of computers linking travel agents with airlines is a Byzantine example of economic cooperation and competition in uneasy truce. The economic tension between travel agents seeking good deals and airlines seeking to maximize profits has led to amazing software wars. Anyway, it got us here, and I paid $379, and the guy over there pecking at his PowerBook paid $723. The two women in front of me are taking a trip that includes this Saturday night, so they paid $119 each. Software wars make for Byzantine price-setting mechanisms, it seems.

To make our reservations, we all used the phone. You lift the receiver off the hook and get a dial tone. Press eleven buttons, and one phone rings out of 151 million. Just the person you want to speak to is on the other end (or her answering machine or voice mail, but let's not get into that). An amazingly complex, richly connected net of switches opens and closes just for you, and it is quick about it—another impressive achievement of the century, whose most recent frill appears on the seatback in front of me, the AirFone. Using the infrastructure of the cellular phone system, you can now send and receive phone calls on an airplane.

No computer invented the cute spelling of AirFone, but the embedded capital letter is brought to you by computer programmers, anyway. Sometimes in a program, a programmer wants to name something—a variable, say—to suggest what it's being used for. For example, a commodities tracking program might have a variable called "the price of eggs in China." Computers want these things to be typed without spaces in them; compilers are fussy that way and must be catered to. But programmers would like to perceive the individual words, not an undifferentiated smear of letters. This problem gets solved several ways, and it is a commentary on the essential humanity of programmers that it's a matter of taste and, occasionally, pseudoreligious dispute. Folks programming in C tend to use underscores, thus: `the_price_of_eggs_in_China`. It gets awfully long to type. To shorten it, some programmers will make mysterious secret names using rules they invent, such as the first letter of each word: *tpoeic*. This gets them enthusiastically loathed by anyone who has to come along later and figure out how their programs work. Another approach embeds capital letters: thePriceOfEggsInChina. Marketing types think this looks stylish and name the products that way. Software is infiltrating on all fronts.

We're descending into Portland now—the view out the window goes woolly gray with the famous Portland clouds, and then I see cars whizzing below us on Marine Drive. These days, they whiz along aided by a wide variety of software: computerized braking, fuel injection, suspension, cruise control, transmission, four-wheel steering, and maybe even navigation systems use software. It astonishes me that software has so thoroughly colonized the car *with practically no public discussion*. Software makes it cheaper to manufacture items—cars, for example—because it eliminates many specific little pieces that must be machined to precise tolerances. But what a decision to leave to the manufacturers!

Below us now I see the runway. On our behalf, a guardian angel peers into the radar screen, while another in the tower communicates with our pilot over the radio. The complex, software-intensive system has worked again—thanks, everyone. We are down. I am home. It is raining.

## THIRTEEN TALES OF DIGITAL WOE

This book is about how things can go wrong. In the next few pages, I'll tell you thirteen stories of things going wrong. Sometimes the outcome is comic; sometimes it's tragic; sometimes it's both. It isn't that the people who design, build, and program computers are any less careful, competent, or conscientious than the rest of us. But they're only human, and digital technology is unforgiving of human limitations. So many details must be tracked! Even the tiniest error can have an enormous effect. Of course the stuff is tested, but the sad truth is that a properly thorough job of testing a software program could take decades . . . centuries . . . sometimes even millennia.

Frankly, developing software is not the easiest way to make money. A careful job is expensive, and even the most careful process can leave that tiny, disastrous error. So even after the product is "finished" and for sale, developers issue constant upgrades to correct some of the mistakes they've been hearing about. Unfortunately, sometimes the upgrade is late.

Failures happen all the time. The consequences of failure depend on what we were using the flaky machine for in the first place. We put computers into all kinds of systems nowadays. Here are some of the things we choose to risk:

- reputations,
- large sums of money,
- democracy,
- human lives,
- the ecosystem that sustains us all.

And yet, some of these systems don't really benefit us much. Some of them are solutions to the *wrong* problem.

The truth is that digital technology is brittle. It tends to break under any but stable, predictable conditions—and those are just what we cannot provide. Life is frequently—emphatically—unpredictable.

You can't think of everything.

### 1. Tiny Errors Can Have Large Effects

On July 22, 1962, a program with a tiny omission in an equation cost U.S. taxpayers $18.5 million when an Atlas-Agena rocket was destroyed in error.[1]

The rocket carried *Mariner I,* built to explore Venus. The equation was used by the computerized guidance system. It was missing a "bar": a horizontal stroke over a symbol that signified the use of a set of averaged values, instead of raw data. The missing bar led the computer to decide that the rocket was behaving erratically, although it was not. When the computer tried to correct a situation that required no correction, it caused actual erratic behavior and the rocket was blown up to save the community of Cocoa Beach. (This unhappy duty falls on the shoulders of an unsung hero called the range safety officer, and we are all glad he's there.)

*Mariner I,* all systems functioning perfectly, surprised the denizens of the Atlantic Ocean instead of the Venusian.

### 2. Thorough Testing Takes Too Long

Because such tiny errors can have such large effects, even the best efforts can miss something that will cause a problem. In late June and early July of 1991, a series of outages affected telephone users in Los Angeles, San Francisco, Washington, D.C., Virginia, W. Virginia, Baltimore, and Greensboro, N.C. The problems were caused by a telephone switching program written by a company called DSC Communications. Their call-routing software had several million lines of programming code. (Printed at 60 lines to a page and 500 pages to a volume, one million lines equals about 33 volumes of bedtime reading.) They tested the program for 13 weeks, and it worked.

Then they made a tiny change—only three lines of the millions were altered in any way. They didn't feel they needed to go through the entire 13 weeks of testing again. They knew what that change did, and they were confident that it did nothing else.[2] And presumably, the customer wanted it *now.* So they sent off their several-million-line program that differed from the tested version by only three lines, and it crashed. Repeatedly. *Sic transit software.*

### 3. Developing Software Is Not the Easiest Way to Make Money

Sometimes it's the software, and sometimes it's the process itself that is buggy—developing software can be a nightmare even for someone who has succeeded at it before.

Mitch Kapor is a gentleman whose name never appears in the software press without the words "industry veteran" in front of it. It's a fine title, and he wears it well: Mitch Kapor is the fellow who wrote the first spreadsheet for the IBM PC. He founded Lotus Development Corporation and made a fortune on Lotus 1-2-3. Then he left Lotus "because the company had gotten too big."[3] In early 1988, he started another company called On Technology and began work on an ambitious project to make personal computers easier to use. He got some venture capital, hired a bunch of bright young programmers and a former Lotus associate to oversee their work, and spent $300,000 a month for thirteen months. When it became obvious that they were years away from a prod-

**Figure 1-1.** Searching for Information the Hard Way

uct, Mr. Kapor scaled back his ambitions considerably, starting development instead on a nice little product called On Location.

On Location is not a major paradigm shift in personal computing, but it *is* handy. It would have been hard to write this book without it; it provides me with meaningful access to over twelve megabytes of information. To show you what I mean, Figure 1-1 shows a little bit of my computer's "desktop."[4] Each one of those little pictures represents a file; the text underneath is the name of the file. They all look the same, don't they? Yet each contains all kinds of different information. If I am searching for a snippet about Mitch Kapor, for example, how do I know where to look?

The answer is that I use this product. It allows me to search through the whole computer for any word or words, and it will tell me which files contain those words. Some of the files on the list still turn out to be irrelevant, but the haystack in which I search for my needle of information is now much, much smaller.

This is handy, but it isn't earthshaking; it's only a modest application of computer technology. And if anyone was in a position to appreciate how long development of this product was going to take, it ought to have been Mr. Kapor. He started development in April 1989 and expected to ship the product in November. The target date for shipping was revised three times; the third time involved a full-blown management crisis, with the head of engineering storming out the door. The product finally shipped at the end of the following February, but only by throwing four more bodies at it. Several people quit. Twice they changed product direction, and twice they abandoned a feature they had planned. A seven-month schedule stretched to eleven months and involved an extra visit to the venture capitalists.

Software development projects are notorious for cost overruns, missed schedules, and products that do less than originally specified. A lot of corporate ships have foundered on these rocks. Their captains can feel a bit better now, though, because they're in excellent company.

### 4. Even a Careful Process Can Leave a Problem

Bugs are troublesome, but so is removing them. The process can leave detritus that will cause serious problems when the system is in use. On July 20, 1969, in the critical final seconds of landing the first manned spacecraft on the moon, Neil Armstrong was distracted by just such left-over detritus—two "computer alarms."[5]

Apollo 11 was a software-intensive undertaking for its time, and it suffered its share of development problems. To debug the software running on the onboard computer, programmers inserted extra bits of computer code which they called "alarms" (nowadays they'd be "debugging aids") to help them determine what happened inside the computer when their programs misbehaved.

As preparations for launch approached maximum intensity, a programmer happened to mention the computer alarms to the fellow who programmed the simulations that trained the mission controllers. The alarms had never been intended to come to the attention of anyone other than the programmers, and the mission controllers had never heard of them. "We had gone through years of working out how in the world to fly that mission in excruciating detail, every kind of failure condition, and never, ever, did I even know those alarms existed," said Bill Tindall, in charge of Mission Techniques. Nevertheless, the Apollo personnel had an understandable passion for thoroughness. Even though the alarms could not reasonably be expected to occur during an actual mission, the mission controllers were promptly given simulations that included them. This turned out to be fortunate; sometimes the backup works.

The onboard computer had several functions. Its primary function was to help land the lunar module on the moon, but it also helped it meet and dock with the command module in lunar orbit after leaving the moon. Obviously, it was not going to perform both functions at once, so original procedures called for flipping a switch to disable the rendezvous radar during descent. However, about a month before launch, it was decided to leave the switch in a different setting to allow the rendezvous radar to monitor the location of the command module during the descent. The programmers felt it would be safer for the crew if the rendezvous software could take over immediately, in case the landing had to be aborted for any reason.

But one change to a complex, delicately balanced system leads to others. In this case, it led to too many others, too close to the launch date. When the extent of the changes became apparent, the software engineers decided to return to the original procedures. But the appropriate software changes had already been loaded into the lunar module's computer, and it was a ticklish job to back them out. They decided instead to withhold the radar data from the rendezvous software, figuring that therefore it wouldn't track the command module during descent. It seemed like the simplest solution.

But computers don't know that no angle has both a sine and cosine of 0. As the lunar module approached the surface of the moon, the computer gamely attempted the impossible task of tracking the command module with mathematically impossible data and landing the lunar module at the same time. Both tasks proved to call for more processing than it could perform simultaneously, so it issued an alarm indicating an overflow. Moments before the historic landing, a twenty-six-year-old mission controller had to decide whether to abort the mission. It was a tough call—some alarms indicated a serious problem, others could safely be ignored, but other factors complicated the picture. The mission controller had nineteen long seconds to think it over before deciding to continue. Then a new alarm occurred and he had to make the decision all over again.

Meanwhile, during crucial moments in the lunar lander, the astronauts were distracted from seeing that their chosen landing site was strewn with boulders. With twenty-four seconds of fuel, they were maneuvering around rocks. They landed with no margin for error.

### 5. Sometimes the Upgrade Is Late

On February 25, 1991, an Iraqi *Scud* missile killed twenty-eight American soldiers and wounded ninety-eight others in a barracks near Dhahran, Saudi Arabia. The missile might have been intercepted had it not been for a bug in the software running on the *Patriot* missile defense system.[6] The bug was in the software that acquired the target. Here's how the system is supposed to work:

1. The *Patriot* scans the sky with its five thousand radar elements until it detects a possible target. Preliminary radar returns indicate how far away the target is.

2. Subsequent radar data indicate how fast the target is going.

3. Now the *Patriot* must determine its direction. The *Patriot* starts by scanning the whole sky, but it can scan more accurately and sensitively if it can concentrate on just a small portion, called the tracking window. Now it needs that improvement. It calculates where the *Scud* is likely to be next, using calculations that depend (unsurprisingly) on being ultraprecise. Then it draws the tracking window—a rectangle around the key portion of the sky—and scans for the *Scud*. If it sees the *Scud*, it has acquired the target, and can track its progress. If it does not see the *Scud*, it concludes that the original blip was not a legitimate target after all. It returns to scanning the sky.


The equation used to draw the tracking window was generating an error of one 10-millionth of a second every ten seconds. Over time, this error accumulated to the point where the tracking window could no longer be drawn accurately, causing real targets to be dismissed as spurious blips. When the machine was restarted, the value was reinitialized to zero. The error started out insignificant and gradually began to grow again.

Original U. S. Army specifications called for a system that would shut down daily, at least, for maintenance or redeployment elsewhere. The Army originally did not plan to run the system continuously for days; it was only supposed to run for fourteen hours at a stretch, and after fourteen hours the error was still insignificant. But successful systems nearly always find unanticipated uses, and by February 25th, the Patriot missile defense installation near Dhahran had been running continuously for a hundred hours—five days. Its timing had drifted by 36-hundredths of a second, a significantly large error.

The bug was noticed almost as soon as the Gulf War began. By February 25th, it had actually been fixed, but the programmers at Raytheon also wanted to fix other bugs deemed more critical. By the time all the bugs had been fixed—

and a new version of the software had been copied onto tape,

and the tape had been sent to Ft. McGuire Air Force Base,

and then flown to Riyadh,

and then trucked to Dhahran,

and then loaded into the Patriot installation—

—well, by that time it was February 26th, and the dead were already dead, and the war was just about over.

### 6. We Risk Our Reputations

In the summer of 1991, a company called National Data Retrieval of Norcross, Georgia, sent a representative to Norwich, Vermont, looking for names of people who were delinquent on their property taxes. National Data Retrieval wanted this information to sell to TRW, a large credit-reporting agency. The town clerk showed the representative the town's receipt book. Because of a misunderstanding, the representative copied down all the names in it—*all* the taxpayers of Norwich. Back in Georgia, the names were keypunched in and supplied to TRW, which then began to report: "delinquent on his/her taxes" in response to every single query regarding a Norwich property owner.[7]

Credit information is not routinely sent to those most keenly affected, such as these maligned property owners. So the information spread from computer to computer, trickling into many tiny rivulets of the Great Data Stream. The town clerk began receiving a series of suspiciously similar inquiries, asking for confirmation of imaginary tax delinquencies. It did not take her long to trace these queries to TRW. After a mere week or so of phone calls, and only one story planted in the local newspaper, someone at TRW undertook to correct their records.

Now suppose that TRW promptly and faithfully does so. The barn door swings slowly shut. In the meantime, how many computers have queried the credit status of how many Norwich residents? Applications for loans, credit card transactions, even actions taken months previously can spark such queries. Due to one error, other computers have already received the false reports of tax delinquencies. TRW may correct its own records, but no Proclamation of Invalidity will be sent to those other computers. Probably, no one even knows where the data went. Though officially dead, the zombie information stalks the data subjects, besmirching their data shadows and planting time bombs in their lives, maybe forever.

### 7. We Risk Financial Disaster

On Wednesday, November 20, 1985, a bug cost the Bank of New York $5 million when the software used to track government securities transactions from the Federal Reserve suddenly began to write new information on top of old.[8] The event occurred inside the memory of a computer; the effect was as if the (digital) clerk failed to skip to a new line before writing down each transaction in an endless ledger. New transaction information was lost in the digital equivalent of one big, inky blotch. The Fed debited the bank for each transaction, but the Bank of New York could not tell who owed it how much for which securities. After ninety minutes they managed to shut off the spigot of incoming transactions, by which time the Bank of New York owed the Federal Reserve $32 billion it could not collect from others.

A valiant effort by all concerned got them up to a debt of only $23.6 billion by the end of the business day, whereupon a lot of people probably phoned home to say: "Honey, I won't be home for dinner tonight. . . Well, uh, probably *really* late . . ." Pledging all its assets as collateral, the Bank of New York borrowed $23.6 billion from the Fed overnight and paid $5 million in interest for the privilege. By Friday, the database was restored, but the bank also paid with intangibles: for a while, it lost the confidence of investors.

Another consequence, however slight, is that an unknown number of econometric models received incorrect data for a couple of days, thereby possibly skewing whatever decisions were based on them.

### 8. We Risk Democracy

In the spring of 1992, the Liberal Party of Nova Scotia, Canada, held a convention. They used a computerized telephone voting system to allow any convention delegate with a touch-tone phone to vote from home by dialing the telephone number for the candidate of his or her choice.[9] (Those without touch-tone phones could go to any of several locations where banks of phones were set up.) All registered Liberals received a PIN which, when entered, verified that they were entitled to vote. A thank-you message verified that their votes had been recorded. Maritime Tel & Tel, the local telephone company, persuaded the convention organizers that a backup voting system using paper ballots was unnecessary. After all, they handled hundreds of thousands of calls a day. What could go wrong?

Everything. The software turned out to be too slow to handle the volume of calls, so many votes were not recorded. In the ensuing confusion, voting was suspended and resumed, then the deadline was extended—twice. Some people reported that their PINS were rejected. Others were able to vote more than once.

Adding the final touch to this election-day chaos, a kid with a scanner called up the Canadian Broadcasting Corporation and announced that he had recorded a cellular telephone conversation between the telephone company and the party, giving the results so far. Representatives of the CBC, uncertain whether this was a hoax, discussed whether to air his story with an executive producer—also over a cellular telephone. When the kid called back with a recording of *that* conversation, the CBC decided to run the story. Needless to say, this did not improve matters.

A week or so later, the dust settled and the Liberal Party decided to try again. This time they required the telephone company to post a $350,000 performance bond. They also made available a backup system that allowed people to vote with paper ballots. The backup system turned out to be unnecessary—the second time around, voting by phone worked fine.

### 9. We Risk Death

In the spring and summer of 1986, two cancer patients in Galveston, Texas, died from radiation therapy received from the Therac-25, a computer-controlled radiation therapy machine manufactured by Atomic Energy of Canada, Ltd.[10] AECL was hardly a fly-by-night outfit—it was a crown corporation of the dominion of Canada, charged with managing nuclear energy for the nation.

A machine such as the Therac-25 can deliver two different kinds of radiation: electrons or X-rays. To deliver electrons, the target area on the patient's body is irradiated directly with a beam of electrons of relatively low intensity. This works well for cancerous areas on or near the surface of the body, such as skin cancer. For cancers of internal organs, buried under healthy flesh, a shield of tungsten is placed between the patient and the beam. An electron beam one hundred times more intense bombards the tungsten, which absorbs the electrons and emits X-rays from its other side. These X-rays pass part of the way through the patient to strike the internal cancers.

What you want to avoid is the hundred-times-too-strong electron beam accidentally striking the patient directly, without the intervening tungsten shield. This unsafe condition must be forestalled. But it was not—under these circumstances:

The operator selected X-rays as the desired procedure, the tungsten shield interposed itself, and the software prepared to send the high-intensity electron beam. Then the operator realized that she had made a mistake: electrons, not X-rays, were the required therapy. She changed the selection to electrons and pressed the button to start treatment. The shield moved out of the way, but the software had not yet changed from the high- to the low-intensity beam setting before it received the signal to start. Events happened in the wrong order.

Previous radiation therapy machines included mechanical interlocks—when the tungsten target moved out of the way of the beam, it physically moved some component of a circuit, opening a switch and preventing the high-intensity beam from turning on. On the Therac-25, the target sensor went from the tungsten directly to the computer. Both the target position and the beam intensity were directly and only under software control. And the software had a bug.

As if in a bad science fiction movie, the Therac-25 printed `Malfunction 54` on the operator's terminal as it gave each man a painful and lethal radiation overdose. One died within a month of the mishap; the other became paralyzed, then comatose, before he finally died several months later.

These were not isolated events. Of eleven Therac-25 machines in use, four displayed these or similar problems. Over a two- to three-year period, three other serious incidents involving the software occurred in clinics in Marietta, Georgia; Yakima, Washington; and Ontario, Canada.

### 10. We Risk the Earth's Ability to Sustain Life

It's not surprising that erroneous data can cause problems, but correct data doesn't guarantee that there will be *no* problems. As anyone can tell you who has spent time in public policy think tanks, computer models can be created to provide any answer you want. One way to do it is to specify ahead of time the answers you do not want.

In the 1970s and 1980s, NASA satellites orbiting the earth observed low ozone readings. The readings were so low that the software for processing satellite results rejected them as errors.[11] Checking to determine whether a value is in an expected range is a common form of "sanity check" to include in a program. Such a check would be useful in a grading program, for example: if student grades are expected to be within the range of 0.0 to 4.0, inclusive, then checking for that range can help you find places where someone made a mistake entering a grade.

It's easy to incorporate a sanity check for a grade, because those limits are set by people, using terms that are straightforward and unambiguous to a computer—real numbers. People sure don't set the ozone levels—well, not directly. As it turns out, we do, in a way, but that was precisely the question NASA was investigating, and they weren't prepared to believe the answer.

In 1986, a team of earthbound British scientists reported the decline in ozone levels. NASA reexamined its old data and confirmed their findings. The world may have missed a chance to get a jump on the ozone problem by a decade or more—without an independent source for data, it is risky to reject a reading because it doesn't meet your preconceptions. (On the other hand, maybe we just missed an additional decade's worth of argument.)

### 11. We May Not Gain Much

In February 1990, an article appeared describing "a seeming reversal of progress": the Washington State ferry system announced that it planned to replace the electronic control systems of the large, Issaquah-class ferries with pneumatic controls.[12] Ferries with electronic controls had rammed the dock, left before being told to do so, or unexpectedly shifted from forward to reverse. The folks in charge had had enough.

Washington State Ferries is the largest ferry transportation system in the United States; thousands of people in western Washington live on the Olympic Peninsula or the beautiful islands across Puget Sound from Seattle, and take the ferries daily to and from work. Under the circumstances, Washington State responsibly decided it did not need to run a poorly controlled experiment with the latest technology. Older pneumatic control systems, which require a physical connection from the control cabinet to the propellors and engine governors, had been doing the job before, and they'd been more reliable.

### 12. We May Be Solving the Wrong Problem

In the early 1980s, General Motors embarked upon an enormous investment in automation. In 1985, it opened its showcase: the new Hamtramck factory in Detroit, Michigan, had 50 automatic guided vehicles (AGVs) to ferry parts around the plant, and 260 robots to weld and paint.[13] It turned out not to be such a hot idea.

> . . . Almost a year after it was opened, all this high technology was still so unreliable that the plant was producing only about half the 60 cars per hour that it was supposed to make. . .

> . . . The production lines ground to a halt for hours while technicians tried to debug software. When they did work, the robots often began dismembering each other, smashing cars, spraying paint everywhere, or even fitting the wrong equipment. . . . AGVs . . . sometimes simply refused to move.

In his headlong rush to beat Japan to the twenty-first century, GM chairman Roger Smith failed to notice that GM's biggest problems lay not with its production processes, but with the way it treated its employees. A thoughtful look at his Japanese competitors revealed that the training, management, and motivation of workers was the source of their successes, not high technology. Not only was the technology expensive and unreliable, it was a solution to the wrong problem.

### 13. Life Is Unpredictable

Despite President Reagan's pledge to get government off their backs, the folks living near March Air Force Base in California had to tolerate his interference with their garage door openers from January 1981 to December 1988.[14] Air Force One had some powerful and inadequately shielded electronics. The consequences to nearby communities were never adequately explored, so when Ronald Reagan rode into town, his neighbors always knew.

## WHAT SOFTWARE HAVE YOU USED TODAY?

Software, or systems with software in them—*digital systems*—come in a variety of guises. Software can be running on a microprocessor embedded inside an appliance or on a computer hidden in the basement—or across town. It might be used to interact with you, to control a physical process, to tie other computers together, to retain huge amounts of data, or to create an abstract model of some part of the world. It might be used for a humble business application or for cutting-edge aerospace technology.

The following are some concepts that, though neither exhaustive nor mutually exclusive, can help us build a vocabulary for thinking about software—a vocabulary that will be useful when we consider how digital systems can fail, and what the the ramifications of those failures might be.

### Microprocessors

The entire category of consumer electronics products is defined by the presence, somewhere within the machine, of a tiny microprocessor running some software. Microprocessors are embedded in clock radios, televisions, VCRs, tape recorders, microwave ovens, dishwashers, washing machines, and compact disc players. I recently bought a toaster for $15 that has a microprocessor in it. It allows me to produce dozens of identical sets of toast, I think. It's hard to say because I am always fiddling with the controls.

Software runs on these microprocessors. It is developed, for the most part, on ordinary computers. When it is deemed ready, it is loaded into the read-only memory of the microprocessor. From then on, it is for all practical purposes fixed. It accepts input from you (what songs on this disc do you want me to play? what television shows do you want me to record? how brown do you want your toast?) and produces its output (playing the music, taping the show, burning—uh, *toasting*—the toast).

If it proves buggy or unreliable, the memory can be modified by technicians with PCs and the right kind of cable, but for all practical purposes,
it is inaccessible to users.[15] Ordinarily, the software does not change for
the lifetime of the product—you don't have to load Version 2.01 into
your microwave oven, for example. But when you bring your '93 Saturn
to the dealer for service, the technicians may do just that, and the car
you drive out may not behave in the same way as the car you drove in.

### User Interfaces

Electronic gadgets are fun, but they're less fun than they might be because they're often hard to use. All kinds of machines are suddenly getting a reputation for incomprehensible controls, and of course, VCRs
have become a standing joke. The fact that these machines include software is not a coincidence. Machines that include software can offer the
user lots of choices—that's why we like them. But this places the burden
of offering comprehensible choices, and clarifying how they are to be selected, on the "user interface."[16]

User interfaces are often hard to learn or to use. In part this is because they are also hard to design. Programmers have no idea who you
are, what other systems you've had experience with, what you expect of
this one, or what else is on your mind. It is surprising how hazy they
can be on such basic information as what you're actually trying to accomplish when you use their programs. Programmers also usually fail to
appreciate the extent to which *you don't care* that you have to press the
# sign to terminate data entry, or that you have to press <CLEAR>
while in STOP mode to clear the previously stored program, or that
the network has to be up to send e-mail, or that you have to press
<ESCAPE> to tell the system that the previous product code was a terri-
ble mistake and you're truly sorry about it but you want to start all over
again now, please. Instead, the system, locked inflexibly into its own sequence, beeps because it expects something else next.[17]

Tyrannical user interfaces abound because programmers, like the rest
of us, are poor at standing in another person's shoes, and even worse at
predicting the future. Humanity has been deficient this way since long
before software was a gleam in the Countess of Lovelace's eye.[18] But software exacerbates the problem because it is so flexible, and because there
are now so many more systems to interface with. Indeed, a poor user interface probably contributed to the deaths of 290 civilians on July 3,
1988, when the U.S.S. *Vincennes* shot down Iran Air Flight 655 over the
Persian Gulf. The system had a lot of information to present to its operator, and critics charge that it presented it in a form that was cryptic, clut-

tered, and sometimes misleading. An operator saw data he misinter-
preted as a descending aircraft. The aircraft was in fact ascending. This
misunderstanding contributed to the perception that the plane was an F-
14 on the attack, rather than an Airbus on a commercial route.[19]

In the wake of this tragic mistake, the U.S. Navy recommended various changes to the Aegis display, including a direct, possibly graphical,
indication of whether an aircraft is descending or ascending. (An upward-
or a downward-pointing arrow would do it, as former Defense Secretary
Frank Carlucci pointed out. Maybe this guy should design user interfaces.)

### Business and Commercial Software

The software you are most commonly aware of using is business or commercial software: applications you buy, or that your boss buys, or custom programs written especially for a business.

Spreadsheets and word processors (and, in fact, the operating system
that keeps the office PC running) are most likely made by a company
whose main product is software. It employs an army of programmers,
whom it calls software engineers.[20] The cafeteria serves reasonably priced,
healthy food. The company may provide coffee, tea, or soft drinks. The
programmers are paid good salaries—the kind you can use to buy a
house and a car and raise a family. On the whole, they are smart people
who work their tails off.

Spreadsheets or word processors don't ordinarily crash, but still the
first thing you learn when you start to work on a computer is how to
back up your work. Why is this, do you suppose?

In order to facilitate sharing information—spreadsheets, memos, letters—the office PCs are connected using a network. The network and an
e-mail system are also products of the burgeoning commercial software
industry. The network makes all the computers in the office one distributed system.

In addition to what is often called "end-user" commercial software,
business software also includes a lot of accounting and auditing software,
such as payroll systems or software used for invoicing and billing. It may
be commercial or homegrown. Banks, for example, are heavy users of
transaction processing software that is nearly always produced in-house,
or on a contract to their specifications.

Phone bills are the end product of another example of such software.
When you make a phone call, one circuit connects you to the telephone
you called. Another circuit notes the connection for billing purposes—it
produces not the connection but the phone bill. I think I am an ordi-

nary user of the telephone system, but the phone company has made three mistakes on my long distance bill in the past six months. One of them was pretty clearly the result of some poor but dishonest high school kids creatively solving the problem of how to make an out-of-state call from a phone booth. This is a flaw in system security, but it is not news that the phone system isn't secure. Nor need it be. The phone company has made a cold-hearted financial decision that it is cheaper and easier to spread around the cost of the phone calls people complain about than to pay programmers to improve the auditing. They are probably right.

The other two mistakes were deeper mysteries, bearing no clue as to their origins. Commercial phone service has been available in the U.S. since the first telephone exchange began work in New Haven, Connecticut, on January 28, 1878. Collecting information for billing purposes has been a requirement for nearly as long. Yet over a century later, no one is surprised enough at phone billing errors to investigate them. For one thing, they know how hard a hunt it could be. Similarly, after more than thirty years of commercial data processing, the $6.3 million electric bill or the $22,000 water bill is still an amusing cliché of local television newscasts or *Reader's Digest* items.[21]

### Databases

When you use your credit card to buy something, the information is in digital form and the transaction is recorded in a database on a computer. Digital information is easy to collect; credit agencies, your bank, your employer, your health insurance provider, your doctor, fund-raisers, and mass-marketing firms all keep databases with lots of information about you. So does the government at various levels—in the United States, the IRS knows how much money you've been making, the Selective Service Bureau hopes it knows if you are a man between the ages of eighteen and twenty-five, the Census Bureau has an idea how many toilets are in your house, your state Department of Motor Vehicles knows your driving record, and your county tax assessor's office thinks it knows the value of your house. Perhaps the FBI has your name, as well—I couldn't say.

From lists of magazines you subscribe to and products you've bought by mail, various organizations infer your political and charitable leanings, and bombard your mailbox with solicitations. From political and charitable donations you've made, they infer which magazines you might subscribe to and what products you might buy. Who knows what they imagine about you?[22]

Banks and commodity markets keep databases of their transactions, hospitals keep databases of their patients, and pharmacists can buy a database that will tell them if a medication that someone is currently taking will interact badly with the one they are about to dispense.[23] Recently, Lotus Corp. was dissuaded from selling a CD-ROM database of consumer information for direct-mail advertisers. The public protested what many felt to be an invasion of privacy for which they had no effective recourse. Lotus and TRW killed the product and swallowed the development costs.[24]

The risks can go far beyond an overflowing mailbox. The amount of freely available information is fostering growing concern over privacy.[25] In recent years, stories of clean credit histories stolen by "credit doctors" have become a staple of the evening news. According to many estimates, there is a fifty-fifty chance that your credit record contains errors. (Mine has one error, although fortunately for me it's insignificant.) A recent UPI article even described a man who falsely obtained others' social security numbers, collecting retirement and disability checks under at least twenty-nine names.[26] And, of course, there are the maligned property owners of Norwich, Vermont.

### Aids to Decision-Making:
### Modeling, Simulation, and Expert Systems

Once someone starts collecting all this data, they (and others) are tempted to use it. For this, you need tools. Software information tools include modeling and simulation, expert systems, and query languages for databases. There is a lot of leeway in making, choosing, or using them. The process of extracting information from data is not straightforward, and no two people will go about it the same way.

The airline discounting practice known as *yield management* is an example of modeling software at work. It uses statistics on passenger travel to determine how many seats on which flights to sell at a discount, when to upgrade a passenger to first class, and so on. The performance of this system can make the difference, under certain circumstances, between profit and loss.

Travel agencies have computers, too, and they have responded to yield management by implementing programs that scan continuously for good deals. Naturally, this throws off the airlines' calculations, and they have begun to respond by charging the travel agencies for each inquiry. (Travel agencies used to pay a simple fee to access the service.) The travel agencies have responded to *that* by rewriting their programs to make fewer inquiries and charging their customers for the service.[27] Kind of like a computer chess tournament, isn't it?

Modeling and its close cousin, simulation, are like recipes for reality. They try to take into account all relevant parameters of a problem (add ingredients), and then see what happens when the world behaves as it usually does (stir, bake at 350°). Two obvious sticking points are:

1. Which parameters are relevant? How do you know? How can you measure them?

2. What is usual behavior? How do you know? How do you model it?

The model or simulation is helpful to the extent that these points have been addressed with intelligence, insight, and skill. Nevertheless, it is a simplification of reality. It *has* to be—that's what it's for: if the map contained all the details in the territory, it would be as large as the territory and therefore useless. The model's job is to boil down an infinitely detailed world to just a few key details, rather like a printer reduces an infinitely detailed scene to 300 dots per inch.

The programmers who made the model or simulation might be able to tell, if asked, exactly what has been simplified. But they are seldom asked, the simplifications are seldom visible, and sometimes they are just plain ignorant of an important factor. If revealed, the simplifications might cast the results in doubt, requiring the policy implementor to cast aside the computational fig leaf and display the naked use of human judgment.

The weather report is another commonplace result of computer modeling. The fact that it's wrong so often indicates the results of relying on oversimplified models—the atmosphere is a terribly complicated set of phenomena; we do not understand it. Nevertheless, a weather report is an excellent example of a basically benign and useful system. It comes with its own confidence rating—"A 50 percent chance of rain tonight," the broadcaster says. When it's right, you get a warm, fuzzy, false sense of security. When it's wrong, well, what were you going to do about it, anyway?

Well, maybe you would have stayed home. The National Oceanic and Atmospheric Administration maintains a system of weather buoys along the U.S. coastline. The ocean is a harsh environment, and weather buoys sometimes need repairs. NOAA failed to repair one for three months once; the National Weather Service, missing its reports, failed to predict a storm. Three lobstermen set out to sea and were lost. Their families sued; in 1985 they were awarded $1.25 million.[28]

Expert systems are different from models and simulations. They were probably born when someone wanted to clone an expert and send him

or her to both Chicago and Seattle at the same time. You ask an expert
to tell you everything that she (or he) knows about a subject. You tell it
all to a computer in the form of a decision tree, a series of logical rules
and steps, or a flowchart. The machine is then supposed to ask a user
the same questions about a problem that an expert would ask and, given
the answers, emit the same expert advice. To Chicago and Seattle, you
send a floppy disk. Much cheaper.

Expert systems have been used with some success for certain applications, such as repairing machinery or determining the peripherals and ac-
cessories needed by a particular computer installation. These domains
are relatively small and clearly delimited; the rules, once discovered, are
not likely to change. Expert systems for such applications as medical diagnosis present deeper problems. When ongoing research sheds new
light on a disease, for example, the diagnostic procedure can change.
Doctors discover the fact from reading their medical journals. Modifying
the software, however, is harder than just informing it. The new knowledge can impact the structure of the rules themselves, requiring extensive
change to the expertise captured by the program.

Query languages are software to allow business executives, who cannot
program their VCRs any better than anyone else, to ask a database a
question, perhaps even in something like natural English, and get an answer, although maybe not to the question they thought they asked. I
know of one product that will give a different answer to the same query,
depending upon whether the naive user types in a "%" sign or spells out
the word "percent." Both answers, of course, are delivered in uninflected
machine style—the executive has not a clue that a trivial change in the
question will yield a completely different answer. The next time you read
an annual report, wonder.

One successful database vendor had the marketing wit to name its
product Oracle, but the danger is that people believe it. People who use
decision-making aids have to make decisions, often public ones. And people who have to make decisions are unhappy. They usually want someone else to make the decisions for them. Best of all, they want to be able
to point to some completely disinterested, objective source—and what
could be more disinterested and objective than a computer, the disem-
bodied brain?

### Distributed Systems

A system is not always found in just one place. For example, an airplane
is a complex system by itself, but it can also be viewed as a component
in a much larger system, the commercial air traffic control (ATC) system. The ATC system is an example of a *distributed system,* so called be-

cause pieces of it are distributed all over the country. Over seventeen thousand airplanes depart daily from over five thousand airports in the United States, and the air traffic control system is charged with making sure that they leave from, and land on, the proper runways and don't bump into each other on the way. Aircraft pass from the control of their airport of origin to the next air traffic control sector, then from sector to sector, and finally to the control of their destination airport. Computers track each aircraft within a sector and help manage the hand-offs between sectors.

Distributed systems abound. Automated teller machine networks distribute access to your checking account. They connect to banks; banks connect to the system of point-of-sale terminals that allow you to use your credit card to buy lunch at a restaurant you've never been to before. The point-of-sale terminals, the banks, and the automated teller machines form a huge, complex, and critical distributed system—the banking and credit system. Billions of dollars in trillions of transactions are shunted around daily through this system in electronic form.

For the winner in the distributed system sweepstakes, I'd nominate the vast and awesome distributed system that is our international telecommunications network. AT&T handles 75 million calls per day within the United States, and of course it is not the only carrier. People or fax machines call from the United States to overseas over 1.6 million times daily.

And 100,000 calls can be disconnected at once when one backhoe blade severs one fiber optic cable. In Newark, New Jersey, on January 4, 1991, an AT&T crew was trying to remove an old cable when it cut another. Approximately 60 percent of the attempted long-distance phone calls from New York did not get through that day (and New Yorkers do not need another source of frustration). The New York Mercantile Exchange and several other commodities exchanges were shut down. Air traffic control communication was disrupted (the systems overlap), resulting in flight delays from New York, Boston, and Washington, D.C.

Although this disruption is frustrating and maybe even expensive, most of it can be tolerated. But a phone call can be about anything. Some people may have died, or will, because of such a hitch in the system get-along. For example, doctors are now talking about being able to send each other patient X-rays over the phone lines. When a patient in a small community has what doctors call (with characteristic linguistic flair) "an equivocal X-ray," it would be a lot easier on everybody to send the X-ray rather than the patient to the big-city diagnostician.[29] If the phone system were down, and it was your child who therefore died on the long ambulance trip from summer camp to the nearest big hospital, would you sue the phone company? Or would you accept that having the system was better than not having it, despite its occasional egregious failures? Or would it be a better use of resources to encourage doctors to serve remote communities? We're going to have to make more and more of these kinds of choices.

A city's system of traffic lights is another common distributed system. Portland, Oregon (City of Roses), boasts 890 traffic lights, each with its own local (and relatively simple) computer and system of sensors in the pavement. As of mid-1991, 283 of them (about 32 percent), mostly downtown, were controlled from a central computer, working in concert to keep traffic flowing as smoothly as possible. This central computer, the 283 intersections it controls, and their local computers and pavement sensors form another big distributed system. As you would expect, the system incorporates a number of fail-safe mechanisms. If the central computer fails, the traffic lights it's supposed to control can fall back on their own local computers. If those computers too should fail, the light reverts to flashing red in both directions, and some people revert from maniacs to careful, thoughtful drivers.[30] (At least in Portland, some do.)

### Integrated Systems

The flip side of distributed systems are integrated systems; sometimes they can be two ways of looking at the same thing. Distributed systems often consist of many similar components (automated teller machines, traffic controllers) that were always intended to be spread across the countryside. Integrated systems, by contrast, usually consist of various different components that started out as separate systems until someone saw the benefit of tying them together.

Take a manufacturing business, for example. The accountants use a computer to track cash flow, sales, profits or losses, and to report this information to the managers. The manufacturing folks use a computer to keep track of the inventory—how many parts they have on hand, what kind, how quickly they are being used, and which parts need to be reordered. Meanwhile, the designers are using a computer-aided design system to design the next widget. The computer-aided design system knows what parts will be used to manufacture this new product, but the other computers don't. The accountants want that information to compute the profit margin for the new product. The inventory system needs it, too. Wouldn't it be great if the design computer could talk directly to the accounting and inventory computers, thus automating these steps? If the business succeeds in getting these systems to communicate with each other, it has a computer-integrated manufacturing system.

Integrated systems need not be large or ambitious. A fax machine
with a built-in modem can be considered an integrated system. So can a
television with a built-in VCR. An automobile may have a microprocessor controlling its antilock braking system, another for the fuel injection
system, and yet another for the suspension system. If the manufacturer
then introduces an electronic controller to coordinate them all, the automobile contains an integrated system.

Integrated systems are possible because at bottom, all computers deal
with the same "stuff": electronic ones and zeroes. No matter what it represents, digital information all looks the same to a computer. It is therefore not too difficult to pass the information from one computer system
to another, and sometimes (as with the manufacturing business above)
the advantages are compelling.

The universal product code (UPC) and its associated system of scanners, cash registers, computers, and inventory control software integrates
many aspects of a retail business. It is a result of the insight that a customer purchase is more than just money coming into a store, it is also
an item leaving the shelves. If the same system that rings up the cash
register can also keep the books and track the inventory, one system
efficiently provides lots of information: how much money you took in
today, what products you need to reorder, which items are hot sellers
and which are duds. Nothing less than a system so overarching can support a chain of hundreds of supermarkets carrying tens of thousands of
items apiece from thousands of local and distant suppliers.[31]

The UPC system is a fine example of how these software categories
overlap. Each cash register contains an embedded microprocessor. Store
clerks interact with the user interface. A store represents a distributed system of cash registers and (perhaps) a central computer. Some franchises
or chains use modems to link their various outlets to another computer
located far away, extending the distributed system or integrating the outlets, depending on how you see it.

### Process-Control Software

When the computer goes down in a heavily computerized retail store,
store clerks may still be able to take your money and write up sales by
hand. If they can't—well, customers are inconvenienced and the store
loses some business. But when software is being used to control an ongoing physical process, an interruption is just *not* acceptable. The physical process will continue whether the software controls it or not. Therefore, process-control software puts a premium on not dropping the ball,
and it's hard to write.

Process-control software probably lurks in your garage; the average 1990s automobile has more software than the lunar lander, and a lot of it controls processes. Software may control an antilock or antiskid braking system, a fuel injection system, an idle stabilizer system, or a cruise control system. Some cars even use software to fine-tune the suspension.

Process-control software is used in manufacturing, chemical plants, and power plants, nuclear and otherwise. Software makes fabrics, pharmaceuticals, and other products that require chemical reactions to be kept within certain bounds. It determines when and how a nuclear reactor must be shut down. It controls the operation of subway systems, transoceanic freighters, and commercial aircraft.

Flight control systems are a good example of how software has taken over an enormous number of once-manual functions. In newer commercial jets, software is told the destination and determines the route and altitude. It reads the loaded weight of the aircraft, compares the current cost of fuel with the current cost of crew time, and determines if it's economical to go fast on this trip. It balances the plane by drawing fuel from the various tanks symmetrically. In the newest commercial jets, the Boeing 747-400, the MD 12, and the Airbus A320, software also controls the hydraulically boosted mechanical systems that used to connect the pilot's controls to the control surfaces of the wings and the tail. Software ignites or shuts down engines, raises or lowers the landing gear. A pilot's gestures are no longer physically connected with any of these events. The connection is now only digital and symbolic.[32]

To see how software can be used to control a physical process, let's examine a hypothetical (and simplified) automotive fuel injection system. Fuel and air mix in the engine, and the spark plugs spark, causing the mixture to burn. The energy from the combustion process moves the ton of metal down the road. The amount of energy available to move the car depends on the engine speed (its RPM) and the efficiency of the combustion. The combustion can be made as efficient as possible by producing the spark at the optimum instant and by maintaining an ideal air-to-fuel ratio.

Naturally, the amount of energy required varies according to what the driver is trying to do—climb a hill or coast down one, accelerate onto a freeway or stop at a red light. The driver conveys a request for a specific amount of acceleration by selecting a certain gear and pressing the accelerator a certain amount. (For the sake of this simplified discussion, we are ignoring several things, including, at the moment, the use of the brakes.)

From the point of view of the fuel-injection system, every trip taken in a car can be seen as a sequence of requests for different amounts of energy, each request lasting a certain amount of time. Each trip is, at some level of detail, a unique sequence of such requests. It is obviously impossible to predict all the trips someone will ever make in the car. The system, therefore, has to respond to requests as they occur. The microcontroller must obtain information about the current state of the system—speed, engine temperature, fuel temperature, combustion efficiency, air flow, voltage available for the spark, requested acceleration. It gets this information from a variety of sensors, measuring battery voltage, engine RPM, temperature of water in the cooling system, temperature of fuel at the fuel pump and elsewhere, air mass in the intake manifold, the amount of unburned oxygen in the exhaust, pressure on the accelerator. Then it must calculate how much fuel to squirt, and when, and how much current to apply to the spark plugs, and when. Then it must send the commands to perform these actions. Figure 1-2 shows a simplified diagram of the control process.

By itself, this is reasonably complicated—sensors must be read, computations performed, controls operated—but nothing out of the ordinary. What makes the system really challenging are the rigid real-time deadlines for each step in the process, as well as for the entire loop. How

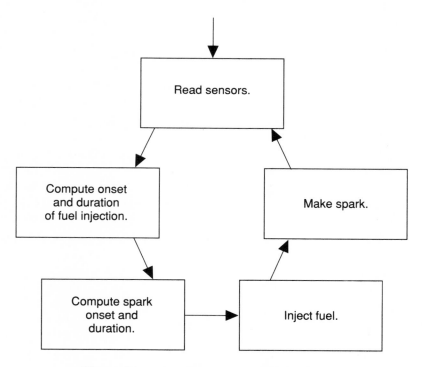

**Figure 1-2.** Very Simple Fuel Injection System

many times per second must the entire loop repeat in order for the driver to adequately control the ton of metal that can so easily mow down the child on the tricycle? The answer depends on the engine RPM; 5–10 microseconds is a typical time budget for the entire loop. (A microsecond is one millionth of a second.)

How long does it take to read each sensor and retain the readings? Given the inputs, how long does it take to compute the results? How long does it take to send the signals to the controls, and for the controls to respond? Do all these add up to more than the time available? What if we use a more powerful processor, one that can do more computations per second? How will that affect the cost of the car?

Process-control software must meet unforgiving real-time deadlines. The phrase *real time* bothers some people. I can understand this. For people who don't write software, it seems superfluous to describe the constraints of simply living one's life: growing older, unable to unsay the regretted remark, undo the regretted action, unmake the consequences we failed to compute. But programmers have the opportunity, sometimes, to slip into another time mode known as *batch*. When batch rules apply, the user asks a question and the program crunches its way through the computation, spitting out the answer when it gets there. If you don't like the answer, you change something and try the whole exercise again. This is acceptable for computing the internal temperatures of type G stars from their spectra, perhaps. It isn't even too awful for typesetting, as long as the report isn't due in an hour and you don't mind wasting paper along the way. It is, of course, impossible for fuel injection and other process-control systems to run in batch mode. The car will not wait for the answer.

Interactive applications such as spreadsheets must also respond in real time, but humans are far more flexible than unconscious physical processes such as combustion. Because of the tradeoffs among such factors as execution speed, cost, and program clarity (necessary for debugging), as well as the often critical nature of the mission (such as keeping the airplane in the air, or ensuring that the car doesn't leap forward when you change gears), process-control software is constraining and demanding to create.

### Military and Aerospace Systems

The most ambitious of digital systems, however, those that push the technology to (or beyond) the limit, are those built by the military. The most extreme example of this, of course, is the Strategic Defense Initiative (SDI), a.k.a. Star Wars. The proposal to cover the United States with a "nuclear umbrella" was the single most expensive project ever seriously proposed by someone in a position to do something about it.[33] It was also probably the least understood by its proposer. In a nutshell, SDI proposed a system that would:

- identify, track, and shoot down targets of unknown ballistic characteristics;

- use sensors whose characteristics were initially unknown and would change as the system develops;

- use weapons whose characteristics were initially unknown and would change as the system develops;

- be computed by machines vulnerable to electronic countermeasures as well as the usual system glitches;

- be executed within a time frame that allows no one to intervene; and

- be put into service without the opportunity for a meaningful system test.[34]

But SDI is an extreme case. A fair amount of the hardware and software that the military dreams up gets implemented and used. Some even proves useful, although the military often exaggerates on this point, as the aftermath of the Gulf War demonstrated.[35] Certain high-tech weapons, such as the laser-guided bombs, got rave reviews from the Pentagon for their accuracy. Similarly, the radar-evading stealth technology incorporated into the F117A fighter jets may have played a role in allowing the United States to fly over and bomb Iraq without being detected, tracked, or shot at. Stealth technology is a function of the aircraft shape and the materials of which it is made, and does not use much software directly, but the aircraft could not have been designed without computers. However, a number of the most successful weapons, such as the A10 and the B-52 airplanes, were not particularly high-tech. And some of the high-tech stuff wasn't particularly useful. For example, the Iraqis built decoy tanks and missile launchers from wood, canvas, and paint, and fooled the spy satellites. The Tomahawk cruise missiles (which rely on software for guidance and target recognition), at $1.3 million each, were also disappointing; 18 percent failed to launch or crashed on the first day they were used.[36] And a recent Israeli report suggests that "[t]he Patriot air defense missile system may have been responsible for more damage and casualties than it prevented . . . less damage might have been done if Iraqi *Scud* missiles had been allowed to fall."[37]

The military's lust for the latest and highest technology functionally underwrites a fair amount of the development costs for many commercial systems. For example, the digital flight control systems in the latest commercial jets could not have been developed without the years of experience with fly-by-wire controls provided by the F8, the F16, the Northrop YF-23, and other military jet fighters and helicopters. The communication satellites we now use for telephone and television rely on technology developed for the space program.

Satellites used for reconnaissance, navigation, and communications all require software. They also require rockets to get them into orbit in the first place, and the rockets need software, such as for the flight plan that went awry at the first *Mariner* launching. Such rockets have boosted a long string of unmanned space explorers on their ways, such as *Galileo, Voyager, Viking,* and *Magellan,* to name just a few. Many scientists feel that the unmanned space missions have been the most successful and cost-effective space science we have accomplished. *Voyager,* in particular, stunned the scientific community with its never-say-die performance, sending back pictures of Neptune years after its creators imagined it would be defunct.

In the summer of 1990, *Magellan* arrived at Venus for the purpose of mapping its surface. About 1 percent of its data was lost, however, because of a bug that caused the spacecraft intermittently to lose contact with the earth. It took NASA engineers almost a year to fix the bug, and then they radioed the corrected version of the software to the craft. Actually, what took them so long was not fixing it, but reproducing it in their *Magellan* duplicate on earth so they could determine how to fix it. And a second error had to manifest itself before they managed to reproduce the problem.

*Magellan* has two computers. Each time the first experienced its problem, the engineers were able to use the second to start the first one over again. In doing so, however, they erased its memory, and with it all traces of the problem. During the successful laboratory re-creation of the bug, the memory of the first computer was not erased—a flaw in the system's fault-protection. They were then finally able to determine what had been going wrong.[38]

But *Magellan's* two computers are nothing to the space shuttle's *five.* Why does the space shuttle need five computers? Well, technically, it doesn't. The shuttle can fly with only one computer. But if that computer failed at the wrong time, the orbiter and all on board would be lost. The "fail-operational/fail-safe" system avoids disaster thus.[39]

One computer can perform all the functions required for a shuttle mission. But if it fails, a backup computer is needed. Furthermore, the backup computer must already be running, aware of the mission status, and ready to take over instantly. After all, reentering the atmosphere (for example) is no time to have to initialize the system. So the backup computer must monitor the primary computer.

But if you have two computers monitoring each other, and one of them disagrees with the other, how can you tell which is correct and which in error? In order to determine which computer is wrong, you need at least three computers. This allows a process called *voting*. Just as in human elections, the majority wins; the computer that disagrees with the other two is presumed to be the one with the problem. Of course, just as in human elections, it is possible that the minority is right, and that two computers have failed in the same way. But you have to make some assumptions, and the official procedure assumes that identical failures are less likely, and that the minority computer is wrong. It is then taken off-line, leaving the other two to back each other up. So three computers constitute an officially "safe" system.

If three computers are required for a safe system, then in order to allow for a "fail-safe" failure, you need four computers. (In fact, it isn't just computers—the space shuttle has four of everything, one way or another.) Four computers constitute an "operational" system.

But how unlikely is it, *really*, that two computers fail in the same manner? Since the four computers are identical, and run identical software, it's possible that they might all suffer from the same flaw. Therefore NASA charged a completely different organization to develop an entirely different computer system that could perform all the necessary functions. Hence the fifth computer. The four computers run software developed by the IBM Federal Systems Division in Houston, Texas. Rockwell International of Downey, California, developed the software for the fifth.

The safety features added complexity. Complexity causes problems. You will come to recognize this theme. The fifth computer, in the full glare of publicity, postponed the first launch for hours when it could not be synchronized with the others. The bug had been there for years, waiting to happen. For a variety of reasons, it was unlikely to occur during simulations, but was likely to delay the first launch.

## UNRELIABLE SYSTEMS, UNMET DESIRES

As a society, we have our strengths. Most houses have electricity and indoor plumbing, most roads are in pretty good shape, and the bridges ordinarily don't fall. (Well, there was that one on the Connecticut Turnpike.) People sometimes suggest that the problems suffered by digital systems are so extensive because we have been building them for so short a time. We've been building physical systems such as roads and bridges for centuries, the argument runs. When we first started, doubtless people experienced this same level of failure and frustration.

This theory is hard to test, if only because it's impossible to remember a time when we didn't know *something* about, for example, building bridges. But we do have a good historical and photographic record of the process of learning to build bridges from concrete, chiefly as documented in the life, work, and passion of a Swiss engineer named Robert Maillart (1872–1940).[40] In fact, the first bridges to be built of this new material developed cracks after a few years, but they didn't come crashing down. By the end of his life, Maillart had learned how to engineer such bridges reliably. Many of them are still in use in Switzerland today. His later bridges are not only sturdy and reliable, they are graceful and beautiful as well.

The software industry hasn't fared so well. Before the end of the 1990's, we will be able to celebrate the golden anniversary of developing commercial software. In 1968, at a NATO Conference on Software Engineering, software professionals coined the term "the Software Crisis" to describe the difficulties they were having in building reliable systems.[41] Since then, a lot of books and papers have been written about it, and a lot of seminars with titles such as "Managing Complexity" have been held. The crisis itself will soon be celebrating its silver anniversary.

This isn't the way we thought it was going to be. We once had a far more optimistic view of our ability to build and maintain complex systems. This view is nicely illustrated by two science fiction stories written about sixty years ago. They purport to describe two opposite events—the computer that crashes and the one that doesn't. Yet they both describe systems far more ambitious than any we could now hope to build, maintained for far longer than we could ever dream of. And as we shall see, they have other things in common as well.

### The Machines Will Take Care of Us
The first story, "Twilight," was written by the patron saint of modern science fiction, John W. Campbell, Jr. It was first published in 1936.

In "Twilight," a time traveler visits a city somewhere on earth in the far future. He finds no one—the population of the earth is now considerably diminished, and whole cities have been abandoned. Nevertheless, in an inspirational display of system robustness and reliability, the machines are up and running:

*I don't know how long that city had been deserted. Some of the men from the other cities said it was a hundred and fifty thousand years. . . . The taxi machine was in perfect condition, functioned at once. It was clean, and the city was clean and orderly. I saw a restaurant and I was hungry. . . .* [42]

The protagonist eats the millennia-old food, which is still wholesome, and cruises around the city in the taxi. In true Campbell fashion, he stops next at a subterranean level to watch the machinery:

*The entire lower block of the city was given over to the machines. Thousands. But most of them seemed idle, or, at most, running under light load. I recognized a telephone apparatus, and not a single signal came through. There was no life in the city. Yet when I pressed a little stud beside the screen on one side of the room, the machine began working instantly.*

(By the way, that phone system has an excellent user interface. Campbell's hero knows exactly which button starts the system, despite missing millions of years of cultural history. Likewise, will those engineers who worked on the taxi service please call their offices? Raytheon, Boeing, the Bank of New York . . . they'd all like to talk to you.)

But Campbell's man doesn't stay forever down among the machines:

*Finally I went up to the top of the city, the upper level. It was a paradise.*

*There were shrubs and trees and parks, glowing in the soft light that they had learned to make in the very air. They had learned it five million years or more before. Two million years ago they forgot. But the machines didn't, and they were still making it.* [43]

It should be evident by now that a system that can operate for five million years, maintaining itself without human help for two million years, is simply miraculous. But it's a fruitless miracle. The machines still function, but the people can hardly manage to. They are declining, energies sapped, vision spent, victims of their success.

"The men knew how to die, and be dead, but the machines didn't," Campbell wrote sadly.

### The Machines Won't Take Care of Us

In 1928, E. M. Forster, a writer of deeper insight, wrote a wonderful tale of system breakdown called, "The Machine Stops." The story depicts a society in which each person lives in a small underground room. All needs and wants are furnished by "the Machine," so there is no need ever to leave one's room. The Machine provides ventilation, plumbing, food and drink, movable furniture, music, and literature. Secondhand, machine-mediated experiences of all kinds are universally available through a worldwide multimedia communication network. Automated manufacturing and transportation systems provide a stunning array of commodities. This has gone on for so long that people remember no other life; they are utterly dependent; even breakdowns have been repaired automatically by the "mending apparatus."

However, one day the Machine begins to disfigure its musical renditions with "curious gasping sighs." Soon thereafter, the fruit gets moldy; the bath water starts to stink, the poetry suffers from defective rhymes. One day beds fail to appear when sleepy people summon them. Finally:

> *It became difficult to read. A blight entered the atmosphere and dulled its luminosity. At times Vashti could scarcely see across her room. The air, too, was foul. Loud were the complaints, impotent the remedies, heroic the tone of the lecturer as he cried, "Courage, courage! What matter so long as the Machine goes on? To it the darkness and the light are one." And though things improved again after a time, the old brilliancy was never recaptured, and humanity never recovered from its entrance into twilight.*[44]

Ultimately, the Machine breaks down completely, and with it, the entire society on which it is based. But on the earth's surface, homeless, half-barbaric rebels still live. Humanity is not wholly lost, after all.

Forster's story may seem to take a more modern, skeptical view of technology, but both stories assume a degree of reliability and robustness far beyond anything we can seriously imagine achieving. We build systems representing only a tiny fraction of this size and complexity, and they break all the time.

### Either Way, We Won't Like It

The point is not, however, that Forster or Campbell were lousy futurists. Everyone is a lousy futurist; Real Life™ is too chaotic, complex, and rich in detail to predict. These writers' concern is not accurate prediction, but the human soul; their stories are about our primal yearning to be cared for.

The temptation to make machines our caretakers is a modern form of a basic human desire. These stories warn of the consequences of succumbing to this temptation: we lose touch with our natures. Our bodies continue living, but our souls die.

The scenarios are far-fetched, but the warning isn't. The urge to let the machines take care of us is still with us; software, we feel, can do it. Software is flexible, it responds to us, it adapts to the situation. The digital systems we are now building really were unimaginably complex just a decade ago. Some of them perform functions that have never before been performed, because they could be accomplished no other way. With the advent of digital systems, we seem at last to be on the verge of building machines big and complicated and smart enough to take care of things. This is an illusion.

Digital systems are capable of a lot of flexibility. Many are even capable of reasonable robustness. They can add a lot to our lives. But they are not 100 percent reliable, nor will they become so in the foreseeable future. Of course, perfection isn't always required. It's nice to get a weather report, even if you know you can't count on it. But nothing less than perfection will do for running a nuclear power plant; the consequences of even a small failure could be just too disastrous.

Of all the software we rely on daily, none of it is bug-free. It's natural to want the machines to take care of us. But it isn't wise. As we'll see in the next chapter, it is not in the nature of software to be bug-free.

## NOTES

1 Ceruzzi, Paul. *Beyond the Limits: Flight Enters the Computer Age.* Cambridge, MA: MIT Press, 1989, pp. 202–3.

2 Andrews, Edmund L. "String of Phone Failures Perplexes Companies and U.S. Investigators." *New York Times,* July 3, 1991. "Theories Narrowed in Phone Inquiry." *New York Times,* July 4, 1991, p. 10. Markoff, John. "Small Company Scrutinized in U.S. Phone Breakdowns." *New York Times,* July 5, 1991, p. C7. Andrews, E. "Computer Maker Says Flaw in Software Caused Phone Disruptions." *New York Times,* July 10, 1991, p. A10. Rankin, Robert E. "Telephone Failures Alarming." *Oregonian,* July 11, 1991, p. A13. *Science News* "Phone glitches and software bugs," Aug. 24, 1991, p. 127. Also, *comp.risks,* 12:2, 5, 6, and more.

3 Carroll, Paul B. "Painful Birth: Creating New Software Was Agonizing Task for Mitch Kapor Firm." *The Wall Street Journal,* May 11, 1990, pp. A1, A5.

4 What I see when I turn on my computer (a Macintosh, as you may have guessed) and open a few windows. Many of you have already guessed that my desktop is showing me *comp.risks* archives. Thank you again, Peter G. Neumann, for the incomparable service this forum provides.

5 Murray, Charles, and Catherine Bly Cox. *Apollo: The Race to the Moon.* New York: Simon and Schuster, 1989, pp. 344–55. The quote is from p. 344. The story and additional analysis can be found in Ceruzzi, *op. cit.* pp. 212–218.

6 Hughes, David. "Tracking Software Error Likely Reason Patriot Battery Failed to Engage Scud," *Aviation Week and Space Technology,* June 10, 1991, pp. 25–6.

7 Schwartz, John. "Consumer Enemy No. 1" and "The Whistle-Blower Who Set TRW Straight." *Newsweek,* Oct. 28, 1991, pp. 42 and 47. Miller, Michael W. "Credit-Report Firms Face Greater Pressure; Ask Norwich, Vt., Why." *The Wall Street Journal,* Sept. 23, 1991, pp. A1 and A5. Also reported in *comp.risks,* 12:14, Aug. 19, 1991.

8 Berry, John M. "Computer Snarled N.Y. Bank: $32 Billion Overdraft Resulted From Snafu," *Washington Post,* Dec. 13, 1985, p. D7, as reported in *comp.risks,* 1:31, Dec. 19, 1985. Zweig, Phillip L. and Allanna Sullivan. "A Computer Snafu Snarls the Handling of Treasury Issues." *Wall Street Journal,* Nov. 25, 1985, reprinted in *Software En-*

*gineering Notes,* 11:1, Jan. 1986, p. 3–4. Also Hopcroft, John E. and Dean B. Krafft. "Toward better computer science." IEEE *Spectrum,* Dec. 1987, pp. 58–60.

9 *comp.risks,* 13:56 and 58, Jun. 9 and 15, 1992. Items contributed by Daniel McKay, to whom thanks is due for his thorough reporting and thoughtful analysis.

10 Jacky, Jonathan. "Programmed for Disaster: Software Errors That Imperil Lives." *The Sciences,* Sept./Oct. 1989, pp. 22ff; Also "Inside Risks: Risks in Medical Electronics." *Communications of the ACM,* 33:12, Dec., 1990, p. 136; also personal communication, Seattle, WA, Jan. 14, 1991. An excellent and thorough technical report covering all aspects of the subject is: Leveson, Nancy G., and Clark S. Turner. "An Investigation of the Therac-25 Accidents." Univ. of Washington Technical Report #92-11-05 (also UCI TR #92-108), Nov. 1992.

11 Forester, Tom, and Perry Morrison. *Computer Ethics: Cautionary Tales and Ethical Dilemmas in Computing.* Cambridge, MA: MIT Press, 1990, p. 75; also, *New York Times* Science section, July 29, 1986, p. C1.

12 Fitzgerald, Karen. "Faults and Failures: Ferry Electronics Out of Control." IEEE *Spectrum,* 27:2, Feb., 1990, p. 54.

13 "When GM's robots ran amok." *The Economist,* August 10, 1991, p. 64–65.

14 Forester and Morrison, *op. cit.* p. 73.

15 To modify memory is to *write* on it. To access memory is to *read* it. If memory can be accessed but not modified, it cannot be written on—hence the term *read-only.*

16 "User interface" is a classically engineer-centered term. The engineer is building a system that requires inputs from its user. Her or his task is to make it clear when inputs can be accepted, what inputs are expected, and what effect they will have. The term "user interface" refers to the portion of the system that presents this information to the user and accepts the input. It is an interface between the user and the system— that is, the "real" system, the part that doesn't have to deal with the user. Dealing with the user is a necessary nuisance. Hmmph.

17 A number of articles have recently lamented how hard it is to use software-related products. For example, Nussbaum, Bruce, and Robert Neff, et al. "I Can't Work This Thing!" *Business Week,* April 29, 1991, pp. 58–66. Although the article focuses on difficult user interfaces in consumer electronics, it could apply to an enormous variety of commercial and military digital systems as well. (For example, the Therac-25 discussed earlier had a clumsy user interface that unfortunately tended to increase the likelihood of one fatal error.) The letters to the editor section of the May 20, 1991, *Business Week* contains many interesting and rather emotional responses to the article. A similar article appeared in *Newsweek.* Rogers, Michael. "The Right Button: Why machines are getting harder and harder to use." *Newsweek,* Jan. 7, 1991, pp. 46–7. See also Neumann, Peter G. "Inside Risks: Putting on Your Best Interface." *Communications of the ACM,* 34:3, March 1991, p. 138. A wonderful book by Donald Norman, entitled *The Design of Everyday Things* (previously published under the title *The Psychology of Everyday Things*)—New York: Doubleday, 1988—ought to be required reading for every working designer and student of design. It is full of insight and examples, both good and bad.

18 Augusta Ada Byron, Countess of Lovelace, was the world's first computer programmer, daughter of the poet Lord Byron, and a close friend of Charles Babbage, the world's first computer designer, for whose machines she wrote programs. Sadly, Babbage kept having "a better idea" and abandoned each of his designs before it reached a functional state. Therefore, Lovelace's programs never had a real machine to run on.

19 Adam, John A. "Fixes to Aegis system recommended by Navy," *The Institute* (news supplement to IEEE *Spectrum*) 12:11, Nov. 1988, pp. 1–2. Also discussed in *comp.risks,* 7:16, 17, 67, and 9:67.

20 Terms proliferate to describe the process of making software, and the people who do it. Software is written (the literary metaphor), built (the construction metaphor), coded (the cryptographic metaphor). This work is done by computer programmers, software engineers, or systems analysts. The past decade has seen the rise of the term "software engineer" as part political statement, part mantra: the design of a software system is like the design of a bridge; we know how to do it; we are engineers following established rules. It isn't; we don't; we aren't. These are scary truths for us all—makers, buyers, and users of the system. It is only human to want to deny it.

Software professionals are also not immune to the human desire for advancement, and the craving for a grander job title. Thus it is that those who work with IBM systems have for years started out as programmers and advanced to systems analysts. "Programmers" are those lowly drones who crank out the code they are told to. "Systems analysts" are supposed to be the ones who do the telling—they see the big picture, they design the whole system of which each programmer makes only a part. Non-IBM worlds inherit this definition of "programmer," sometimes to such an extent that they don't employ any! Instead they hire "software engineers," a more egalitarian term that can apply to everyone, from the drone writing a small piece to the designer of the whole system. The difference between plain old computer programming and serious, professional software engineering is discussed in greater detail in Chapters 3 and 4.

21 For several more examples, Neumann, Peter G. "Inside Risks: Aggravation by Life, Death, and Taxes." *Communications of the ACM*, 35:7 July, 1992, p. 122.

22 If you want to know, you can find out. It will cost you $15 per report, possibly less. The three largest credit-reporting agencies are: TRW (P.O. Box 5450, Orange, CA 92667), 714-991-5100; Equifax (5505 Peachtree Dunwoody, Suite 600, Atlanta, GA 30358), 404-252-1134; and Trans Union Corporation Consumer Relations Dept. (P.O. Box 119001, Chicago, IL 60611); 312-645-6008.

Other credit bureaus exist locally. If you send two dollars to the Bankcard Holders of America (560 Herndon Parkway Suite 120, Herndon, VA 22070), they will send you a kit including the name, address, and phone numbers of other credit-reporting agencies across the country.

23 *comp.risks*, 1:35, Jan. 5, 1986.

24 "Lotus—New program spurs fear privacy could be undermined." *The Wall Street Journal*, Nov. 13, 1990, p. B1. Copious discussion in many computer bulletin boards, including *comp.risks*, fueled the campaign to withdraw the product. *cf. comp.risks*, 10:61, 62, 63, 68, 79, from Nov. 16, 1990 through Jan. 23, 1991. A follow-up *Wall Street Journal* article of Jan. 23, 1991, announced the product's withdrawal.

25 Schwartz, John. "How Did They Get My Name?" *Newsweek*, June 3, 1991, pp. 40–42.

26 "Miser held in record Social Security fraud." UPI, Aug. 31, 1991. Extracted in *comp.risks*, 12:23, Sept. 4, 1991.

27 "Agents rankle airlines with fare-checking programs." *The Wall Street Journal*, May 20, 1991, p. B1. Also *comp.risks*, 11:70, May 22, 1991.

28 *New York Times*, Aug. 13, 1985, as reported in *comp.risks* 1:2, Aug. 28, 1985.

29 Dr. Robert Beck, Biomedical Instructional Computing Center, address to Software Association of Oregon, Beaverton, Oregon, June 28, 1991.

30 For these statistics and other information, I am indebted to Mr. William C. Kloos, P.E., Signal Systems Manager, Bureau of Traffic Management for the City of Portland Office of Transportation. Personal communication, Aug. 22, 1991.

31 Stroll through the largest supermarket you can find. Walk up and down each aisle. The air is fresh and, if they know what they're doing, smells appetizing; music plays softly; the displays are colorful and appealing. In its way, it is grander than a palace. A

supermarket chain is a gargantuan, ambitious, and more or less successful creation of the twentieth century. Too bad you can't bury an entire Safeway, Thriftway, or A&P in a time capsule.

32 Stix, Gary. "Along for the Ride?" *Scientific American,* July 1991, pp. 94–106.

In the Airbus A320, the pilot has direct control, unmediated by software, over pitch using the trimmable horizontal stabilizer, and direction using the rudder. It is unclear whether these controls alone are adequate to fly the airplane in the event of a total computer systems failure.

33 See, for example, the September 1985 issue of IEEE *Spectrum,* which is devoted to SDI.

34 For this analysis I am indebted to David L. Parnas, in his lucid, thorough, and closely reasoned article "Software Aspects of Strategic Defense Systems," in *American Scientist,* 73:5, Sept./Oct. 1985, pp. 432–40. Also published in *Communications of the ACM,* 28:12, Dec. 1985, pp. 1326–35. This article is technical, but it is also highly readable. Dr. Parnas is not an uncritical dove; he has a long career of doing research for the military. He was appointed to the SDIO Panel on Computing in Support of Battle Management, and the paper is his letter of resignation from it.

35 Gannon, Bill. "Evaluations kick sand into military might." *Oregonian,* Sept. 8, 1991, pp. A5–6.

36 Schwartz, John, et al. "The Mind of a Missile." *Newsweek,* Feb. 18, 1991, pp. 40–43.

37 Bill Gannon, *op.cit.*

38 Sawyer, Kathy. "Magellan 'bug' killed by NASA." *Oregonian,* Aug. 18, 1991, p. A16.

39 Garman, John R. "The 'Bug' Heard 'Round the World." *Software Engineering Notes,* 6:5, Oct., 1981, pp. 3–10.

40 See Billington, David P. *Robert Maillart's Bridges: The Art of Engineering.* Princeton, N.J.: Princeton University Press, 1989.

41 Dijkstra, Edsger W. "Programming Considered as a Human Activity" in *Classics in Software Engineering,* Edward Yourdon, ed. New York: Yourdon Press, 1979, pp. 3–9.

42 "Twilight" John W. Campbell, copyright 1934 by Street and Smith Publications, Inc. First published in February 1935 *Astounding Stories,* and reprinted in *The Best of John W. Campbell.* Garden City, N.Y.: Doubleday, Inc., 1976, pp. 28–29.

43 *ibid.*

44 Forster, E. M. "The Machine Stops." From *The Eternal Moment and Other Stories,* Orlando, Fla.: Harcourt Brace Jovanovich, Inc., 1928.

# CHAPTER 2

# WHY
# DOES
# SOFTWARE
# HAVE BUGS ?

We didn't
mean to, but in software
we have created the first artifact that exhibits
the human duality of
body and soul.

The soul of software is invisible, intangible, silent, weightless, deaf, mute, blind, paralyzed. Like a soul, too, it is complex and hard to understand. It is a structure of logical symbols organized in a framework according to someone's model of some aspect of the world. How do you visualize the invisible? How do you grasp the intangible? How do you hear the silent?

But software also has a body. To be good for something, software must be part of a physical system that can affect some part of the world. The processor incorporates its enormous capacity for arithmetic and Boolean logic. Its sensory organs are keyboard, mouse, or touch pad. Its expressive organs are a display screen, a printer, or perhaps a robotic gripper. And being part of a physical system means being prey to the ills that technology is heir to. Machines break, overheat, get wet, kicked, or dusty; sensors provide flaky readings, or none at all; the printer jams; electromagnetic radiation invades the system with spurious electrons.

Software has bugs because it is made of logic. Such structures are abstract, complex, and outside our direct experience.

Software has bugs because it is used to accomplish something. It is therefore part of a physical system, vulnerable to the vagaries of the environment.

## STUFF OF LOGIC

If software is so unreliable, why do we use so much of it? What is it really good for?

Software can structure enormous amounts of data. By applying some energy, we can extract a fair amount of information from that data. We can find a cheaper way to manufacture something; we can learn more about wind shear at airports; we can match a fingerprint, perhaps while it still matters; maybe we can even learn why so many species of frogs are suddenly dying.[1]

It confers unparalleled flexibility on the structures we build. With that flexibility, we can do astounding things. We can ask the question a different way each time, building imaginary worlds by the millions, each one different. (This is the big appeal of many computer games; rumor has it, for example, that Bud Clark, esteemed former mayor of Portland, Oregon, favors playing SimCity, a game in which the player imagines him- or herself to be the mayor of a city.) You can ask practical, powerful questions: if I spend $50,000 to make a new mold for this part, will it save money in the end? Does anything special happen before an earthquake? Wnat do ozone readings from the upper atmosphere show? How about compared to last year, and the year before that, and the year before that?

Software allows otherwise unimaginable enterprises. Landing a man on the moon is the obvious example, but we should not lose our wonder at such feats as the system that distributes millions of different items to millions of different outlets over entire continents. Or present levels of stock exchange transactions, telephone calls, global banking funds transfers, or commercial air traffic. Such accomplishments are amazing.

The flip side of flexibility, though, is unpredictability. The more different things *might* happen, the less you can say about what *will* happen. The more flexible a system gets, the more complexity its programmers must master and encode in a logical structure.

Logic is the stuff that software is made of. At its heart, therefore, software is:

• invisible, abstract, and discontinuous;

• unconstrained by common sense or physical laws.

These characteristics are responsible for the benefits of digital systems; they are also responsible for their difficulties. Since the same characteristics are responsible for both, bugs are unlikely to go away soon.

### Invisible, Abstract, Discontinuous

Even if you buy a computer with rows of blinking lights across the front panel, watching software execute is less exciting than watching the grass grow. It is not a visual experience. If you could watch the processor with microscope eyes that were sensitive to radiation of the right frequencies, it might look like a time-lapse movie of the entire North American freeway system at night, including all the interchanges in great detail.[2] It might be pretty. It would not mean a lot to you.

What's visible about software is the effect it has on something else. If two thoroughly different programs have the same observable effects, you cannot tell which one has executed. If a given portion of a program has no observable effects, then you have no way of knowing if it is executing, if it has finished, if it got part way through and then stopped, or if it produced "the right answer." Programmers nearly always must rely on highly indirect measures to determine what happens when their programs execute. This is one reason why debugging is so difficult.[3]

This opacity is why the Bank of New York suffered the $5 million software error discussed in the previous chapter. In all likelihood, the programmers responsible were neither negligent nor careless. It is a commonplace story even for an experienced and professional outfit. They almost certainly went to great pains to get it right, but the fact is that any programmer who has worked on any piece of software larger than a Pascal homework assignment can provide dozens of examples of errors that were unforeseen, hard to understand, and hard to fix.

The computer system was composed of several pieces; one piece was the messaging system. When a transaction arrived from outside the bank, the bank's processing system might or might not be able to deal with it right away. Since you cannot predict when a message might arrive, it is not realistic to design a system that must handle each transaction the moment it arrives. Instead, the messaging system received and stored incoming messages in an electronic in-basket, available for processing when the processing system could handle them. (This might be only a few seconds after they arrived, but you still don't want a few seconds' worth of transactions spilling all over the floor every minute.)

The messaging system is complex in its own right. One of its components was a counter—a part of a program that keeps track of how many there are of something, or of how many times something has happened. The counter could hold 16 bits, meaning that it could count up to $2^{16}$, or 65,536. Unfortunately, another part of the program thought it could hold 32 bits, and could therefore count up to $2^{32}$, or 4,294,967,296. Who knows why this was not discovered earlier? Perhaps it took particularly heavy trading for the bug to manifest itself. Perhaps another part of the software experienced an earlier problem. It is entirely likely that no one ever found the answer to that question. In any case, the database holding the messages became "corrupted"—meaning that the information it contained could not be presumed to be correct anymore. In fact, it was not correct.[4]

What happens when software executes often depends on what happened previously. Logic provides the mechanism for capturing these dependencies. For example, a typical if-then-else statement allows the program to choose between two future courses of action, depending upon what just happened: did the processor send a busy signal? If not, give it the message. If so, send the message to the in-basket instead.

Some of these dependencies are designed-in, such as the one above. They are analogous to the chord changes of a folk song, designed in sequences like C F G C; the chord you play depends on the one you previously played.

But some of these dependencies are not designed-in. They are errors, like the unpracticed instrumentalist whose fingers never quite stretch all the way from *this* note to *that* one. But when you hear a wrong note, it's obvious, whereas dependencies in the software can be deeply hidden and hard to spot. The person who decided to make that counter a 16-bit number almost certainly did not realize that the counter would be used by whichever piece of software it was that sent it the number that was too high. The piece of the program that emitted the high number could have been written years after the piece containing the 16-bit register. When the 16-bit register was produced, 16 bits might have been the only choice. Having functioned correctly for years, the register had long since been forgotten; the programmer who coded it long since departed. On most days, perhaps, the numbers don't get up high enough to overflow the 16-bit register, anyway.

Ultimately, the computer holds nothing but zeroes and ones in a certain configuration. A zero isn't even a "0"—it just means that the voltage is lower than a specified threshold.[5] The "1," of course, is really a voltage over that threshold. When the software executes, some values change.[6] You can therefore imagine an 8-bit register in a computer as a sequence of eight ones or zeroes, as shown in Figure 2–1.

What does a zero mean in the leftmost position of a register? What does it mean in the rightmost position? What about over here, in this memory location instead? Depending on where it is, it could mean anything.

| 0 | 1 | 1 | 0 | 0 | 0 | 0 | 1 |
|---|---|---|---|---|---|---|---|

**Figure 2-1.** Zeroes and Ones Peacefully Residing in an 8-bit Register

For example, suppose you are writing a letter using a word processing program on your personal computer. Depending on where it is found, a value of "1" could mean:

- Color this pixel on the display white.
- Yes, go ahead and double-space this paragraph.
- The user just asked to save this file.
- Print only one copy of this letter.
- It could even represent the difference between a lowercase "a" and an exclamation point (!), as shown in Figure 2–2.

A value of "1" can, in fact, mean just about anything, depending on where it is and how the program is structured. What a high voltage represents is essentially an arbitrary decision.

The telephone network failures of late June and early July 1991 demonstrate the problem. By some accounts, all those failures occurred because a "6" was typed instead of a "D."[7] Those characters represent hexadecimal (base 16) numbers; in binary notation, this means that a number that should have been 0110 became 1101. In a file that contained millions of bits (probably at least tens of millions), three of them should have been different—and phone networks toppled. It may be counterintuitive that such a small error could have such massive effects, but with software, you simply cannot tell which errors are the small ones.

This arbitrariness is what makes digital information interchangeable; it is comparatively easy to integrate systems that all use the same representations for information. But such representations must necessarily be highly abstract. The abstract nature of software can make its meaning difficult to grasp.

Discontinuity is another troublesome aspect of software that results from its nature as a structure of logic. The concept of continuity, as we are using it here, is abstract and mathematical, but it is neither exotic

| 0 | 0 | 1 | 0 | 0 | 0 | 0 | 1 |   !
|---|---|---|---|---|---|---|---|

| 0 | 1 | 1 | 0 | 0 | 0 | 0 | 1 |   a
|---|---|---|---|---|---|---|---|

**Figure 2-2.** Binary Code for the ASCII Characters ! and a

nor difficult to understand. It means that changes to inputs produce cor-
responding changes to outputs. In other words, if the input to a system
doesn't change, then neither will its output. When the inputs change a
little, the outputs change a little. When the inputs change a lot, so do
the outputs. For example, the gas pedal in an older car is mechanically
linked to a spring, which is linked, in turn, to a throttle that permits gas
to flow into the engine. If there is no pressure on the gas pedal, the
throttle permits only enough gas to flow for the engine to idle. A small
amount of pressure on the pedal opens the throttle a little bit more, and
lets a bit more gas through. A lot of pressure on the pedal opens the
throttle a lot, and lets a lot of gas through. This system can be graphed
by a continuous line, as in Figure 2-3.

Mathematicians call these things *continuous functions* because a graph
of the function continues without gap. (Of course, the graph of the function ceases abruptly at the point at which the accelerator is pressed to
the floor and the throttle is wide open and the siren wails behind you,
but between zero and that point, the function is continuous.)

Continuity is a property of many familiar physical systems: The fire
burns hotter when we give it more oxygen; the ax bites deeper when we
strike with more force; the needle points to a higher number when we
place more weight on the scale. The fact that software lacks continuity
may be its most confusing and unfamiliar characteristic. We are accus-
tomed to interacting with continuous systems. But change the input to
software in the smallest possible way—change just one "1" to a "0"—
and major changes can happen.

Such discontinuities can be startling. For example, let's revisit the digital fuel injection system. Suppose that the system reads the pressure on
the accelerator and converts it to a 7-bit number. This means that the
system can distinguish between $2^7 = 128$ levels of pressure on the accel-

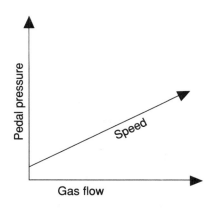

**Figure 2-3.**
A Simple Continuous
Function—Stepping on
the Gas

erator—accurate enough for the purpose, certainly. Now imagine the driver pressing very slightly on the accelerator. This slight pressure should be represented by the number 00000011—the binary notation for "3."

But let's say that because of electromagnetic interference from someone's cellular phone, the seventh bit flips from 0 to 1. The number is now 01000011—the binary notation for "67."

The chip inside the engine has no way of saying, "Gee, that's odd. We just jumped from 3 to 67 with no intermediate values. There's very little pressure on the accelerator. I doubt the driver *really* wants me to accelerate that much. Maybe I'd better ask." No, the throttle opens wide, spurts fuel, and the car lurches forward. The graph of pedal pressure against gas flow (Figure 2-4) now shows a discontinuity.

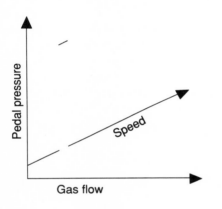

**Figure 2-4.**
A Discontinuous Function
Made Possible by Digital
Fuel Injection

## Unconstrained by Common Sense or Physical Laws

A lot of the predictability of the world comes from knowing that physical laws will be obeyed, because physical laws greatly constrain the sorts of things that can happen. Bridge builders must know the strength and rigidity of the material they are using, the length of the abyss they must span, and the characteristics of the earth in which they will anchor their structure. They do not have to worry about what will happen when gravity is turned off.

Fred Brooks, a pioneer in the field of software engineering, has pointed this out: "Einstein argued that there must be simplified explanations of nature, because God is not capricious or arbitrary. No such faith comforts the software engineer."[8]

Imagine, for example, that you are a programmer working on a program to allow a personal computer to simulate a piano. To produce the notes, you have a synthesizer capable of making almost any sound you can imagine—you can independently control the pitch, timbre, loudness, and all other characteristics of the sound.

You want the pitch to change when the user touches different "piano keys," but the timbre must remain constant. Your program will define the piano's timbre once, and prevent all the relevant parameters from changing, thus precluding all others. Real pianos don't have to be told to maintain their timbres; they can't help it. A software piano, however, could conceivably suddenly start to sound like a cello, if the program were clumsy enough, or if the electronics were flaky. Software knows nothing about real-world physical constraints.

Its ignorance of physical constraints can be a strength as well as a weakness. You can play more interesting tricks than turning a piano into a cello. A fascinating disc called *Secrets of Synthesis*[9] explores the idea of *hybrid timbres:* in sections made possible purely by digital technology, Wendy Carlos plays the bowed piano and a cello struck with piano hammers. The instruments sound completely convincing. Exploring alternate realities is definitely one of the things software is good for.

Software has no knowledge of the real world—nothing we term "common sense." Therefore you can take nothing for granted where software is concerned. When the physical coupling between the gas pedal and the fuel throttle has been replaced by a symbolic one—a digital one—the built-in physical constraint against discontinuous behavior is gone, and must be replaced by an explicit artificial constraint.

To constrain an event, however, one must foresee it. Numerous systems misbehave because the designer did not foresee a contingency. For example, early versions of the navigation software written for the F16 caused the jet to flip when it crossed the equator. Fortunately, no pilots had to tear through the sky upside-down unless they wanted to; this bug appeared in a simulation and was caught and corrected before the airplane ever flew.[10] In spite of all the stories I'm telling you, a lot of bugs are caught and corrected while building a system. It's just that even more happen later.

Here is one situation that was not foreseen by the system designers. In August 1983, United Air Lines Flight 310 from Los Angeles, a Boeing 767, was approaching the Denver airport on a computer-controlled descent. The computer was programmed to conserve as much fuel as possible, so it slowed the engines to the minimum rate that would have been safe under normal conditions. But the plane was flying through a storm. It was cold, and the engines ran so slow and cool that they were unable to prevent ice from forming on them. When ice accumulates on a jet engine, it interferes with the flow of air and the engine overheats. The ice caused both engines to fail this way, and the passengers enjoyed a four-minute powerless glide before the pilots could restart the engines.[11] Perhaps that conserved even more fuel.

If an entity with more real-world knowledge (such as a pilot) had been controlling the engine, he or she might have taken into account a factor—the outside temperature—that is not ordinarily relevant, but was so right then. A software engineering view of this is that the engine control program has an inadequate model of the world—and it does. Interpreted in this manner, the problem becomes: the programmers failed to include a check of the outside temperature in their calculations of engine speed and fuel economy. In one sense, that's a valid analysis.

But the real world throws an infinite set of unique situations at such programs. It is hard to imagine a model of the world that will be able to handle all of them. Software designers wrack their brains over each system, trying to abstract all the real-world factors that could ever matter, and to accurately capture *how* they matter. But no model of the world is ever 100 percent correct.

Abstracting the right model is recognized as a fundamental difficulty of system design. Some artificial intelligence researchers have therefore tried to build a system that already knows everything it could ever need to know.

Roger Schank, a well-known artificial intelligence researcher, has described and implemented software systems that embody "scripts." A *script* is a piece of real-world knowledge that enables you to navigate through the situation it describes. The script allows you to make assumptions, and not to be fazed by missing or unclear information. For instance, Dr. Schank explained to his program in painstaking detail what was involved in a visit to a restaurant, so that it would know that if it went, it could expect to have to pay a bill. (There is no record of it treating its creator to a night out in gratitude for this knowledge.)[12]

More recently, a dedicated group in Austin, Texas, has been trying to enter the full database they call "common-sense knowledge"—which they estimate to be about 100 million bits—into a computer program called Cyc. This effort, backed by the research consortium MCC, has been given ten years of funding, the assumption being that it will take at least that long to spoon-feed a computer all the underlying things that an average adult knows "that allow us to reject as untrue an article about the discovery of a human skeleton on the moon," for example. The process, like most digital endeavors, is slow and painstaking. "After all, Cyc can't learn about automobiles by going for a ride in the countryside."[13]

But I'm willing to predict that, even with ten years and $35 million, they don't think of everything. Writing software is not only an exercise in predicting all possible futures, it is also an exercise in *constraining* all possible futures. How many things must you prevent? Normally, the physical world or the common sense knowledge in a person's head takes care of a lot for us. But when the system goes digital, this can no longer be taken for granted.

Bugs are in the system to start with. They are a natural consequence of software's nature as a symbolic, logical construct. But this is not the only source of bugs. Software is also part of a physical system, affecting and being affected by the real world. And boundaries between software and the physical universe are also rich sources of bugs.

## PART OF A SYSTEM

Any software that matters is part of a physical network of machines embedded in the real world. It has brains, eyes and ears, a mouth and fingers made of hardware. It has input devices such as keyboards, keypads, touch screens, microphones, wires, lasers; and output devices such as CRT screens, loudspeakers, microphones, wires, valves, telephone lines. The system has a physical incarnation that must be pressed, pedaled, pushed.

What are the properties of software as part of this larger physical system?

- The software executes on a digital processor.
- It receives inputs and produces outputs.
- People are users or operators of the system.
- It takes up space in a noisy, busy, messy, physical environment.
- It takes time to perform its task.
- If it is a distributed system, its components must be properly connected.

Each of these characteristics implies bugs.

### Processors

The processor is the portion of a computer that performs the computations we mean when we say that software executes an instruction.[14] A processor is itself a system with various components. The arithmetic logic unit does the computing. Registers store values required for the present computation. Memory holds data and instructions to be fetched and placed into the registers, computed upon, and then returned, perhaps modified.

48 DIGITAL WOES

**Figure 2-5.** MC68020 Processor, Used to Write This Book, Magnified 20X[15]

There are fewer chips to choose from than there are computers. A lot of familiar computers these days use chips from Intel (IBM PCs and their clones use Intel 80286, 80386, and 80486 processors) and Motorola (Macintoshes and various UNIX workstations such as Suns, HP Apollos, and NeXT machines use 68020, 68030, and 68040 processors). Figure 2-5 shows a 68020 processor, magnified 20×. All this complexity is actually found on a square of silicon about 1/4" on a side.

The chip provides a physical substrate on which the software expresses its ones and zeroes as voltages traveling down wires.[16] Certain voltages traveling down certain wires cause other voltages to change in obedience to the logical rules laid down by the software designer. What a programmer does for a living, essentially, is to design the situations under which electrons flow down this or that pathway.

Obviously, these designs must rely on the chip behaving as it was designed to. Most of the time, that is a reasonable thing to rely on: software bugs easily outnumber hardware problems. Still, hardware failures *have* been known to occur—for example, early versions of the the Intel 80486 chip had faulty trigonometric functions. Compaq found the bug while testing the system it was developing for an 80486-based PC.[17]

Fortunately, the bug was found before the chip was incorporated into millions of PCs (of many brands) used for everything from running a business to modeling the weather. Intel was responsive; corrected chips appeared within weeks. Bugs in chips occur less often, are found more frequently, and are sometimes easier to fix because hardware designs are usually simpler and incorporate repetitive structures, such as memory, that are less confusing to understand. Still, chip designs are getting more exotic. In certain critical applications some customers, such as the U.K. Ministry of Defence, are insisting that even the basic chip design be proved correct using mathematical methods.[18] Chip designs may soon become complex and problematic enough to rival software.[19]

### Input and Output

If you hang the chip on your bathroom wall, it won't make any difference whether it's correct or not. But if you want software to do something, the processor must be physically connected to the outside world. The chip rests inside a cellular telephone, a Macintosh PC, a microwave oven, an automobile engine, an automated teller machine, a cash register, a telephone switch, the flight control computer of an Airbus A320, or a CD player. Inside this device, it receives *input:* waves sensed by the antenna, pressure on keys or touch pad, noise, heat, light, X-rays, incoming voltages, the depth of the pits as read by the laser.

The processor responds to this input by shunting electrons down certain wires in elaborately choreographed patterns, so the device produces *output:* phosphors on the screen glow white or green or blue, showing pictures or text; microwave radiation of a specific strength is produced for a specific amount of time; twenty-dollar bills are rolled out; bank account balances are incremented or decremented; sound is emitted from the speaker; valves open and close to precise tolerances; lists of numbers appear representing prices, units, UPC codes, or the spectrograph of a G-type star.

Input and output are the two ends of the thread that ties the system to the world.

But requiring input opens the possibility of receiving bad input—the wrong input, or input provided too fast, too slowly, too forcefully or not forcefully enough. Inputs come from people or the environment, including other systems. Either can produce bad input.

### People

Software systems include *people* as operators and users. Operators press keys, touch screens, push buttons, press pedals, talk into the microphone. Users read the text, view the pictures, receive the calls, collect the cash, listen to the music. With software such as video games or word processors, operators and users are the same people. With software such as that used in the telephone system or an ATM machine, they aren't.

People as sources of input are as unreliable as you'd expect. They make mistakes, they change their minds, they arrive late and get impatient. This sort of behavior leads to keys labeled CANCEL, ESC, UNDO, or CLEAR. Although it's better to have such keys than not, they certainly don't cover all cases.

Naive users, in particular, do things that programmers don't anticipate. They ask for results before they have specified causes; they press keys no one ever expected them to press. Although it is no substitute for thorough testing, it is a good idea for programmers to allow naive fools to use their programs before releasing them for general use, to ensure that the programs can withstand the violation of the programmers' assumptions.

Even experienced users can be absentminded. Once, a fellow mistakenly inserted his telephone credit card into an ATM machine, and it responded by spewing out cash at him.[20]

Naiveté, absentmindedness, or error aren't the only problems: people can also be mischievous, hostile, or criminal. For a fee, you can fix bad grades, bad credit records, bad driving records. ATM cards can be counterfeited using cardboard and audio tape.[21] Disgruntled ex-employees can sabotage their former employers' systems. Captain Midnight can publicly protest cable rates. Clever adolescents can break into secure military computers.[22] It is extremely difficult to control access to any computer system connected to a network. A computer system is as secure as its weakest link, the software that controls access and authorizes actions. That software is no more reliable than any other.[23]

### The Environment

People are one problem; the *environment* is another. The environment is a rich source of bad input, and therefore of bugs. It's noisy, dusty, too hot or too cold, too wet or too dry. The air is full of electromagnetic radiation from lightning, police radios, cellular phones, security systems, VDTs, high-tension power lines, television and radio broadcasts, CB or shortwave radio transmission, sunspots, or the Big Red Eye of Jupiter. Sometimes the earth quakes. Sometimes people kick the machine. Sometimes pigeons deposit a "white dielectric substance" in the antenna horn.[24] The environment, in short, is the Big, Bad World.

As you travel down a city street, there is electromagnetic radiation in the air around you not only from all the aforementioned sources, but also from garage-door openers, model airplanes, walkie-talkies, micro-wave ovens. . . . All these machines must be shielded from each other. They all take input in the form of electronic signals. If they start getting electronic signals from anywhere and everywhere, who knows what could result? All the circuitry of all the systems within some arbitrary radius would become inadvertently integrated, one giant system of randomly connected components without the unifying vision even of Rube Gold-berg. Some shielding works well, some poorly; some signals are stronger than others. People who live closer than they wish to broadcast transmis-sion towers (strong sources of electromagnetic radiation) have reported such phenomena as television interference, garage doors opening and closing, and children's toys barreling along the carpet by themselves.[25] "They hear rock and roll on their toasters," as one report says.[26] Rea-gan's neighbors were also familiar with the problem. But you don't have to live next door to a transmission tower or an air force base to experi-ence it.

The San Francisco Muni Metro has also seen electromagnetic ghosts: according to the signaling system, a ghost train blocked a switch outside Embarcadero Station for two hours during the morning rush hour on May 23, 1983. When the signaling system sees a train that isn't there and won't go away, switches must be cleared and trains moved manu-ally. This slow, finicky process continued for two hours until the train "vanished as mysteriously as it had appeared . . ."[27]

Ghosts have even haunted a McDonald's drive-thru.[28] Once upon a time in Los Angeles, a McDonald's restaurant began receiving orders from its drive-thru window when no one was there. This troubled the restaurant staff, who did not have the authority simply to cancel orders. Instead, the orders had to be cashiered out of the system, "thereby ren-dering all product mix and sales information invalid and creating a po-tential security/theft problem, in addition to slowing customer service in the drive-thru."[29] The ghost orders were easy to spot—apparently, ghosts travel in packs and lack imagination; they all want the same meal as the previous customer. So the restaurant would get orders for eleven cheese-burgers, eleven large orders of fries, eleven chocolate shakes.

The ghosts turned out to be electromagnetic interference from nearby radio and television transmission towers, but this was not discovered un-til the entire system of networked, computerized cash registers was replaced, along with all the software that ran on it. The wiring for the point-of-sale system was acting as an antenna, capturing signals from the towers. These signals corrupted the data in the network.

The interesting point about this, besides the poor dietary habits of ghosts, is that the network, when corrupted, neither shut down nor announced that it had been corrupted. It had no way of doing that. Instead, electromagnetic radiation intended to be interpreted as sound or television pictures was picked up by a system looking for cheeseburger orders. Each system used electrons to represent different things; when spurious electrons entered the McDonald's system, they were interpreted in the only way they could be.

Of course, the system also included highly fault-tolerant components capable of correcting the situation. Human beings, masters of pattern recognition, recognized spurious orders when they got them. But they were unable to correct the problem because the system designers had designed in solutions to other problems—employee fraud, neglect, or incompetence. This says more about McDonald's management practices than it says about software: if a digital system needs human operators, it may as well make use of their uniquely human abilities—pattern recognition, imagination, initiative.

The most amazing things can enter a system, such as the tomato that cried for help. In early November 1990, law officials in Montgomery County, Virginia, were testing their new 911 emergency response system. They received repeated calls from one address, so the police went to investigate. But when they entered, the house was empty. The calls were initiated by an overripe tomato that hung over the answering machine, dripping juice. The startled owners of the answering machine did not even know the machine could dial out.[30]

When tomato juice drips into an analogue machine, the machine either breaks or continues to operate. It may get progressively worse in some way before it breaks (perhaps by requiring more force as the internal mechanism gets sticky). If tomato juice falls onto an electrical component, a short circuit could start a fire. But the machine is unlikely suddenly to demonstrate some capability it was never known to have.

It is a hallmark of a digital system that this tomato causes *behavior.* The answering machine doesn't break, exactly. Nor does it continue as usual. Instead, tomato juice in the mechanism reveals a hitherto unknown dial-out capability, and the machine calls 911 (presumably because a button was programmed to do so, and it shorted out).[31]

The creature that gave its name to software bugs was the quintessence of bad environmental input. It is familiar computer lore by now. The

late U. S. Navy Admiral Grace Hopper was working with the Mark II
computer in 1945. The machine used racks of relays that closed to create
circuits as required. (There were no integrated circuits in 1945, of
course.) But the relays were exposed to the environment, and one day a
big fat moth settled on a relay contact just before it closed. Its body prevented the circuit from closing, of course, since moths are poor conduc-
tors of electricity, and so the computer did not behave as expected and
the system had a bug in it.[32]

System designers go to great lengths to keep the environment out, if
they can. If they can't, they have to make sure that the system can cope
with it. For example, somewhere near each intersection in Portland, Oregon, is a metal box containing the electronic equipment that operates the
traffic light. The boxes are tightly sealed to keep out Portland's famous
rain. Keeping a constant temperature would be prohibitively expensive,
however, so the designers "bake 'em and freeze 'em" to ensure that the
traffic lights will continue to function no matter what the temperature.[33]

However, you cannot preclude what you cannot foresee, as British
Rail found out one wet, leafy autumn. To improve safety, British Rail
changed their trains from external clutch brakes to disc brakes. The new
brakes work fine, but the change confused the signaling system, of all
things. The signaling system is safety-critical, since its purpose is to prevent train collisions. It therefore uses *three* redundant computerized systems to detect the location of each train from the contact its wheels
make with sensors in the track. The position of all trains is available to
the signals staff with a glance at a display.

The problem arose in autumn, when leaves fell from the trees and the
weather was wet. Wet leaves get mashed on the track and form an insu-
lating paste that builds up on the wheels, which (with disc brakes) are
never scraped clean. As the paste thickens, the trains cease to make contact with the sensors in the rails; as far as the signaling system is concerned, trains simply vanish. On Monday, November 11, 1991, hundreds
of passengers waited and waited for train service while the British Rail
authorities tried to sort out which trains were where. They finally added
one of the older clutch-braked cars to each train, just to get things rolling again. Eventually, they had to modify the trains with some form of
wheel-scraping mechanism.[34]

This problem is classic. To its passengers, British Rail is one system.
But every system, no matter how big or small, is made up of others.
British Rail has a signaling system, a scheduling system, a financial system. . . . Each train has a propulsive system, a braking system, and interfaces to the larger British Rail systems (neither of these lists pretends to

be exhaustive, of course). It is not always clear what depends on what. Before they improved the braking system, nobody had any idea that the signaling system was using one aspect of it—the fact that clutch brakes scrape the wheels clean of wet leaves every autumn. This was not a feature that was designed in. But it was used, nevertheless.

### Time

A vulnerable physical system implies one set of bugs. But software is embedded not only in space, but in time as well. Software takes time to execute, and time creates its own potential for failure.

Simply allowing for the interaction with humans—accepting the inserted card, the button push or key presses—takes a certain amount of time. The physical act of producing the result also takes time—opening the valves, closing the switch, rolling out the twenty-dollar bills. Between these events, the electrons must be shunted around. This takes a certain amount of time, too. In fact, a fair amount of programmer sweat goes to reducing the amount of time this takes. But sometimes it can't be helped, because a lot of electrons have to go to a lot of places.

*The Thread of Execution.* The basic temporal concept associated with software is neither the second nor the nanosecond. It is the *thread of execution*—the specific sequence of instructions that the software executes. Just as a musician plays a fixed sequence of notes and silences, each of a specified duration, so software executes a sequence of instructions, each taking some time.

In classical music, the thread a musician plays is specified in advance by the score. If software spelled out its sequence of instructions ahead of time in that manner, it would lose flexibility, its great advantage. Software is more like jazz: the instruction sequence is specified in advance only in a general way. With jazz, the specific sequence of notes and silences occurs at least partly in response to outside stimuli occurring as the musician plays—the music of the other musicians, the whistling and clapping of the crowd. With software, the actions of operators, users, or other systems influence the turn of events.

You can experience a thread of execution for yourself, by imagining that you are a compact disc player.[35] You awaken to the universe when someone presses your ON button. First, you scan your disc holder to see if it holds a disc.

You find a disc and read its header. You learn how many selections the disc has, where each selection starts, how long it lasts, and the total playing time of the disc. Then you display the number of selections and the total playing time. Then you start playing the first selection, displaying the number "1" and its playing time.

When someone opens the disc holder, you stop playing and clear all the header information from your memory and from the display. When the disc holder closes, you read the new header. Then you wait until someone pushes PLAY. You begin to spin the disc. When it spins at the correct speed, the laser shines. You read the pits in the surface, converting them to binary digits. You then convert the binary digits into the electrical signals that the amplifier is designed to accept.

When the disc has been played to the end, or when someone presses STOP, the disc stops spinning, the stream of bits ends, the electrical signals end. Then someone presses OFF, and your present interaction with the universe ends.

That's one thread through the system. In another, the user pressed REPEAT, and when the disc reached the end it started playing all over again. In yet another, the user pressed PAUSE midway through a song (the phone rang), and the disc kept spinning but the laser stopped moving and remained where it was. The stream of bits stopped coming, and the software that transforms the bits to electrical signals decoded its last bit and then waited for the next bit, which did not come. It kept waiting until PAUSE was pressed again. Then the laser began moving, bits started flowing, electrical signals started flowing, and the music resumed.

All of these are possible threads of execution through the system: a *thread* in the sense of a path, and *execution* because the software is *executing* its instructions. At any given moment, only some of the software is executing. That is, electrons flow down some paths on the chip, but not others. While the music is playing, the instructions responsible for reading the header, or pausing the music, or stopping the disc, are not executing.

When the programmers[36] wrote the software for the compact disc player, they had to design all possible situations. They had to spell out precisely what should occur when someone presses ON, OFF, PLAY, STOP, PAUSE, NEXT, BACK, OPEN, CLOSE—when a disc is present, and when one is not.[37] When a disc is already playing, and when it is not. And what should occur if the laser cannot read a pit because the disc is smeared or dusty? And how are the bits decoded into electrical signals?

What should the player do if it cannot read a disc header? Where should it look? How many times should it try? All these situations must be designed completely before the player is usable.[38]

Systems that have just one thread of execution, such as a compact disc player or a spreadsheet, can experience problems if the software executes too slowly, too fast, or if it executes instructions in the wrong order. You may have experienced an ATM machine that responds too slowly after you insert your card. You wait, contemplating the introductory screen enticing you to apply for a loan. Just as you decide that the machine has gone south and press CANCEL to retrieve your card, the system displays its first menu of choices—but only long enough to frustrate you as it responds promptly to your button press, ejecting your card, beeping, and returning to the initial screen.

On the other hand, systems that execute too fast can also cause problems. For example, an F18 can launch a missile from its wing. A computer is supposed to launch the missile by opening the clamp that holds the missile to the wing, firing the missile, then closing the clamp. One day in 1983, the computer-controlled launching system was being tested. The computer opened the clamp, but closed it too quickly, before the missile had built up sufficient thrust to leave the wing. The pilots then had to contend with a missile with 3000 pounds of thrust clamped to the airplane. The plane plummeted 20,000 feet; the pilots nearly ejected before they managed to regain control.[39]

But it isn't always the pace of execution that causes trouble—sometimes it's the order in which the instructions execute. The Therac-25, for example, killed or injured several patients because the tungsten shield moved out of the path of the radiation beam, and the beam switched on before the software switched from the high- to the low-intensity radiation setting.

On January 15, 1990, the AT&T long-distance telephone system in the United States experienced a major disruption of service because instructions executed in the wrong order.[40] The slowdown was ultimately traced to a few lines of programming code that were too complex—indeed, deeply confusing. One statement (called a *switch* statement) was supposed to determine which of several different possible cases had occurred. The statement would pass the execution baton to the appropriate set of instructions, depending upon which case was in effect. One of the sets of instructions for one of those possible cases had an *if* statement to determine if another condition was true. Inside the *if* statement was another statement called a *break*. If something else happened, the *break* was supposed to cause execution to break out of the *if* statement back to the original instructions for that particular case. Instead, it broke out of the entire *switch* construct within which the *if* statement was nested.[41] This thread of execution (illustrated in Figure 2-6) is as wild as a roller coaster ride—it's no wonder it caused confusion and, ultimately, trouble.

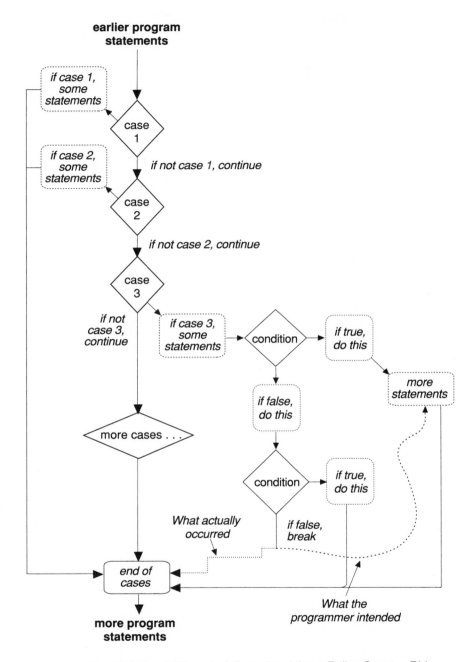

**Figure 2-6.**  A Thread of Execution Like a Roller Coaster Ride

*Concurrency.* Even so, a single-thread system is simpler to program and debug than a concurrent system. Systems that exhibit *concurrency* are ones in which more than one thread can be executing at any given time (as measured on a real-world clock). A symphony orchestra or a rock group are perfect examples of concurrency. Before the start, silence. Then, as the clock says BEGIN, the musicians start to play. Each executes his or her thread, playing the prescribed sequence of notes and silences. A conductor coordinates the orchestra, making sure all the musicians keep to the same clock.[42] Each musician concentrates on only one thread; the output from all their threads is the input to the conductor's thread; and the audience hears what they have come to hear, the glory of concurrent sound.

Concurrent software systems are, as usual, more complex than this example suggests. In a concurrent software system, each thread could be accessing different data at any given moment, or executing different instructions.

For instance, imagine all the people who, this instant, are operating any of hundreds of MagiCash automated teller machines. Right now (*beep*) the MagiCash network is processing thousands of transactions. The customers are counting on each thread accessing unique data—that is, their own unique bank accounts. They expect their transactions to be reflected on their own monthly statements, not someone else's.

(Well, at opposite ends of the same mall, one husband and one wife are each trying to access the same account. The one who started first has gained access, and the other is being bedeviled by a display that reads:

```
                        Sorry.

    We  are  temporarily  unable  to  process  your  transaction.
```

No explanation is given, because the programmers have designed this situation only incompletely. This generic message comes up for a lot of reasons—a lot of situations were lumped into one. This is now worrying one frustrated spouse unnecessarily.)

The MagiCash ATM network is a good example of a concurrent distributed system. Many distinct copies of the same software are executing at the same time on many different processors connected by wires that allow them to exchange data. They are executing different parts of the same software when they check account balances, or add to or subtract from an account. Some are just starting—prompting for the user's PIN—while others are ending—printing out the receipt and beeping at people to remind them to take their cards.

In most concurrent systems, the different threads depend on each other more. Can you imagine what a symphony orchestra or rock group would sound like if each musician played any sequence of notes and silences without reference to what the others were playing? The fact that each thread depends upon the others, and creates its share of a glorious whole, is what makes the music. The specific kinds of dependencies between the threads (as well as other factors, of course) determines the style: Beethoven or Berry.

Musical dependencies are usually captured before the music is ever played, when the composer writes the score. For software, the programmer is supposed to provide the same function. But software has to respond flexibly to a variety of situations, and so a lot of these issues are harder to specify ahead of time.

Concurrency comes in three main flavors:

- One processor runs on one machine.
- Many processors run on one machine.
- Many processors run on many machines (like the MagiCash ATM network).

Concurrency can be a factor even on one machine with just one processor, if many threads must be in progress all at once. This is typically what happens on a mainframe with many users. Since there is only one processor to execute all the threads, they must somehow take turns. How they do so is frequently a matter of earnest debate during the design of a system, because the implications can be far-reaching. Scheduling tasks properly is difficult and error-prone, even for one processor on one machine. Many processors on one machine (called *parallel processing*) only make matters more confusing.

*Parallel Processing.* Parallel processing aims for the computational equivalent of the adage: "Two heads are better than one." Some problems require a lot of processing power. A naive newcomer might suppose that if a single-processor machine takes eight hours to crunch all the numbers, then an eight-processor machine should take just one hour. Because the computation goes so much faster, you can compute more difficult problems in the same amount of time.

Not even human teams work *that* well. First comes the inevitable overhead of the coordinator—something has to keep track of which processor is working on which part of the problem. But more difficult is figuring out how to divide up the work in the first place.[43]

Two issues make this problem difficult: load-balancing and dependencies within the task. Understanding load-balancing is relatively straightforward—if you cannot keep all the processors busy at least most of the time, then obviously a parallel program will not provide the speed advantage that is supposed to make the extra work worthwhile.

When some portion of the computation depends on results from other independently computed portions, the problem worsens. The processors proceed in parallel until one of them reaches a point where it can go no further without an intermediate result from another processor. While it waits for the result, the computation is not going as fast as it could be. More important, though, communication between processors must now take place. How will the halted processor find out when the result it awaits is available? When it is available, will the other processor send it the result, thus storing the data twice? If so, what if the data changes in one place but not the other? Or do both processors share access to the same region of memory? If so, then how is that region of memory protected against both processors trying to change it simultaneously, which could cause any sort of bizarre behavior?

When the program runs, and the processors all seem to be crunching, you must still be certain that the program is working as it should, and that the answer you are getting is the right one. Debugging parallel programs can be suspenseful. To quote from a paper on the subject:

*Most notable are the following problems:*

- *Non-repeatable problems will occur often,*

- *Correct answers* do not *imply a correct program [emphasis theirs],*

- *Conventional debugging techniques can yield misleading information. . . .*[44]

The human mind thinks sequentially; it is difficult to hold even a few independent threads of events in your mind at once. (Musical composers are remarkable because, in one limited domain, they are so good at it.) When the number of threads increases, and the actions they take can influence each other, the problem quickly grows beyond the ability of the mind to grasp. Parallel programs are worst cases; each time a program executes, events can occur in a different sequence. Results are therefore unpredictable; the situation is as described in the above-quoted report: "Each time a program is run, different answers can appear—even with identical inputs."

Particularly pernicious is the case when most event sequences yield the expected result, and misbehavior occurs only as a result of one specific sequence out of many. If this sequence is improbable, a program can run correctly for weeks, months, or even years, when one day the latent bug manifests itself. Clearly, this presents difficulties for testing. When you finally find and fix such a bug, you will want to test it to ensure that the fix works as intended. But it will be nearly impossible to make events reoccur in the same sequence for a meaningful test.

*Determinism* is a concept that describes a system in which the same actions always lead to the same results. If a system is deterministic, we can predict what it will do. Software is not necessarily deterministic; given the same inputs, the same program can nevertheless behave as it never has before. Parallel programs often show nondeterminism. For critical applications, such unpredictability can be quite risky.

*Synchronization.* Many processors running on many different machines can have even more kinds of synchronization problems. Indeed, in April 1981, the very first launch of the space shuttle was delayed due to a synchronization problem.

Four of the space shuttle's five flight control computers use the same software; they schedule tasks according to their relative priorities. The four computers are intended to back each other up in the event of computer or other hardware failures.

The fifth computer serves as the ultimate understudy for space shuttle flight control: it backs up the other computers in case of software failure. The fifth computer uses completely different software, therefore, so that the same bug to hit the four will not affect it.

However, in order for it to be able to take over in an emergency, the fifth computer must start each flight synchronized with respect to the other four. It has to listen to the same data that the other computers are receiving, much as an understudy must follow the performance of a play, or else it would have no idea what to do if suddenly called upon to take control of the flight. And in order to listen to the data and make meaningful use of it, it has to know when to expect it. Synchronizing the two systems turned out to be harder than anyone realized.

The four primary computers all started running and checked out fine. Thirty hours later, the fifth computer could not be made to synchronize with them. Without a synchronized backup computer, the launch was delayed while all the experts assembled in one room to thrash it out. The problem turned out to have been caused by a change made two years previously to a seemingly unrelated part of the program. It was exacer-

bated by another change made to the same place about a year later. The
problem still had only one chance in sixty-seven of actually occurring,
which made it unlikely to crop up during testing.

The problem was: "Time! That nemesis of real-time systems and concurrent processing, that concept which though pervasive in our lives is
so difficult to conceptualize in so many contexts."[45] It turned out that,
because of a two-year-old change to an initialization routine, the four
primary computers had had an inaccurate idea of the current time when
they were first started up.[46] It was only very slightly inaccurate, but that
was enough to delay the launch from Friday, April 10 until Sunday,
April 12. The bug that had been planted two years previously had sur-
faced twenty minutes before the shuttle was scheduled for its first flight.
At that, a delay of only two days was lucky. "This problem had all the
characteristics of bugs that can take weeks of analysis to really 'nail
down.'"

### Connectivity

The AT&T long-distance slowdown on January 15, 1990, was also a synchronization problem, but one with more disturbing long-term implications. The 4ESS long-distance switching system consists of more than
one hundred switches all over the United States. Each switch can connect to many others, allowing many possible routes for any given long-
distance telephone call. In that way, if a switch fails for any reason, a
call can be routed through other switches and still reach its destination.

Software for the 4ESS long-distance switching system consists of about
four million lines of code; of that, fully half is dedicated to recovering
from errors, including initializing a switch.[47] In other words, as Mr. Michael Meyers of AT&T Bell Labs put it, "It's twice as hard to be reliable."[48] This ensures that switches can go down and come back up as
often as they have to without callers even being aware of it.

A few weeks after a change to part of the software, a switch in New
York City reset itself—a routine operation requiring only a few seconds.
It sent messages to the rest of the network, saying it could accept no
more calls until further notice. The other switches would therefore send
it no calls until they heard from it again. When it finished resetting, it
began processing calls again. It sent a message to one of the other
switches indicating that it would be sending along a phone call. This
message constituted "further notice"; it was supposed to tell that switch
that the New York City switch could now accept incoming calls again.
So the second switch began to update its picture of the world to include
the information that the New York City switch was operating again. But

it was an unusually busy day, and before it had finished, it received a second call request from the New York City switch. It had to shunt this second request aside until it had finished with its update, but unfortunately, due to the programming error described earlier, it shunted the second request to the wrong part of its memory. Still, all was not lost—the telephone switching system is built to be robust in the face of errors. The second switch notified its backup to take over while it shut itself down to correct the error.

But it *was* a busy day. The backup had inherited the switch's concept of the state of the world, including the information that the original switch in New York City was still down. And then the backup also got two call requests from the New York City switch, one hard on the heels of the other, and went down just as the second switch had, notifying the rest of the switches on the network that it could accept no more calls until further notice. When the second switch came back up and began processing calls again, its messages affected other switches just as it had been affected by the switch in New York City. Switches went down like dominoes as the error cascaded through the switching system. Nine hours later, fifty million phone calls had failed to get through and AT&T had lost about $60 million because of an obscure error in a few lines of a four-million-line program.[49]

If a network has high connectivity, then each node on that network—each computer, telephone relay switch, or neuron—is connected to many others. If a network has low connectivity, each node is connected to few others. A network consisting of a bunch of computers linked by one cable in a straight line exhibits low connectivity. The neurons in your brain, each linked to its neighbors with thousands of synapses, constitute a highly connected system.

High connectivity is the whole point of the telephone switching system. In this case, it was also its weakness. Connectivity allows "network bugs"—things aren't connected as they should be, or maybe all those connections just help an error to spread. To test for network bugs, you have to test a network. It is no longer enough to run the code on just one switch; now you must hook several switches together and run the code on the resulting configuration as well. In the wake of this incident, AT&T has in fact changed its testing procedures in this manner.[50]

The concept of connectivity is playfully explored in yet another science fiction story, written in 1950, called "A Subway Named Mobius."[51] In it, Boston, Massachusetts, completes a new subway shuttle that ". . . finally tied together the seven principal lines on four different levels." With this stroke, the Boston subway system has achieved ". . . connectiv-

ity . . . of an order so high I don't know how to calculate it," as the
mathematician from M.I.T. explains to the general manager of the subway system. The subway manager is not particularly interested in mathematics, but he needs to determine what has happened to train #86,
which has seemingly vanished when it hit a singularity in the too-highly-
connected network and crossed over into another dimension. (It then
traveled across the continent and into the future, where it sat outside
the Embarcadero Station of the San Francisco Muni Metro system on
May 23, 1983. Two hours later, Elvis finally boarded, and it returned
whence it had come.)

Connectivity is a property of any distributed system. Highly connected
systems are complex and hard to understand. The telephone switching
system probably represents the most highly connected computer network
in the world, and the most complex distributed system. Its occasional
failures should surprise nobody; what is truly surprising is that it works
as well as it does. It is astonishing that I can pick up my phone, dial
fifteen digits, and be connected to nearly any other phone in the world.
One of these days, the phone system will reach the point where a problem in Tokyo will bring down the telephone system in Des Moines.[52]

## WRITING SOFTWARE IS A SUBTRACTIVE EXERCISE

Look at it this way: an infinite number of things can go wrong with any
system in its raw, entropic state. Writing software is a matter of trying
to take out as many bugs as possible. This subtractive exercise is considerably more arduous—and more hopeless—than the aspect we concentrate on, which is adding behavior. After all, if you subtract the finite
number of problems you have solved from the infinite number of problems lurking in the primordial system, an infinite number of potential
problems still remain.

Software has bugs in it because that is its nature. Large structures of
logic are complex and abstract; they have no real-world analogues; they
are often outside the realm of our direct experience. They are, in short,
hard for people to understand. The flexibility of software—the property
that makes it so useful to us—is also its Achilles' heel. Too many things
can happen; it is impossible to imagine and eliminate them all, and we
cannot rely on nature to eliminate the physically absurd.

Time also causes problems. Although the user experiences only one
thread through the system, the system can execute many threads concur-
rently, leading to many potential states of the system. The programmer
must design all the threads that can ever be executed. The tapestry must

be completely woven; every situation designed; every contingency planned for. What inputs are possible? How will the system respond to any combination of these? What sequences should be permitted? From any point in the system, what can happen next? What does it depend on?

And it isn't even that simple. The system designer must also ask, how can the environment affect the system? What must its skin withstand? And how much of it? In short, what else can happen?

This aspect of writing software—the need to prevent every contingency you do not design—requires reducing life to a finite resolution, like a 640 x 480 computer display. You need to know, when you eliminate a detail, that no new details have sprung up to take its place, but it can't be done. The world is full of subtlety and nuance; it has infinite resolution. When you erase one detail, you create infinitely many more. In other words, it's easy to add behavior, but it's hard to subtract the behavior you don't want that came along with it.

Not surprisingly, the process of creating software and keeping it running reflects these difficulties, as we shall see in the next chapter.

### NOTES

1 No, I'm not making this up, and it worries me. See Gould, Stephen Jay. *Bully for Brontosaurus.* New York: W. W. Norton & Co., 1991, p. 306.

2 In that sense, *Koyannisqatsi* (Island Alive/Blue Dolphin, 1983) did more than *Tron* (Walt Disney Productions, 1982) to show people what software could look like, for those who go to the movies.

3 We will discuss debugging in more detail in the next chapter. For now, though, it is of interest to point out that tools to help programmers program—debugging tools, visual programming tools, software development "environments" with a wide variety of programmer aids—account for a significant proportion of the commercial software market. Programmers are not superhuman; they don't find this stuff any easier than anyone else would, really.

4 Trei, Peter G. ACM SIGSOFT *Software Engineering Notes,* 11:1, Jan. 1986, p. 4.

5 About 1.5 volts, if you must know. This is the sort of thing electrical engineers worry about. They are even stranger folks than programmers—but harmless.

6 Penzias, Arno. *Ideas and Information: Managing in a High Tech World.* New York: W.W. Norton and Co., 1989. Pages 97–105 offer the clearest explanation I have encountered of exactly what goes on inside a computer at this level.

7 Collingwood, Harris. "How a typo toppled the phone networks." *Business Week,* Dec. 9, 1991, p. 44.

8 Brooks, Frederick P., Jr. "No Silver Bullet: Essence and Accidents of Software Engineering." IEEE *Computer,* April 1987, pp. 10–19. The quote is from p. 12. If the field of software engineering had its own version of *Bartlett's Familiar Quotations,* this would be in it. This article, which argues that "building software will always be hard" (p. 11), is a classic. Fred Brooks is also the author of another software engineering classic, *The Mythical Man-Month,* in which he shares software project management insights gleaned from his experiences overseeing the development of the operating sys-

tem for one of IBM's most widely used and commercially successful mainframes, the IBM 360. He is not a software optimist.

9 Carlos, Wendy. *Secrets of Synthesis*, CBS, 1987, MK42333.

10 ACM SIGSOFT *Software Engineering Notes*, 5:2, April 1980, p. 5.

11 "Jet Engine Failure Tied to Computer: It's Too Efficient." *Los Angeles Times*, Aug. 24, 1983, p. A1. Excerpted in ACM SIGSOFT *Software Engineering Notes*, 8:5, Oct., 1983, p. 5.

12 Schank, Roger, and Robert Abelson. *Scripts, Plans, Goals and Understanding: An Inquiry into Human Knowledge Structures*. Hillsdale, N.J.: Lawrence Erlbaum Associates, 1977. Pages 36–68 are especially germane.

13 Freedman, David H. "Common Sense and the Computer." *Discover*, Aug., 1990, pp. 65–71.

14 Penzias, Arno. *Ideas and Information: Managing in a High Tech World*. New York: W.W. Norton and Co., 1989. Pages 120–125 offer yet another remarkably lucid explanation, this one of processors.

15 Photograph courtesy of Motorola, Inc. Semiconductor Products Sector, Microprocessor and Memory Technologies Group, 6501 William Cannon Drive West, Austin, Texas 78735-8598. A 68020 is the processor embedded within the computer on which I am writing this book. Thanks, folks.

16 Actually the "wires" aren't wires in the usual sense; they are paths of electrically conductive material etched through a nonconducting layer.

17 Reported by Peter G. Neumann in *comp.risks*, 9:36. He cited the Oct. 27, 1989 *San Francisco Chronicle*.

18 A processor called Viper was developed by the Royal Signals and Radar Establishment for the British Ministry of Defence, primarily for military applications. The MoD insisted that the hardware design be proved correct using mathematical methods. The proof is somewhat controversial. For example, see Hill, Simon. "User Threatens Court Action Over MoD Chip." *Computer Weekly* (U.K.), July 5, 1990, p. 3. The next chapter discusses in more detail using mathematical methods to prove things correct.

19 *Formal Verification of Hardware Design* by Michael Yoeli (IEEE Computer Science Press, 1990) discusses the use of first- and second-order logic, needed because hardware designs are becoming so complex they can no longer be understood.

20 *comp.risks*, 12:6, July 17, 1991.

21 Mercuri, Rebecca. Trip report on the Computers, Freedom, and Privacy Conference, March 26–28, 1991, in *comp.risks*, 11:39.

22 Stoll, Clifford. *The Cuckoo's Egg: Tracking a Spy Through the Maze of Computer Espionage*. New York: Doubleday, 1989. Also see *2600*, a periodical devoted entirely to activities of the sort.

23 Neumann, Peter G. "Inside Risks: Insecurity About Security." *Communications of the ACM*, Vol. 33:8, Aug. 1990, p. 170.

24 Bernstein, Jeremy. *Three Degrees Above Zero*. New York: Scribner's, 1984. Page 202 tells of the role played by pigeons in the Nobel Prize–winning radio astronomy of Arno Penzias and Robert Wilson.

25 Ellis, Barnes C. "Study Finds Radio Tower Beneficial." *Oregonian*, Jan. 30, 1992, p. C2.

26 Holtz, Larry M., and Gray F. Haertig. "Construction of a Multiple User FM facility in an Urban Environment." National Association of Broadcasters *45th Annual Broadcast Engineering Conference Proceedings*, April 14–18, 1991, pp. 448–59.

27 Neumann, Peter G. ACM SIGSOFT *Software Engineering Notes*, 8:3, July, 1983, p. 2.

28 ACM SIGSOFT *Software Engineering Notes*, 15:1, Jan. 1990, p. 14. Contribution from Robert Horvitz.

29 "The Importance of EMC in the Preparation and Selling of Big Macs," Fernando M. Esparza, *EMC Technology*, Sept.-Oct. 1989. EMC stands for electromagnetic compatibility, the opposite of electromagnetic interference, the problem we have been discussing.

30 "911 calls are ripe for trouble" in the *Austin American-Statesman*, Nov. 11, 1990, as reported on-line in *comp.risks*, 10:60.

31 For this suggestion, I am indebted to Tim Steele, *comp.risks*, 10:63.

32 Hopper, Grace M. *Annals of the History of Computing*, vol. 3, 1981, p. 285. It's a familiar tale, but the moth's point of view has been neglected. It gave its life, not for science, but merely for lexicography. And moths aren't even bugs, properly speaking, as any entomologist would love to tell you.

33 Mr. William C. Kloos, P.E., Signal Systems Manager, Bureau of Traffic Management for the City of Portland Office of Transportation. Personal communication, Aug. 22, 1991.

34 *comp.risks*, 12:62, Nov. 12, 1991, and 12:66, Nov. 27, 1991.

35 For the purposes of this discussion, you are a Sony CDP-391. Different disc players will behave slightly differently, but this discussion needs specific details, so I had to pick something; it really doesn't matter what. (When you are finished reading this, you can decide to be any kind of compact disc player you like. Perhaps you'll decide to be a video cassette recorder instead. Fine. Don't blame me when you break.)

36 Commercial software is nearly always a team effort these days. Even the software in a CD player is probably too complicated for one person to produce on schedule.

37 If this strikes you as odd, think about it a moment. You wouldn't want your player to go catatonic because you mistakenly pushed PLAY when no disc was in the holder, would you? Yet this could easily happen unless the programmers specify what the machine *should* do.

38 Furthermore, designing these situations also implies the design of the situation in which the music is recorded, and the one in which the disc is manufactured. For the concept of "designing situations," I am indebted to Ralph Caplan and his interesting book, *By Design* (New York: St. Martin's Press, 1982). Programmers should read this book. It's full of demonstrations of the neglected truism that designing software has a great deal in common with designing other things.

39 ACM SIGSOFT *Software Engineering Notes*, 8:5, Oct. 1983, p. 3. Item contributed by Nancy Leveson.

40 Mason, C., and D. Bushaus. "Software problem cripples AT&T long distance network." *Telephony*, Jan. 22, 1990, pp. 10–11. Rogers, Michael, et al. "Can We Trust Our Software?" *Newsweek*, Jan. 29, 1990, pp. 70–73. Also, *comp.risks*, 9:62, 64, 66, and others.

41 Neumann, Peter G. "Inside Risks: Some Reflections on a Telephone Switching Problem" *Communications of the ACM*, 33:7, July 1990, p. 154. Also, see *comp.risks*, 9:69, Feb. 20, 1990.

42 The other function of the conductor, that of interpreting the music according to an integral vision, has no analogue in this discussion.

43 Carriero, Nicholas, and David Gelernter. "How to Write Parallel Programs: A Guide to the Perplexed," Research Report YALEU/DCS/RR-628, May 1988.

44 McGraw, James R., and Timothy S. Axelrod. "Exploiting Multiprocessors: Issues and Options," in *Programming Parallel Processors*, Robert G. Babb, editor. Reading, MA: Addison-Wesley, 1988, pp. 7–26.

45 My source for this entire wondrous tale is the excellent article by John R. Garman, "The 'Bug' Heard 'Round the World." (ACM SIGSOFT *Software Engineering Notes*, 6:5, Oct. 1981, pp. 3–10.) Both quotes are from p. 8.

46 Here is an interesting example of a situation in which voting would have produced the wrong answer.

47 Initialization sounds like something that is done when a system starts up, but it is a more generally useful function than that. Initialization is like pressing a button marked RESET; a typical initialization function sets whatever it is initializing to a known state from which you can hope to predict its behavior. It is therefore extremely useful for recovering from errors.

48 Wiener, Lauren. "A Trip Report on SIGSOFT '91." ACM *Software Engineering Notes,* 17:2, April 1992, pp. 23–38. The quote is from p. 33, Michael Meyers of AT&T Bell Labs, Naperville, Ill. "The 4ESS Switching System," *Invited Talks on Practical Experiences,* SIGSOFT '91, Dec. 4–6, 1991, New Orleans, LA.

49 Peterson, Ivars. "Finding Fault: The formidable task of eradicating software bugs." *Science News,* vol. 139, Feb. 16, 1991, p. 104. Also Neumann, Peter G. "Inside Risks: Some Reflections on a Telephone Switching Problem" *Communications of the ACM,* 33:7, July 1990, p. 154.

50 Wiener, *op. cit.*

51 Deutsch, A. J. "A Subway Named Mobius." Copyright 1950, Street & Smith Publications, Inc. First published in *Astounding Science Fiction,* Dec. 1950. Reprinted in *Where Do We Go From Here?* Isaac Asimov, ed. Greenwich, CT: Fawcett Publications, 1971, pp. 139–156.

52 Ramirez, Anthony. "Global Phone Systems Act to Avoid Failures." *New York Times,* Oct. 12, 1991, p. 25. Ramirez, Anthony. "Phone Industries Grapple with the New World Order." *New York Times,* Oct. 7, 1991, p. C1. Rankin, Robert A. "Telephone Failures Alarming." *Oregonian,* July 11, 1991, p. A13.

# CHAPTER 3

# THE
# RESOURCE
# SINK

Norman
Augustine, president
of Martin-Marietta, takes a suitably long-term view of
technology,
as befits his
position. Extrapolating from two trends over several decades—electronic
aircraft are growing increasingly expensive and increasingly lightweight—
he asks, how can both these trends continue? "[W]hat is needed is something that can be added to airplanes and other systems which weighs
*nothing,* is *very costly,* yet violates none of the physical laws of the universe . . ."[1] That's software, all right.

Why is software so expensive? It certainly isn't the medium—you can
buy diskettes for less than a dollar apiece. Software is expensive because
it is expensive to develop.

The previous chapter discussed the complexities inherent in software
itself. This chapter discusses the process of developing it—a process
which is ordinarily hurried, *ad hoc* if not chaotic, and rather hard on the
participants. The results of this process are likely to be behind schedule,
over budget, and not quite what was originally wanted, after all. Software may be inherently unreliable, but the typical software development
process is not apt to improve matters.

The U.S. government is perhaps the world's largest single software pur-
chaser. Figure 3-1 shows a chart from a 1979 U.S. Government Accounting Office report on the appalling statistics for nine federal software
development projects:[2]

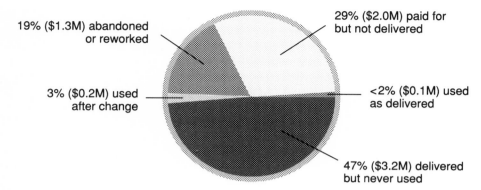

19% ($1.3M) abandoned
or reworked

29% ($2.0M) paid for
but not delivered

3% ($0.2M) used
after change

<2% ($0.1M) used
as delivered

47% ($3.2M) delivered
but never used

**Figure 3-1.** U. S. Federal Software Development Goes Awry

In March 1967, *Fortune* magazine ran an article about the then-novel process of software development.[3] Table 3-1 shows how little has changed since. The left column contains quotations from the 1967 article, and the right column contains quotations from a variety of other sources since then.

■ **Table 3–1.** Software Development, Then and Now

| 1967 | Ever Since |
|------|------------|
| Programming has nowhere near the discipline of physics, for example, so intuition plays a large part. Yet individual programmers differ in their creative and intuitive abilities. | Programmers, unlike foot soldiers, are not interchangeable. (Weinberg, 1971)[4] |
| . . . software poses difficult management problems. On the one hand, a good programmer, like a writer or composer, works best independently. But the pressures to turn out . . . programs within a limited time makes it necessary to deploy huge task forces whose coordination becomes a monstrous task. | The dilemma is a cruel one. For efficiency and conceptual integrity, one prefers a few good minds doing design and construction. Yet for large systems one wants a way to bring considerable manpower to bear, so that the product can make a timely appearance. (Brooks, 1978)[5] |
| . . . there is no way as yet to program a computer to detect semantic errors that can dramatically alter the intent of the program. | I really hate this damn machine, I wish that they would sell it. It never does quite what I want, But only what I tell it. (Folklore, quoted in Shore, 1985)[6] |

■ **Table 3–1.**   Software Development, Then and Now   (continued)

| 1967 | Ever Since |
|---|---|
| Many companies that have invested heavily in the latest model computers find themselves increasingly frustrated by the discrepancy between the fantastic potential of the machines and their own ability to use them with maximum effectiveness. | For large software systems, the cost and complexity of the software typically dominate that of the hardware. (Borning, 1987)[7] |
| Another factor that influences the quality of programming is the frequent inability of business and industrial managers to state fully or precisely the problem they want their programmers to solve. | . . . the client does not know what he wants. The client usually does not know what questions must be answered, and he has almost never thought of the problem in the detail necessary for the specification. (Brooks, 1987)[8] |
| . . . when they buy newer computers, they have to rewrite their existing applications programs to suit the configurations and the logic of the new machines—a time-consuming job that demands battalions of programmers. | . . . successful software survives beyond the normal life of the machine vehicle for which it is first written. If not new computers, then at least new disks, new displays, new printers come along; and the software must be conformed to its new vehicles of opportunity. (Brooks, 1987)[9] |
| And while problems do crop up in hardware from time to time, it is generally agreed that 90% of the troubles that come up in computers today are in programming. | True, faults may exist in the hardware—the chips themselves—but, more frequently, they crop up in the software. (Jacky, 1989)[10] |
| . . . generating software is "brain business," often an agonizingly difficult intellectual effort. | The distinguishing characteristic of industrial-strength software is that it is intensely difficult, if not impossible, for the individual developer to comprehend all the subtleties of its design. (Booch, 1990)[11] |
| Partly because of this communication failure and partly because of deadline pressures, all significant programming problems turn out to be emergencies. | Often, developers of commercial software work under so much pressure to deliver a product that new programs go out riddled with flaws. (Peterson, 1991)[12] |

Developing software has been like this for at least twenty-five years, and the situation is unlikely to change anytime soon. As Fred Brooks said, "The familiar software project . . . is capable of becoming a monster of missed schedules, blown budgets, and flawed products."[13]

## STILL CRAZY AFTER ALL THESE YEARS

The *Fortune* article quoted above was written just a year before the Software Crisis got its name. We can now celebrate its silver jubilee, and software development still absorbs more time, people, and money than we expect.

Mentor Graphics, for example, is a publicly traded software corporation whose products are used to design electronic circuits. They first announced that Release 8.0 (the 8th version of their products to be sold) was to ship in late 1989 or early 1990. They missed that deadline and the next one; most of it finally shipped a year later, although as of early spring, 1992, reportedly a few last pieces had *still* not been shipped.[14] In the meantime, the programmers have had several stressful years of sixty-, eighty-, or even one-hundred-hour weeks, leading to a crop of bumper stickers in the parking lot reading: `I Work 8.0 Days a Week at Mentor Graphics`, while customers began referring to the new version as Release Late.0.

They have plenty of company—the phenomenon is global. In the U.K., custom accounting software for the Foreign Office was budgeted at £560,000. The vendor, Memory Computers, ran into development trouble and failed to deliver on time. When they finally delivered the system, the government ended up paying £937,000. Memory Computers then went into liquidation.[15]

Software that is developed in a hurry and only lightly tested is not to be relied upon, as Montreal Life Insurance Co. found out the hard way. It decided to install a program that would integrate all aspects of the company's operations. Development was rushed and testing was inadequate.

> *Within a year, Montreal Life was losing money. After three years, the company was near collapse. Errors in commission cheques, for example, drove away most of the company's agents. The agents took their clients with them. When agents weren't underpaid, they were overpaid, which accounted for another $1 million in losses.*[16]

The products of these chaotic processes will need changing sometimes. It may not be too hard to make the change you want, but it's seldom simple to make *only* the change you want. For example, on March 3, 1992, the Toronto Stock Exchange closed from 10 A.M. to 2 P.M. because of wild behavior on the part of the computer system used to trade equities. The program recorded wildly inaccurate prices and failed to print trade confirmations. "The bugs appeared after the TSE changed its computer software over the weekend to deal with new trading rules," said a description in the *Toronto Globe and Mail.*[17]

Why is it so hard to write reliable software, on time and to a budget? This chapter will try to answer that question for commercial software or noncritical custom software whose failure does not kill or harm. (*Mission-critical* software, disastrous, often financially, when it fails, and *safety-critical* software, which can kill when it fails, can be developed using a variety of extraordinary measures discussed in the next chapter.) In nearly all organizations, software development is problematic. This isn't a matter of fraud, negligence, or incompetence. Like hardware failure, they exist, but the real problems come in three main flavors: the market pressures, the organization, and the software development process itself.

## MARKET PRESSURES

Compared to other enterprises, the market pressures on software development are extreme. Developing software is a new sort of enterprise, and companies often have no idea what they're getting into; they often have unrealistic notions. It is easy to start a software business, so the field is highly competitive. Driven by hardware, which improves constantly, the pace of change in the software industry is heretofore unheard-of. New products must constantly be announced to take advantage of the latest processor or printer. As if this wasn't tough enough, it's difficult to control costs, as the lion's share of the budget pays for the time and efforts of skilled professionals. And, the final insult, once you sell a bunch of copies of your product, a lot of other people can simply help themselves to it. The result is that no one ever wants to pay what it costs to develop a piece of software, nor wait as long as it takes.

### A Brave New World

Developing software is different in key ways from anything people have ever tried to do before. We've been at it for fifty years, more or less, and some professionals are just developing an appreciation for the properties of software that make it difficult to develop reliably. Companies who are new to the software business often lack such insights, however. They may harbor utterly unrealistic expectations and goals. They may be trying to accomplish tasks with software that have never before been attempted. They routinely underestimate how long something will take or how difficult it will prove to develop reliably. Under the circumstances, even a heroic performance by the grunts in the trenches can look like a poor show to the bigwigs in the boardroom.

Adele Goldberg, pioneer of object-oriented technology, told the following tale to an audience of software professionals.[18] A company decided to invest up front in a library of software pieces customized for the particulars of their business. This software would then be reused by all the company's software projects, thus saving time and increasing productivity. The project took the assigned group one year. In the second year, three projects, reusing 80 percent of the code, were completed on time and without major incident. Dr. Goldberg's audience gasped appreciatively, but top management at the company in question had not been impressed. The programming group was not rewarded.

I don't know what that company expected, but they made a mistake: 80 percent reuse of existing code is quite an achievement for a company. Most programmers would rather write it themselves than rely on anyone else's code, no matter what *it* is. An 80 percent level of reuse is a tribute to the dedication of the group who wrote the original software library, and to the quality of their work. But software development is such a new and mysterious enterprise that a company with an impressive success doesn't even know it.

### Competition

It's easy to start a software business, so a lot of people do. No need to purchase heavy machinery—about $10,000 for a PC and some software, a corner of a room, and a bright idea will do it. So competition exists on all levels. Thousands of loners distribute shareware (small, inexpensive programs for which users, if they are pleased, can mail checks for $20 to the address displayed, for example, when the program starts). The two-developer garage shop is legendary. There are tiny start-ups with minuscule funding; well-funded start-ups; and hotshot companies that were start-ups yesterday but have now shipped a product that sold well. Large corporations establish well-funded research labs, ignore their research, and create another round of well-funded start-ups. The wheel turns.

All that competition keeps things tough. Every day companies spring up, get venture capital, hire some people who work frantically for a few years, fail to make a go of it, and fold. For every Microsoft or Lotus, there are thousands of companies that you have never heard of, and probably never will hear of.

### Rapid Change

All this competition ensures that no one slows down. Processors get faster, memory gets cheaper, displays get larger and finer, printers start printing in zillions of typefaces and colors, and your product had better be able to take advantage of all these new capabilities. The achievements of the computer hardware industry have been remarkable, so nearly every book about computers contains some variant of the following cliché: "If the auto industry did what the computer industry has done, a Rolls Royce would get a thousand miles to the gallon, go a million miles per hour, and cost $99."[19] This is nonsense physics, but the real problem with this statement is that, without software, the computer is just an inert hunk—and the software just can't keep up.

I got my first job working with computers in 1985. The tools I then used to write, edit, and typeset manuals are now utterly obsolete.[20] The tools now used for those tasks are an outgrowth of the personal workstations and large, high-resolution monitors that were then only just starting to be sold. Knowing the old tools qualifies me as a genuine oldtimer in some circles, after just eight years!

Writing tools are the least of it, of course. Fernando Corbató, a pioneer in the development of the time-sharing, general-purpose computer, writes: "A key reason we cannot get ambitious systems right is change. The computer field is intoxicated with change. We have seen galloping growth over a period of four decades and it still does not seem to be slowing down."[21]

A new generation of hardware appears every few years, and software developers scramble madly to crank out *something* that uses the new machines' potential. For a brief time, the market is wide open, but late entrants must play catch-up. So someone with a gleam in the eye borrows money to start a company. Developers give up home life and sanity to get the product out the door while the company can still hope to make money on it. We'll polish the rough edges for the next release, when it's not so crazy, they think.

But for the next release, they are adapting the software to run on a newer computer. In theory, this process—known as a *port*—is simple: copy the program onto the new machine, change a few well-insulated places that depend on specific aspects of the machine (are the registers in the processor 16 bits or 32 bits? that sort of thing), compile it and run it. In practice, a port is never straightforward. The program turns out to depend on the specifics of the computer in all kinds of places. Even if the original programmers made an effort to isolate and mark these dependencies (as they're supposed to), a few surprises always turn up. They are typically hard to find. The interactions they represent are typically unplanned and unexpected. Often, accommodating them to the new machine means solving some difficult technical problem on a production schedule. The difficult technical problem wins, and the schedule limps off to the venture capitalist, hat in hand.

The pace of change in the computer industry is hard on education, too. It takes two or three years to write a textbook that will be out of date when it is published. Nor are there a lot of places to get a computer science or software engineering degree. A lot of the programs that do exist are relatively new; at both the college and graduate level, computer science and software engineering professors continue to argue over the core curriculum—what every graduate should know to be considered a professional. They don't agree on many points; some of the field's leading contributors are also some of the key critics of the present curriculum.[22]

This leads directly to another squeeze on software development: a shortage of qualified, experienced, mature practitioners. The shortage is nowhere near as pronounced as it was twenty-five years ago; it is even possible to be an unemployed programmer for a while, if you are unfortunate enough to live in the wrong part of the world. But on the whole, it's still hard to hire the person you want.

### Hard to Cut Costs

Developing software costs what it costs—it's tough to see what to cut. A manufacturing enterprise can search for a cheaper source of copper, or a way to substitute a cheaper material. It can close the plant in Flint, Michigan, and open one in Monterrey, Mexico, and pay the workers one-tenth as much. Such economies are arguably not impossible with software, but they are much, much harder.

The main budget item for a software development project is educated, trained, well-paid professional brainpower. Some enterprises contract out programming to Asia, where competent programmers can presumably be hired for considerably less than their North American or European counterparts. But often, companies need people with specific backgrounds and skills. A recent book details the disciplined, rigid approach that the more docile, disciplined, and conformist workers of Japanese electronics firms tolerate.[23] Some cost-cutting may be possible, although logistically difficult for the North American or European entrepreneur.

One much-overlooked way to cut costs is to write fewer lines of code in the first place. This requires a disciplined, focused approach, and a willingness to invest money up front in such software engineering activities as thoughtful requirements specification, careful design, and thorough testing. But these are the very activities most often cut under deadline pressures.[24]

### Easy to Copy, Easy to Steal

Another reason why it's hard to make money in the software business is the nature of the product itself: a magnetic pattern on a plastic diskette, 3 and 1/2" on a side. It runs on a computer that can also be used to make another diskette with another copy of the same software. Pamela Samuelson, an expert on the legal aspects of computing, makes this point: "Selling computer programs . . . has become comparable to selling a customer the Ford automotive plant at the same time as selling him or her a Ford automobile."[25] Except that it is a lot easier to copy a diskette than to operate an automotive plant.

When the market for software was just starting, producers tried to protect themselves by selling diskettes that couldn't be copied. But both hard disks and diskettes can die, leaving users without a back-up copy of legitimately purchased software. Users therefore complained loudly and the practice was stopped. This left software vendors with few options. What they do now is to shrink-wrap the diskettes in plastic. The license agreement says that as soon as you tear open the plastic you agree to their terms of use: the license holder has the right to use *one* copy of the software. Short of staffing massive surveillance centers and installing video cameras behind every computer user, I see no way that this license agreement is generally enforceable.

Like other unenforceable laws, it is ineffective: "Shrink wrap licenses . . . are widely ignored by consumers who continue to use and share software as if they had acquired the software without restriction" says Samuelson, and that jibes with my own experience. For instance, an older man I know, a retired engineer, once discussed with me that favorite '80s question, should he buy an IBM PC or a Macintosh? Because he had little experience with software, I suggested that a Mac might be easier to learn and use. But, he said, I have a friend with an IBM PC, and I could use his software. Coming as I do from the software community, I was shocked, but I soon learned that I was out of touch with reality. This man, who has probably paid every parking ticket he ever got, views an act that is technically a crime as mere borrowing. How can anyone dream of making money in a business in which customers can so easily take products without paying for them and feel as if they had done nothing wrong?

### Psychological Resistance

The software development process sucks up resources—time, people, money—to a much greater extent than we ever expect, and no one wants to pay for it. Software is immaterial; you can't knock on it and make it go *thunk*. The product of five years' effort by one hundred people or ten minutes' effort by one person reduces to the same physical object: the plastic diskette. The sweat doesn't show.

But something else is at work as well. I can understand the bemusement people felt twenty-five years ago when their schedules slipped, but it is now harder to see why people are still unwilling to fund software development projects, whether custom or commercial, to the level that they are going to need. Decades of evidence show that wishful thinking is more expensive in the long run, but "gutless estimating," as Fred Brooks called it, remains rampant.

## THE ORGANIZATION

A lot of software is created in corporations, and top corporate management seems to have learned how to organize people for a common goal by watching the same films I watched in college psychology class. They showed the social dynamics of a baboon troop: hierarchies of males with clearly established dominant-subordinate relations. A strict chain of command, yessir.

Dominance hierarchies may not be the *absolute worst* mechanism for getting some sort of work done, but they aren't particularly suited to software development. Invention comes unbidden; subtle stubborn fact cannot be commanded; technical details must not be ignored. Gerald Weinberg complains of the inappropriateness of corporate hierarchy in *The Psychology of Computer Programming:*

> In an engine, for example, the valves are not the "boss" of the cylinders, nor is the crankshaft the "boss" of the valves. The hierarchical organization, which so many of our projects seem to emulate, comes to us not from the observation of successful machines or natural systems, but from the 19th century successes of the Austrian Army. Yet it would be difficult to imagine two groups which differ more than a bunch of privates and a bunch of programmers.[26]

Dominance hierarchies are poor organizational structures for software development projects. For one thing, programmers as a rule respect competence above status; many have nothing but contempt for managers with high-sounding titles and fancy offices who can nevertheless be fooled with technical obfuscation. They are unlikely to respect the decisions of one who does not have the technical background to discuss the consequences of those decisions. Authority, to many programmers, is not real until it has beaten them in a contest of technical prowess. Whoever has the authority to make decisions must understand technical issues.

Technically ignorant project managers are less common than they used to be, but higher up in the corporate hierarchy, technical ignorance remains the rule. People with enough experience of software development to see the difficulties inherent in a project require the authority to make decisions; instead, they frequently have only weak influence. They cannot make expensive decisions; they can only communicate recommendations upward.

Corporate anthropology can be revealing. If you study an organization the way an anthropologist studies a different culture, you can see how the beliefs and behaviors of its participants can make its product better or worse. The structure of an organization can contribute to the quality, safety, and reliability of its software. Yet the weaknesses exhibited by corporate hierarchies are at their worst when undertaking large, complex, and hazardous engineering efforts.

In one study, a researcher examined the construction and operation of offshore oil-drilling platforms to determine the characteristics of an organization that contribute to safety, or its lack.[27] Offshore oil-drilling platforms are not software, but building them requires communicating complex technical information so that intelligent decisions can be made. Therefore the problems she found with corporate reporting structures are also relevant to software development projects. Most pertinent were:

- *No corporate memory.* Failures are likely to be kept secret, so nothing is learned from them. Also, promotions or transfers often ensure that managers do not witness or learn from the results of their actions. In the software industry, frequent job changes serve the same function.

- *Disincentives for accurate reporting.* As the information percolates upward, details vanish that would have qualified or enriched it. The decision-maker receives impoverished information.

The incentive structure is "dominated by corporate goals":

*. . . there are strong incentives to stick to goals and constraints as set. There is relatively little individual penalty for technical failures. . . . There is, however, high individual penalty in the long run for not reaching corporate targets.*[28]

Gerald Weinberg makes the same point:

*It is difficult, if not impossible, to reward [a worker] for accurate report-ing at the same time he is being reprimanded for poor performance. Inas-much as the hierarchical system of organization requires this confusion of goals for its managers, we generally see reporting systems in this type of organization move further and further away from meaningfulness as time goes on.*[29]

Fernando Corbató also echoes the theme: "with more levels of manage-ment, the topmost layers become out of touch with the relevant bottom issues," he observes, and "subordinates hate to report bad news."[30] This puts it mildly.

Dominance hierarchies are notoriously poor at communicating subtle information upward. They're not bad at communicating things down-ward—schedules and goals propagate down the chain of command with relative ease. Top management simply pegs the reward structure to them, and that gets the message across. What's broken is the mechanism for getting the reality-check back up the chain. For software develop-ment, this is a recipe for unpleasant surprises.

Management decisions have consequences; technical information bear-ing on those consequences has to climb out of a gravity well of resis-tance to information from low-status sources. In the process, the information is liable to be distorted and attenuated. Look at what hap-pens to such information-gathering devices as progress reports, for exam-ple.[31] Weinberg writes of an organization with six layers of management hierarchy from the blue-collar programmer at the bottom to the fellow in charge of the whole project. It involved many groups in several loca-tions.[32]

The head of the project told the managers who reported to him that the September progress report was due October 10. These fellows wanted to hand in a spiffy color report, which required twelve days at the printer, so they required their subordinates to hand in September's progress report just before September ended. In order to get the informa-tion on time, *these* managers had to require *their* subordinates to hand in *their* progress reports considerably before the end of the month, and to extrapolate from their due date to the end of September. And so on. The upshot was that the programmers at the bottom were told to sub-mit September's progress report on August 26th. The report thus achieved the status of science fiction.

Moreover, for obvious reasons, extremely bad news was filtered out at each level. But so was extremely good news, because that strategy al-lowed one to show consistent improvement, especially if things didn't go quite right next month. By the time four intermediate levels of managers worked over the information, it was pap.

Corporate hierarchies almost ensure that the consequences of schedules and goals are not well communicated to those whose decisions affect so much, and for software, this is worst-case behavior. The information least likely to make it to the top is the complex, subtle stuff—precisely the information needed to make intelligent decisions about an artifact as opaque as software. The people who make the decisions are therefore using badly degraded information to do so, and it is no wonder if their decisions reflect this.

Poor decisions result in expensive debacles such as that of the Bank of America, which reportedly once spent four years and $20 million to develop a financial system that functioned marginally for less than a year. It cost them $60 million in overtime expenses and late interest charges and $1.5 billion in lost business, and was finally abandoned.[33]

The development of an electronic trading system by the Chicago futures exchanges and Reuters PLC looks as if it may become another expensive mess. The project has experienced repeated delays in its two years of development. A field test conducted on March 3, 1992, failed after only ten minutes, thus deferring a vote on an agreement governing the partnership and postponing the system's inauguration.[34]

Poor decisions also result in canceled projects. This happens more often than you think, because it is seldom discussed. I do not know any programmers who have never worked on a canceled project. I do know some who have never worked on a delivered product, though. I know programmers with twenty years of experience, *none of which* was *ever* incorporated in a product that was sold. Many are like the computer architect described by Tracy Kidder in *The Soul of a New Machine:*

> *Wallach had now spent more than a decade working on computer equipment. He'd had a hand in the design of five computers—all good designs, in his opinion. He had worked long hours on all of them. He had put himself into those creatures of metal and silicon. And he had seen only one of them come to functional life, and in that case the customer had decided not to buy the machine.*[35]

Projects like this are expensive for management, but they aren't fun for the programmers, either. Programmers toil crazy hours for two-and-a-half years on a project that struggles on, falling farther and farther behind schedule, bleeding money and shedding capabilities, until the memo finally comes down from above canceling the thing. After months of increasing stress, initial enthusiasm has become grim exhaustion and finally bitter cynicism. In the aftermath, these people develop a harder attitude toward spending their heart's blood on a project. I know programmers who, wishing to devote their energies wholeheartedly to *something,* have changed professions. More often, though, they simply change jobs. Too many canceled projects turn idealistic kids in love with their jobs into cynical, hard-to-manage job-hoppers.

Yet some efforts can succeed only with wholehearted dedication. Some things are so hard to do that commitment and devotion must be harnessed to skill and talent if they are ever to be done at all. Intelligent, talented, and committed people are a resource, too. We cannot afford to burn them up the way we now do in the software industry.

## THE PROCESS

The pressures on software development are considerable, and the organization is not optimal for the task. But what is the task? The following models of software development define the basic activities.

### Software Development Activities

Over the years, practitioners have developed the following model of how software should be developed. First, the customer and the developers sit down together to specify what the system should be required to do. Next, the software is designed—experienced people plan the program's structure. Determining the program's structure allows you to divide the work up so that different people or teams can each work on a piece. Each programmer or team of programmers then implements the system. (This is the part of the process that everyone thinks of when you say "programming a computer." It involves writing the lines of code—the instructions.) Then the program goes through some quality assurance process, usually testing, and bugs are found and fixed. Finally, the program is released to the customer, who finds more bugs and may also request new features. The process of fixing those bugs and adding new features is misleadingly called "maintenance."

This model of how software is developed is known as the *waterfall model,* shown in Figure 3-2, because each stage is supposed to flow into the next like a series of waterfalls flowing into one pool after another down a mountainside. It's an idealization; projects don't actually work this way.

The problem is that you aren't going to think of everything at just its appointed hour. You may have an unusually articulate and sophisticated customer, and you may believe that together you have specified everything the system is required to do. But as soon as you begin to design the system, you will come up against problems for which the specification provides no guidance. A practical person may wish to ask the cus-

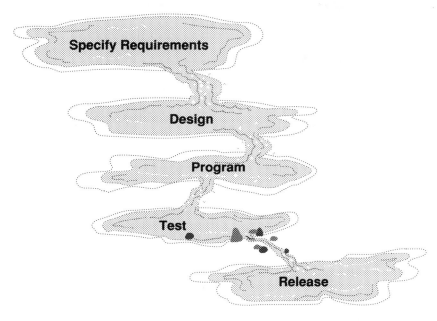

**Figure 3-2.**  The Waterfall Model for Developing Software

tomer more questions, but this is embarrassing if you have already collected your payment for having reached the specification milestone. Then, when the programmers are implementing the system, even more questions come up. They may require further clarification of the requirements, and perhaps some redesign, too. Then a bug found during testing will cause you to question your entire design approach.

One software project is sufficient to drive home the point that a computer program is a big fat welter of interdependencies over which you cannot squeeze the strait jacket of the waterfall process model. So realistic software practitioners of various viewpoints invented another idealization: the spiral model. The *spiral model* of software development, shown in Figure 3-3, simply recognizes the fact that one must continually revisit prior stages as one learns more at later stages.

The most often followed software development model, however, is the Casey model, shown in Figure 3-4. It was named to commemorate a very young vice president of engineering. The chief designer of his next-generation product came to him one day and proposed building a *prototype* of the system—a fully or partly functional system implemented for the twin purposes of teaching the developers more about the problem, and teaching the users more about the solution. He thought this might

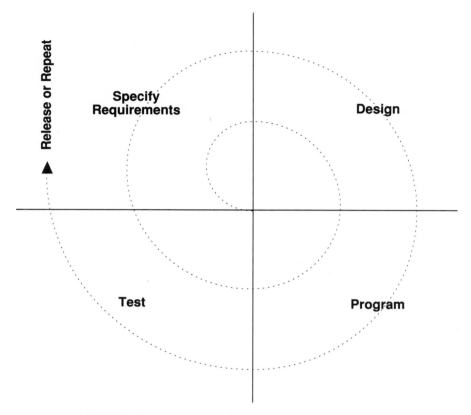

**Figure 3-3.** The Spiral Model for Developing Software

lead to a deeper understanding of the problem and, ultimately, to a better product. The very young vice president, feeling the heat of the schedule, responded by shouting, "No! Start coding, dammit!" Soon afterward, the chief designer quit.

The Casey model can be expressed as follows: the only stage of the software life cycle that doesn't turn out to be optional, in a pinch, is writing the code. This is the difference between programming and software engineering. *Programming* is writing the code. *Software engineering* involves all the other activities—defining the requirements, making a careful and thoughtful design, testing the result thoroughly, and more—that you do in order to get it right.

However seldom it is actually used, the waterfall model defines the major software development activities. Each activity brings problems. It's

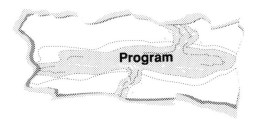

**Figure 3-4.** The Casey Model for Developing Software

hard to specify what you want. Once you do, all kinds of changes will be requested, threatening chaos. The program can be designed and implemented an infinite number of ways. It has to be completed far faster than anyone believes possible. When it is done, it cannot possibly be tested enough to ensure that it will reliably perform as specified. It is sold, duly warranted to be of low reliability. Customers then continue your testing program, finding bugs and paying for them to be fixed.

### What Do You Want, Anyway?

After nearly every software debacle, someone can be counted on to say, "Actually, that's not a bug. The system behaved just as it was supposed to." And they're often right, in a narrow way. Determining how the system is supposed to behave is the hard part.

After a decision to go ahead with a particular software system, the customers, users, and developers should sit down together and talk about what the system is required to do. This is a two-way process:

- The users or the customers (sometimes they're the same people; sometimes they're not) must educate the developers about the *problem domain*—their world. They have to tell them about their business if it's a business system, or about flying if it's an aviation system.

- The developers must educate the customers about what's possible. The customers may have a rosy notion that a particular function would be great, without any clear idea of how much more time and expense it would take to implement. On the other hand, the customers may not ask for a particular function because they may not realize that it would be a snap to add.

The communication that takes place between customers and developers is deeply flawed. They live in two different worlds: the customers are thinking about air flow or accounts payable, and the developers are thinking about data structures and module interfaces. Occasionally even the same word—*file,* for example—can mean two different things.

In general, though, the customers are somewhat more successful in communicating the requirements than the developers are in communicating capabilities and limitations, at least at first. This is true for three reasons: the developers are motivated to get the requirements, without which it is tough to start work (and therefore to send the first bill). The developers' communication task is less well defined—the customers may not even expect to receive much information about technical issues. Finally, the customers speak in the vocabulary of the real world. Money, air pressure, or pieces of sheet metal are things that both customers and developers have experienced. The developers speak in the vocabulary of computers, which the customers are less likely to have experienced, at least to any depth.

What emerges from this flawed process is a specifications document, known from now on as a *spec:* a long, deadly dull document consisting of zillions of paragraphs, numbered hierarchically in the manner of your most boring college texts.[36] A tiny portion of a specification for a flight control system for a simple little Cessna (if you had to write one) might read something like this:

```
18.1.2 Guidance. When the pilot pushes the con-
trol stick of the airplane to the right, the
aileron on the right wing shall lift accordingly,
and the aileron on the left wing shall fall ac-
cordingly. Likewise, when the pilot pushes the
control stick to the left, the aileron on the
left wing shall lift accordingly, and the aileron
on the right wing shall fall accordingly.
```

The point of the numbered paragraphs and the sparkling prose is to dissect the system down to the last detail and identify every behavior required. Armed with a list of requirements, you can identify all the steps you are going to take to satisfy them, so that the system you build will perform as everyone expects, hopes, and has paid for.

If not, at least there will be a document to argue over. The numbered paragraphs are in support of these arguments, among other things. In theory, they help you trace every piece of code in the ultimate system back to the requirement it was put there to satisfy. If a requirement is not satisfied, they allow everyone in the room to reference unambiguously *which* requirement they are shouting about. And they allow one requirement to refer to another.

Writing the spec is difficult for a lot of reasons. It's hard to think of every single detail that you used to be able to take for granted. It's even harder because it's so easy to add new features, thereby creating more details. It's hard to specify how the system is going to interact with users. It's easy to overlook the fact that you might be depending on something outside the system. It's hard to foresee all possible events. Two requirements, separated by hundreds of pages, can contradict each other. An unforeseen pattern of events can cause the system to loop interminably, or to deadlock. And it's hard to write all these details down carefully in imprecise human language.

For example, let's return to the snippet from the flight control system above. At first glance, it seems complete. What more could there be to say? The pilot pushes on the stick, the aircraft follows the push, in the same direction and to the same degree.

You didn't use to have to specify these things, though; you could take them for granted in the course of building the airplane. In small, simple airplanes, the pilot's stick is linked by a mechanical cable to the control surfaces of the wings. Moving the stick moves the ailerons; the pilot's gestures communicate naturally with the wings. In commercial jets (except the newest), the cable is augmented with hydraulics to allow the pilot to control a jet's more massive surfaces with a reasonable degree of muscular effort. In some new commercial jets, however, neither mechanical nor hydraulic cable directly connects the pilot's gestures with the control surfaces of the aircraft. The link is merely symbolic, represented digitally in a microprocessor. And software does not intrinsically "know" that the direction and extent of the pilot's input must correspond to its real-world result. You have to say so. Software has no common sense.

That word "accordingly" in the spec above is therefore far too vague. The requirement needs rewriting:

**18.1.2  Guidance.**

**18.1.2.1 Direction.** When the pilot pushes the control stick of the airplane to the right, the aileron on the right wing shall lift, and the aileron on the left wing shall fall. Likewise, when the pilot pushes the control stick to the left, the aileron on the left wing shall lift, and the aileron on the right wing shall fall.

**18.1.2.2** Extent. Increasingly greater deflection of the stick shall correspond to increasingly greater movements of the ailerons.

This is one small point in a system designed to control an airplane's entire flight behavior. The system's developers have to think of every one of the things that common sense or physics used to allow us to take for granted.

It is hard enough trying to foresee all contingencies in an ordinary physical system, but software adds flexibility to do things you could never do before. An example is the envelope protection feature common in digital flight control systems.

Engineers sometimes refer to the limits of the structural integrity of the aircraft as its *envelope. Envelope protection* assures that the aircraft cannot be flown outside these limits—an ability that could never be implemented until the advent of digital systems. It is equivalent to rewriting paragraph 18.1.2.2 with the following qualifier:

**18.1.2.2 Extent.** Increasingly greater deflection of the stick shall correspond to increasingly greater movements of the ailerons, to the limit of the structural integrity of the airframe.

This in turn spawns a new set of requirements:

**18.1.2.2.1 Safety.** If the pilot pushes the stick too far in too short a time, the aircraft shall execute the steepest turn that does not exceed the tolerances of the airframe for structural integrity.

And therefore:

**18.1.2.2.1.1** The system shall monitor air speed.
**18.1.2.2.1.2** The system shall monitor . . .
*<other factors to monitor—there will be many>*

**18.1.2.2.1.n** The system shall compute the steepest possible banking angle compliant with the constraints of the airframe structural integrity.

The system has just gotten a whole lot more complicated. Demands on its computational resources have just gone up considerably. Many interactions are now possible that may not have been foreseen. And we have just introduced a whole lot of new ways that it can fail.

Adding new features is seductive, and it leads to a disease that digital systems are prone to: feature-itis. You have seen the symptoms on unusable remote controllers sprouting hundreds of buttons.

As I write this, the Boeing Corporation's Commercial Airplane Group is developing a digital flight control system for its next-generation jet, the Boeing 777. The chief engineer in charge of the flight control system recently spoke about the need to resist an endless proliferation of tempting features:

> *The software development has exhibited the usual problems: memory requirements were underestimated, bugs were found, there have been cost overruns and late deliveries. But, McWha emphasized, software is not the problem. The requirements are the problem; in particular, he emphasized the need to resist all the late changes that try to creep in. In most branches of engineering, he said, natural laws limit the growth of the requirements, but software has no such laws. Hence there seems no limit to the complexity one can require. The specs become wish lists, and changes grow "cancerously" until one loses the ability to understand or control the software.*[37]

Figure 3-5 shows a sign that hangs over the desk of the chief engineer of the Boeing 777 flight control system.

It's impossible to specify all circumstances, and unforeseen events can always cause problems. Consider this example of a poorly specified insurance system:

> *. . . a three-step reinsurance cycle where one firm reinsured with a second, which reinsured with a third, which reinsured with the first, which was thus reinsuring itself and paying commissions for accepting its own risk. The computer program checked only for short cycles.*[38]

The problem that British Rail was having with autumn leaves, described in the previous chapter, is another example. When the designers of the signaling system wrote the spec, they did not specify that the wheels had to make contact with the sensors in the tracks. They took it for granted that gravity would not be repealed. They did not realize that another circumstance—wet leafmeal pasting the wheels—could cause loss of contact. It did not occur to them because it had never happened: the clutch brakes kept the wheels scraped clean. The signaling system de-

```
                 NO!
(What part of this don't you understand?)
```

**Figure 3.5**
A Management Tool
for the Boeing 777
Flight Controls

pended on an incidental feature of the braking system to screen an inevitable environmental input.

There's *no way* something like that makes it into the spec. The system designers don't know they're depending on it. The problem it prevents has never happened. The preventive mechanism is outside the system they're designing. If you had to think of every contingency that met this description, how many do you think you'd miss?

Specs don't cause as many problems as they might only because they are seldom written. The spec is begun; people get a feel for the system, and then they feel pressed to start designing and implementing it. They promise to keep the spec up to date as they work. They never do. Many commercial software developers do not go to the trouble to write a spec at all. Some programmers seldom see a spec in their entire careers, much less are asked to work from one. Ordinarily, specs are written and attended to only for large, complex, mission-critical or safety-critical software projects, and not always then, either. As Peter Neumann, an expert on software for critical systems, writes:

> *Casual practice in establishing requirements and in writing specifications supposedly to meet those requirements—or worse yet, designing systems without much attention to requirements and specifications—remains widespread.*[39]

A lot of laser printer toner has been spent bemoaning this state of affairs, but things haven't changed much. Production pressures make the world go around; we had better learn more effective ways to cope with them.

### Fifty Ways to Write a Program

The first program I ever wrote was a homework assignment; it was about a dozen lines long.[40] As we handed in our papers, I glanced at the other students' programs. They looked pretty much like mine.

That didn't last. By the time we handed in the third assignment (about two pages), I was amazed at how much our programs differed. In response to the same problem, no two people will write the same program. A program is a mirror of the mind that wrote it, and human minds vary infinitely.

In essence, the software design problem is that any question can have infinitely many answers. Some answers are better than others, though—particularly if you are worried about such issues as ensuring safe behavior even with incorrect inputs, or making sure that someone else can come along three years from now and understand the program well enough to port it to a new computer.

Even within such limits, no single answer is obviously right, but there are plenty of opinions. Programmers tend to be smart; they have lots of opinions. Furthermore, each is likely to have different histories and to have seen different strategies succeed or fail. Many have been right often enough to cling stubbornly to their points of view, and the situations are so complicated that many viewpoints may be valid. The result is that several intelligent, strong-minded, energetic, opinionated people may argue over every detail. I have attended design meetings that reminded me of rams butting heads for hours. Given the authority, technically savvy managers can make intelligent decisions when their opinionated, intelligent charges argue vociferously over a design decision, and it will take technical savvy to command enough respect to make it stick. In poorly managed projects, such wrangles can go on for months, preventing the system from making any progress whatsoever.

### Structuring the Team

There is considerable tension in software development between the need for a large, complex system that only a team can produce, and the design integrity, clarity, and economy only an individual mind can produce. This tension is resolved in various ways. Sometimes a lone wolf goes off into a corner, and, several years later, has produced something that the marketing department decides they can sell. Because no one expected the product, the schedule has not been a problem. This happens more often than you'd think; managers do not always understand what their subordinates are doing. Nor is it necessarily a bad idea; some useful software has been written this way. Before corporations had a lot of experience with software developers, some would even invite this behavior: a help wanted ad from 1967 promises to train the employee and then "turn you loose."[41] Any corporation that ran such an ad nowadays would be really reckless, though—it happens often enough without asking for it.

A more common approach is to organize smaller and smaller subteams, reflecting the way the design has divided up the problem. Each subteam is responsible for smaller and smaller portions of the work, until an individual-sized contribution is reached. The point is to find the most efficient and sensible way for each programmer to deal with just a portion of the system, since the whole is too complex and too overwhelming.[42]

But every solution is a Pandora's box of fresh problems. Many small teams working on a project means that more communication is required among them, and therefore more opportunity for misunderstanding and miscommunication. Many small modules require more interfaces and therefore more opportunities to pass too much, too little, or the wrong information.

The tug-of-war between the need for an individual contributor and a team is always present. Software that reaches the market today is commonly the product of a team. Just as commonly, key portions of it are the product of one individual: a major contributor, a designated hero, a high-status, well-rewarded person of stunning competence who put in completely insane hours for as long as it took.

For years, certain practitioners have recommended this approach. The designated hero has been called "the chief programmer" by Harlan Mills[43] or the "surgeon" by Fred Brooks.[44] But both recommend formally recognizing the designated hero and providing specialized help. The approach is not often formally implemented, but it often evolves informally, because it's the best compromise between these two contradictory needs. Still, while an informal evolution may produce a "chief programmer," it doesn't provide the special help that can make such a person most effective.

### Optimistic Scheduling

Trouble creeps up unexpectedly just as the project seems about 80 percent or 90 percent done. It is unexpected, but it shouldn't be; as Brooks has pointed out, the schedule has been created absurdly assuming that nothing will go wrong.[45] This is not realistic.

According to Norman Augustine, "Any task can be completed in only one-third more time than is currently estimated."[46] The crucial word in that sentence is "currently." Your current estimate is still off, even after its upward revision by one-third. Like Zeno's hare, you just get closer and closer to an ever-retreating finish line.

A lot of software projects feel like that. That last 10 percent takes forever.

For example, as discussed in Chapter 1, the development of On Location seemed to go smoothly from April (when it started) until September (two months before it was due to ship). Then, with the project's features essentially complete, "everything started going wrong." Several features thought to be pretty simple turned out to be quite hard. The last 10 percent of the project took not two months, but six—adding four to the originally scheduled seven. "It's like a Russian doll," said the director of marketing. "Every time we finally crack open one problem, we find there's another one inside."[47]

Classic reactions to schedule trouble are to reorganize the project or throw more bodies at it. Panicked organizations have done both. Neither is a particularly smart move. A reorganization disrupts established lines of communication and new ones have to be learned; this is not a recipe for improving the schedule. Throwing more bodies at the problem is known to be a lousy idea—as long ago as 1978, Fred Brooks wrote, "Adding manpower to a late software project makes it later."[48] But no one can think of a better solution, so they do it anyway.

To be fair, it isn't intuitively obvious why adding more people should be so little help. If you were trying to produce a certain number of bricks, more people could be a big help, under the right circumstances. But software ain't bricks: the new people must first learn about the existing code, and teaching them absorbs some of the project veterans' time. Then they have to figure out how to accomplish their allotted tasks while having as little impact as possible on the existing system. Over the years, software engineers have propounded a number of mechanisms to help with the problem.[49] A lot of research has been done because the problem crops up again and again. If a project is well-designed to start with, such mechanisms can prove useful. If it just grew like Topsy, it's going to be much more difficult for the new people to stay out of the rest of the team's way. In either case, it's a dubious experiment.

For example, in October (at the proverbial eleventh hour: one month before the original shipment date), a new programmer was added to the On Location development team. She was supposed to write the code that, as far as I'm concerned, makes the whole system worth using: it allows me to request files that include the words "shipping software," for example, and get all the files that include "shipped" or "ships" or "shipment" as well. The code she had to add can be described by the phrase *fuzzy searches*.

But just because the functionality can be described by a discrete phrase does not mean that it can be added without affecting any other code. It was unrealistic to expect that such a change could be added at the last minute without affecting anything else—and, of course, it didn't. The code collided with someone else's code, and the resulting bug took yet more time to find and fix.

Schedule pressures are common in most large endeavors. Nevertheless, caving into them can be tantamount to organizational insanity. The paper on offshore oil-drilling platforms reports the following amazing incident: "In 1969, a platform slid in the mud of the Gulf of Mexico because the design of the foundation was completed before the results of soil tests were known."[50] Management was aware of the potential problem, but schedule pressures dictated pressing ahead with the design for a *foundation* for a structure. The structure weighs many tons, it rests in mud in a restless sea, and they couldn't stop to find out what kind of mud it was to rest in?

This insanity is not even in the best interests of the organization, let alone its employees, the rest of us, or the fish. An offshore oil-drilling platform costs about $400 million. To patch an inadequate structure to make it safer may cost approximately $9 million more. Holding a timely design review, on the other hand, costs about $100,000. This is a general characteristic of complex engineering endeavors. An exactly analogous situation holds for software—the sooner you find and fix the bug, the cheaper it is to fix.[51]

### Planning to Throw One Away[52]

Another decision is whether to build a prototype or not.[53] A *prototype* is a model of the system that shows some, or even all, of the functionality of the final system, but is not a product. Even if a prototype incorporates all the functionality of the system, it isn't a product because a product has to do a whole lot more than simply fulfill the functional requirements. It must be testable, for example; and the code must be comprehensible to programmers who have not worked on it (so they can fix bugs or add new functions). The prototype might perform too slowly for a real product, or it might not be robust, crashing in response to an input that differs in even the slightest way from the input the developer expected.

Nevertheless, a prototype can be quite useful. Building a prototype teaches the developers a lot about both the problem domain and the issues involved in implementing it. In order to build a prototype, the developers have to communicate with the people who understand the problem, be it corporate finance, automotive transmissions, or cardiac diagnosis. The prototype reveals, as nothing else can, where the misunderstandings lie. It may also reveal which technical issues are going to be the tough nuts to crack.

Prototyping was the design strategy chosen by Mitch Kapor for On Location. It was a good choice. There is no way of knowing what it did to the schedule, but I can personally vouch for the fact that it helped sales. It was after seeing a prototype that an "industry guru" suggested that the product should be able to "find any word in a file, not just the file names as originally intended."[54] That's what *I* bought the product to do, all right. On a Macintosh, several free utilities allow users to find files by name—I wouldn't spend $75 for another.

Another aspect of the system for which a prototype is incomparably useful is the user interface. To test a user interface, you don't even have to implement most of the system. You just have to develop the part that a user sees—the windows, the menus, the questions that the user must answer, and the mechanisms that will be available to answer them. Then you round up some people who represent the typical user population and let them poke at it. You watch what they have trouble with; you watch the mistakes they make; you see the assumptions you made that turn out to be false; you ask them to report their perceptions; perhaps you time them. This exercise can improve a user interface in a number of ways, but only if you choose representative guinea pigs, listen to what they tell you, and change things as a result. Dreadful user interfaces abound, and a lot of systems would have been improved if their developers had chosen this route. But it's time-consuming, and expensive, and it can be difficult to build just the user interface.

Prototyping is often resisted because it can seem like a giant step sideways. Why go to all that trouble to build a system that you may never use? You are behind schedule already. Even if you know, on an intellectual level, that it will teach you what you need to learn to deliver a high-quality product, it still feels like madness in the gut. If a prototype is built, the temptation can become overwhelming to fix its defects and declare it the product. After all, it functions, and you're late. If it isn't good enough, you can fix it for the next release. This is folly, but it has been done.

The decision to prototype the system, and then use what you've learned to build the real system, is virtually impossible for the manager of any software project unless top management supports it. It will take longer to specify, design, and code the final system. You will then have far fewer bugs to fix, but, as Weinberg notes, "It will always be difficult to appreciate how much trouble we are *not* having . . .".[55]

For this reason, you rarely see the word "prototyping" in the software engineering literature without the word "rapid" in front of it. This is an attempt by the underlings to brainwash management into taking the correct risk.

### Testing Till the Seas Run Dry

No product of human intellect comes out right the first time. We rewrite sentences, rip out knitting stitches, replant gardens, remodel houses, and repair bridges. Why should software be any different?

QA—*quality assurance*—is the thankless, unglamorous job of making sure that the system works. The QA function is a perfect example of co-operation disguised as competition. But the folks involved seldom see it that way. QA has little prestige among software developers. The QA team usually feels underpaid and underappreciated and forced to work under schedules even less realistic than those of the developers, and for the most part they are right. It is a shame.

One reason for the relatively low prestige of QA work is that, unlike development, QA seldom provides the opportunity to glorify the contributions of a single individual. Thus it is difficult, if not impossible, to achieve hero status. Instead, QA is the quintessential team effort. This is actually a benefit, as it is often much easier to divide up the work of testing than the work of development.

What with ever-changing goals and eleventh-hour crises, the average QA program for commercial software consists of whatever the schedule will allow. Management certainly isn't going to give the QA team their originally allotted four months, because development has long ago swallowed those four months and more. They might be lucky to get two weeks to hammer on the product before shipment is scheduled. The result is that the testing team seldom has time to do its task properly.

To test software, you need to get representative test data and run the program with it. To test a program thoroughly, you should test every thread of execution, but this takes forever. So you bang on it unthinkingly, and hope you hit all the important stuff. You won't, though. A more systematic approach is to test each requirement in the spec; at least you'll know the product does everything it's supposed to. But you won't know what else it does that it shouldn't.

Testing software thoroughly is simple—and impossible. You determine and gather all possible inputs. For each, you test all possible sequences of instructions—all possible threads through the system that could be executed. In each case, you determine that the program behaves as it should. If it does not, you find the problem, fix it, and retest the fixed system from scratch.

That's all there is to it. It will take somewhere between forty and forty thousand years, depending on the size of the system, how much help you can afford, and how reliable you want it—how much is at stake if it fails.[56] Trying to test every possible thread through the system is like being the hapless janitor who must sweep every cranny of the Minotaur's labyrinth. It is a very large labyrinth. To test every thread of execution requires testing every possible sequence of commands (remember, one part of the system can affect another in subtle, obscure ways). Even for small simple systems, the number of such sequences is enormous.

For example, imagine testing all possible threads of execution for the following simple system:

- A thread of execution consists of a sequence of between one and ten commands.
- Any of twenty different commands can be used to make up the sequence, in any order.
- A command can be repeated any number of times.

For sequences one command long, 20 different threads of execution are possible, one for each command. For sequences two commands long, each of those 20 commands can be followed by twenty others (20 × 20), yielding 400 possible threads of execution. The numbers in Table 3-2 show what mathematicians call, rather delightfully, a combinatorial explosion:

■ **Table 3-2.** The Size of the Minotaur's Labyrinth

| Number of commands | Number of possible threads | | |
|---|---|---|---|
| 1 | 20 | = | 20 |
| 2 | 20 × 20 | = | 400 |
| 3 | 20 × 20 × 20 | = | 8000 |
| 4 | 20 × 20 × 20 × 20 | = | 160,000 |
| 5 | 20 × 20 × 20 × 20 × 20 | = | 3,200,000 |
| 6 | 20 × 20 × 20 × 20 × 20 × 20 | = | 64,000,000 |
| 7 | 20 × 20 × 20 × 20 × 20 × 20 × 20 | = | 1,280,000,000 |
| 8 | 20 × 20 × 20 × 20 × 20 × 20 × 20 × 20 | = | 25,600,000,000 |
| 9 | 20 × 20 × 20 × 20 × 20 × 20 × 20 × 20 × 20 | = | 512,000,000,000 |
| 10 | 20 × 20 × 20 × 20 × 20 × 20 × 20 × 20 × 20 × 20 | = | 10,240,000,000,000 |
| **Total** | | | 10,778,947,368,420 |

There are 31,536,000 seconds in a year (60 × 60 × 24 × 365). If each thread of execution takes (on average) one second to test, your testing program will take over 300,000 years (10,778,947,368,420 ÷ 31,536,000 = 341,798). Of course, you could test faster: 100 tests a second allows you to test the entire corpus in only 3000 years, instead. But faster computers might give you different results.

You can test several copies of the system at a time: testing a hundred copies gets the testing time down to a mere 30 years. Testing a hundred copies is feasible for commercial software, perhaps, but one seldom has more than one or two copies of an F-16 aircraft or a new electronic funds transfer computer network.

And when you find a bug, you have to fix it and then start the entire testing regime over from scratch. Fixing the bug has changed the software, thereby invalidating all previous test results.

If you want very highly reliable software, you have to continue this process for quite a while, because each successive bug has a lower failure rate and thus takes longer to appear. You eventually reach the point of diminishing returns. These theoretical calculations are supported by empirical findings: one investigation has shown that over 30 percent of all bugs reported for a particular widely used operating system caused a failure on average of only once every 5000 years of system operation.[57]

Under the circumstances, software is almost never tested rigorously and thoroughly. People would rather put it into service while their organization still exists to profit from it. Recognizing this, Peter Neumann says: "It is impossible to guarantee your system is going to be dependable. No matter how much testing you do, you're still going to have vulnerabilities."[58] Under the circumstances, testing must be narrowed down.

In despair, you can take your two weeks and just bang on the system. This technique is resorted to when no one has any test plan, because everyone was too busy cranking out bits of the program to think about how they were going to test it. This is pretty bad; most software developers are doing better than this nowadays. But it still happens.

The basic idea of this method is: after the program is running, run it. Get your friends, family, and colleagues to run it. Try doing different things. See what happens.

This approach has the virtue of simplicity. No one has to spend any time or brainpower planning it. The drawbacks are several, however:

- Some testers know too much, because they helped develop the system. They know, for example, what they assumed the inputs would be. They are likely to respect such unenforced assumptions, although their novice users won't.

- Some testers know too little, and have even less commitment to the enterprise. Testing was not planned, so there are too few people to do it in the time allotted. Therefore people throughout the company, with production pressures of their own, are pressed into service. They are untrained in the domain, and their reports of the details of a bug are not reliable, leave out relevant facts, or stress irrelevant ones. Some of these "testers" may not even be able to recognize anomalous behavior when it happens.

- The process is hit-and-miss, a prisoner of probabilities. Threads of execution that are likely to be traveled will be; less likely threads will not be tested.

A related testing strategy uses what are called *beta sites*. A preliminary functional version of a program is called an *alpha* version. After it has been tested inside the development organization, the program becomes a *beta* version. Wise organizations then distribute the *beta* version to other organizations. At these sites, users do what they would ordinarily do and report the bugs they find. *Beta* users are usually chosen to be either representative of the user population, or even more rigorous and demanding in their use of the software.

The search is on for intelligent ways to test software. Researchers study such exotic topics as the topology of programs. Another approach uses the spec.

If written carefully and completely (a big *if*), the spec should contain a finite list of behaviors and features required of the system. We can insist that each requirement be written so that it can be tested. Testing requirements is appealing because it is done from the point of view of the user, and allows us to plan the testing program as we write the spec.[59]

Testing the requirements, unlike testing every thread, is a finite, doable process, at least in theory. But it allows you to test only the specified behavior. Unwanted behavior that must be subtracted from the system (the quintessential "bug") may or may not appear.

Serious testing can involve such herculean effort that, once done, an organization may be tempted to skip it for "minor" changes. The spate of telephone service outages suffered around the United States in the summer of 1991 provides an example of the perils of this approach. The software run by the call-routing computers (signal transfer points, as they are known) was a program consisting of millions of lines that took thirteen weeks to test. The software vendor changed "only a few lines."[60] (You may wonder why, but there are zillions of reasons why it's necessary to make small changes now and then. They may even have done it in response to a customer request.) Since the upgrade represented barely any change at all, the company did not feel that the full thirteen-week testing regime was required.

"In hindsight, that was a huge mistake," said Mr. Frank Perpiglia, vice president of DSC Communications for technology and product development.[61] His commendably forthright admission adds to the growing lore of bug fixes or other "minor" changes that introduce new bugs. It happens all the time.

The developers for the Docklands Light Railway routing software took another approach. After their system passed its tests, they simply refused to change it, no matter what. Therefore, in London in 1989, the Docklands Light Railway habitually stopped pointlessly on an empty portion of elevated track. The train sat for a few minutes with its doors closed and then moved on. The original specifications had called for a stop there because a big development had been planned. For financial reasons, the development was canceled, but not the railway stop. "DLR had already included it in the software which, having been tested, they were unwilling or unable to modify."[62]

If it is impossible to test software long enough to assure ourselves that it is highly reliable, what can we do about it? In practice, what we do is: we accept low reliability, and we pay for the bugs that we find to be fixed.

### We Warrant This Software to Be Unreliable

The average warranty for commercial software acknowledges that software is essentially unreliable. It warrants, basically, nothing. The software is not warranted to be fit for any particular purpose. The company that sold it to you is not liable for any damages you suffer as a result of using their software. They are not liable even if you suffer damage as a result of some bug that they already knew about.

Compared to any other consumer product, this is pathetic. Certainly, nobody would buy a car under a warranty such as this, but some software purchased under a comparable warranty costs as much as a car. We put up with this simply because it is the only game in town. All commercial software is sold under this kind of warranty, or a similar one, because the warranty reflects the realities of software development. It's hard enough to make money developing software without having to promise that it's bug-free when you know it isn't; or that you'll instantly fix every bug you hear about and distribute the fixes immediately, when you know you can't.[63]

### Living with the Results

So users find bugs and pay to have them fixed. This process, and the related one of adding new features, is called *maintenance*.

In February 1991, a software professional told of his frustration in dealing with a subsidiary of an automobile manufacturer. They insisted on periodic scheduled preventive maintenance for the software they were buying.[64] Stories like this make the rounds every so often.

But if practitioners have to overcome these poignant misapprehensions, the software industry has no one to blame but itself for using the blatantly misleading term *maintenance* to describe what happens to software after someone has bought it. Unlike cars or other physical systems, software does not wear out with use. It need not combat friction or overcome inertia; it does not accumulate dust or soot. It therefore does not require cleaning or lubrication—the term *maintenance* is a fig leaf. What software needs after it has been sold is not maintenance, it's repair.

When maintaining software, programmers often add new features, too. Perhaps the program must be upgraded to run on a computer that uses a new version of its operating system. Perhaps users have asked for certain features. Perhaps the company simply needs to stay competitive with a new product, or wishes to sweeten the mood of users who have to pay for and install the upgrade.

But when you pay for software maintenance, what you are mostly paying for is for the company to fix the bugs it did not find during its own testing. Nothing flushes out bugs like a whole bunch of people using the software under realistic, unforgiving conditions for years. Actual use by real users finds more bugs than any testing program ever does.

When users find and report bugs, someone must discover why the software is misbehaving. After finding the cause, some part of the software must be rewritten so that it behaves as it should.

*Documentation.*  Finding the cause is at least as hard as fixing it. It is hard to read a program and figure out what it does. So software professionals generally acknowledge that a program should be documented.

If documentation is done properly, it's a big job. The spec is a formal document that needs updating for each change in the requirements. We also need a formal design document, and the program itself should have lots of helpful comments sprinkled throughout to document how the design was coded. We need a test plan, a set of test input data, and the test results. All these documents are supposed to help the maintainers figure out what the code is doing, why it is doing it, how it was tested, and what happened then. Decisions are documented so that you can keep project history and learn from it. When bugs crop up, the web of dependencies will be traceable; you need not sow new bugs while fixing the old.

In practice, few of these documents are available in a useful form. For example, the requirements have changed dozens of times. Maybe the developers found it too hard to do what they originally set out to do, and made the system less ambitious in order not to slip the schedule too drastically. Other features changed to reflect a deeper understanding of the problem.

Even if there was a formal spec, no one has been updating it. They've all been too busy with other, less onerous chores, because any chore is less onerous than updating the spec. Similarly, the design document is incomplete, because as soon as the design reached the point where programming could begin, it was dropped in favor of the pleasanter activity. Programmers like to program, but they are notorious for hating to write. As one practitioner puts it:

> In my experience, most programmers work best during the rewarding problem-solving and coding phases of a project. When it is time for tedious testing and mindless paperwork, their enthusiasm dwindles, and with it their effectiveness. Sermons about rigor make them feel guilty, but rarely affect work habits. This is not scandalous irresponsibility, it is just human nature.[65]

Nor is the program properly commented. Every programming language has a typographical convention that allows programmers to intersperse the program with helpful explanatory remarks—comments—for people to read, and that the compiler will ignore. Comments help others figure out what the program will do. Theoretically, this information is available from reading the program itself, but in practice it can be exhausting to read more than a few pages of code that you yourself have not written recently. One's own old programs can be confusing; other people's, impenetrable.

Computer science students are therefore taught from their first programming classes that it is good style to place comments in their programs. However, commenting programs turns out to be one of those salutary ideals, like a balanced diet, regular exercise, and eight hours of sleep, that few of us live up to for long. It is usually one of those things that people promise to get back to later when, under production pressures, they let it slide. Most commercial programs are sparsely commented, if at all.

When managers, paid to avert problems, try to enforce a commenting convention on their charges, they can get less than illuminating results, as shown in Figure 3-6.[66]

Of course, some organizations do better than others. Application developers at Microsoft, for example, use a convention called Hungarian to name variables, constants, procedures, and structures so that any other programmer in the group can divine the purpose and use of the item from its name.[68] After all, these items must be named *something;* thus, before a single comment has been written, the program is already informative to the initiated. This piece of common sense is what one might expect from a company whose CEO can program.

**Debugging.** With or without documentation, software maintainers have a tough struggle; it is seldom quick or easy to find the cause of a bug. A bug is often the result of such a precise set of interactions that it is difficult or impossible to replicate. People who report bugs are exhorted to report everything they did up to that point, and every bit of detail about the state of their system. But often the users do not remember a crucial fact, or the bug is a result of an interaction with such a seemingly unrelated part of the system that it occurs to nobody to men-

```
/* Fixed some bugs. JBH */

#define OFF 7
#define ON  7 /* This is the same as OFF now to prevent confusion*/

/* $Header: write_metafile.c,v 1.5 91/07/22 16:19:18 garry Exp $ */

CCCCCCCCCCCCCCCCCCCCCCCCCCCCCCCCCCCCCC

C////////////////////////////////C

C/                               /C

C/    Here is subroutine HRMNC    /C

C/                               /C

C////////////////////////////////C

CCCCCCCCCCCCCCCCCCCCCCCCCCCCCCCCCCCCCC

;; Added an extra set of parentheses, 6/17 krc[67]
```

**Figure 3-6.** Five Comments That Probably Helped Nobody

tion it. Like the funny engine sound that disappears when you drive your car to the shop, no one can make the bug happen again.

Even when a bug can be induced to reoccur, it is frequently the result of such a subtle set of causes that it is the work of hours, days, even weeks to figure out what is happening. (After all, if it hadn't been subtle, the interaction might have been foreseen and prevented in the first place.) Sometimes, in an effort to track down the bug, programmers insert special instructions to make events inside the machine apparent. These instructions can themselves cause problems, as the crew of *Apollo 11* discovered. The alarms that distracted Neil Armstrong as he tried to land the lunar module were just such instructions, inserted to aid debugging.

***Personnel, Round One.*** Under the circumstances, familiarity with the software helps a lot. The person most likely to grasp what is happening is the person who wrote the program. Unfortunately, this person is least likely to be doing this work. The person who must maintain a piece of software is usually someone who has never seen it before. Developers seldom maintain their own software for two reasons: prestige and job mobility.

Like testing, software maintenance is an unglamorous job with few opportunities for glory. The people who developed the software are not maintaining it, they are off developing other wonderful things. The person stuck with maintaining it is often a kid just out of college.

The developers don't work for the same outfit anymore, anyway. Programmers who work for big companies and perform well often wish to move from project to project, because each move offers a promotion or a raise or at least the opportunity for fresh challenges. Others get the same benefits from changing employers. When maintenance programmers become familiar with a system, therefore, they become quite valuable—sometimes valuable enough to insist on a job doing development work.

It can work the other way, too. Sometimes a member of the development team is the only person who knows enough about some software to maintain it. Sometimes this employee, knowing how valuable he or she is, quits to become a consultant. The company, over a barrel, can be forced to pay four or five times the employee's former salary to retain access to information that exists only in this person's head. This happened to the U.K. Foreign Office with the ill-fated Memory Computers accounting software. The situation was made urgent by sheer bad luck:

*... a hard disc shattered inside the old computer, destroying all the information [in the old system], and leaving officials to rely on the new untried system. Within months it started shutting down unexpectedly, and inexplicably posting money to the wrong accounts. All the bookkeeping staff left and their replacements were not able to familiarise themselves properly with the system to prevent further errors.*

*A consultant from the bankrupt software company is now working for the FO [Foreign Office] at a salary of 53 thousand pounds a year to try to solve the problems.*[69]

And just as with the original development, the upgrade is often late, as any number of personal computer users can tell you. The situation is so common, it has its own acronym: RSN, for Real Soon Now, the standard answer organizations give to the query, when will my upgrade arrive? The problems suffered with the Patriot missile installation in Dhahran are atypical solely in that the upgrade arrived only one day later than it was needed. In this case, alas, a day made all the difference.

**The Hell of Constant Upgrades.** After software is deployed, it does not cease to be a resource sink. Bugs keep appearing long after the software is put into service, and someone must pay a battalion of skilled and trained professionals to fix the bugs the users find, and possibly to add new features as they are requested. Peter Mellor, a widely regarded authority on software reliability from the Centre for Software Reliability at City University in London, described the appearance of two old bugs:

*I was told by a colleague, who was a computer engineer, about a UK site which required its operating system to be enormously reliable. . . . They had learned the hard way that each new version brought with it its own crop of new bugs, and so had stayed resolutely out of date for many years. Running a stable job mix and not updating, they eventually achieved four years of failure-free running. At the end of that time, a new, serious, bug was discovered. This had lain dormant all that time.*

*The Air-Traffic Control system at West Drayton has recently been replaced. The previous system had been in use for many years. A software engineer who had studied this system told us that a new bug was recently discovered in a piece of COBOL code which had not been changed for 20 years.*[70]

Other reports have described ancient bugs in the digital flight control system of the X-31[71] and the code that adjusts the system clocks for workstations that run another widely used operating system.[72]

If a system is to remain in use, it needs ongoing maintenance. As these old bugs attest, remaining in use for a long time is the only sure way for software to attain high reliability. If a system can be maintained by those who understand it, they can fix the bugs intelligently and can hope to introduce few new ones. They can then retest the system and return it to service. The bugs get shaken out—progressively fewer appear less often. The system becomes reliable; people learn to trust it. This state of grace is attainable only by mature, widely used products whose maintainers work for a stable organization. Employee turnover mitigates against it. AT&T, for example, explicitly recognizes this when it lists "long-term staff stability" among its techniques for achieving software reliability.[73] In software, the cliché "tried and true" applies as in no other field.

If no one is left who remembers how the system was designed, however, those assigned to maintain it respond to bugs with *patches*—inadequate local fixes and makeshift accommodations. The more patches it accumulates, the harder it is to fix the next bug, as the system grows larger and murkier each time. After a while, it is possible that the person who last fixed the software cannot even explain why the fix worked. Eventually, it succumbs to its accumulated patches with erratic, unpredictable behavior. This means trouble, and corporations struggle with it regularly: an article in *Datamation* describes the problem, and proposes one of many expensive solutions—rewriting all the applications in a new, supposedly clearer language.[74]

After a while, each fix seems like taking more and more of a risk. Programmers cannot even dream of predicting the effects a patch will have, and the fact that it seems to have no undesirable effects today spells nothing for certain about what may occur tomorrow. Under these circumstances, fixing a bug or adding a feature is quite likely to introduce another bug, if not several. Eventually, the only answer is to throw out the entire system and start over again. The Toronto Stock Exchange seems to have hit this wall:

> . . . *Don Unruh, a former TSE vice president who helped develop the system eight years ago, said the problems run deeper than yesterday's malfunction. A patchwork of different software and hardware has emerged over the years, he said. "The people who are making the changes eight years later have no idea what was done by the people who went before them. You end up with these bizarre logic problems." Mr. Unruh, now a consultant who recently wrote a report on the TSE's computers for the Professional Traders Association, said the whole system should be scrapped and a new one developed.*[75]

This ditty, known as "The Maintenance Programmer's Drinking Song," sums it up:

100 little bugs in the code,
100 bugs in the code,
Fix one bug, compile it again,
101 little bugs in the code.
101 little bugs in the code . . .
(Repeat until bugs = 0)

Organizations that develop software have a lot of problems that traditional manufacturing enterprises don't have. They cannot gauge the productivity of their employees by counting words typed per minute or widgets made per day. In an effort to find an objective measure, they have traditionally counted lines of code per programmer per month. But the more code you have, the more it will cost to develop and the harder it will be to maintain. The way to save money on software development is to develop less software. Lines of code are a debit, not an asset.[76]

## WHAT IF IT ABSOLUTELY, POSITIVELY MUST WORK RIGHT THE FIRST TIME?

The software community is not ignoring these problems; they are a key impetus for research, discussion, and a variety of commercial software engineering tools. The Software Engineering Institute was formed to improve the situation. In an attempt to determine where things stand right now, it conducted a five-year survey of a variety of organizations. It spent about a week at each organization and asked over a hundred questions about its software development process. The results were graded on a scale of 1 through 5, where 1 represents *ad hoc* chaos and 5 represents the best we can do. Over 80 percent of the organizations surveyed were at level 1. Fourteen percent had reached level 2. *One* organization, the producers of the Space Shuttle flight control software, had reached level 5.[77] And we know that software has caused problems on several occasions,[78] for example during the May 1992, shuttle flight that had to attempt *three* rendezvous with a communications satellite.[79]

Clearly, we have a long way to go. In 1991, the Pacific Northwest Software Quality Conference sponsored a committee to give a Software Excellence Award to an organization with a high-quality development process and a superior, defect-free product.[80] So who won the Software Excellence Award? Who won the monster beauty contest? Nobody.

We expect new systems to fail; they become reliable only after many years of use by many users. But what if the software controls a critical function? What if it must work reliably from the start? The next chapter discusses how we face these challenges in the development of critical systems.

## NOTES

1 Augustine, Norman R. *Augustine's Laws.* New York: Penguin Books, 1986. The quote is from p. 150.

2 Neumann, Peter G. RISKS Forum, ACM SIGSOFT *Software Engineering Notes,* 10:5, Oct. 1985, p. 6. Item contributed by Nancy Leveson.

3 Bylinsky, Gene. "Help Wanted: 50,000 Programmers." *Fortune,* March 1967, pp. 141ff.

4 Weinberg, Gerald. *The Psychology of Computer Programming.* New York: Van Nostrand Reinhold, 1971.

5 Brooks, Frederick P. *The Mythical Man-Month.* Reading, MA: Addison-Wesley, 1978, p. 31.

6 Shore, John. *The Sachertorte Algorithm and Other Antidotes to Computer Anxiety.* New York: Penguin, 1985.

7 Borning, Alan. "Computer System Reliability and Nuclear War." *Communications of the ACM,* Feb. 1987, 30:2, p. 119.

8 Brooks, Frederick P. "No Silver Bullet: Essence and Accidents in Software Engineering," IEEE *Computer,* April 1987, pp. 10–19. The quote is from p. 17.

9 Brooks, *op. cit.,* p. 12.

10 Jacky, Jonathan. "Programmed for Disaster: Software Errors That Imperil Lives." *The Sciences,* Sept./Oct. 1989, p. 24.

11 Booch, Grady. *Object-Oriented Design With Applications.* Reading, MA: Addison-Wesley, 1990, p. 3.

12 Peterson, Ivars. "Finding Fault: The formidable task of eradicating software bugs." *Science News,* vol. 139, Feb. 16, 1991, p. 106.

13 Brooks, *op. cit,* p. 10.

14 Manning, Jeff. "Mentor Graphics ships product—finally. Company upbeat after ordeal of 'Late.0,' but earnings may not rebound until June." *Business Journal* (Portland, Oregon), March 25–31, 1991, pp. 1, 11.

15 Hencke, David. "High tech blackout." *Guardian Weekly,* Manchester (U.K.) edition, Feb. 7, 1991, p. 27.

16 Bryan, Jay. "Taking care of computer; without knowledgeable system managers, some firms would be step away from disaster. The experts are treated as technological high priests by baffled management at many corporations." *Montreal Gazette,* Feb. 22, 1992, pp. C1 and C4. Also see Govindan, Marshall, and John Picard. *Manifesto on Information Systems Control and Management: A New World Order.* New York: McGraw-Hill, 1990.

17 Leitch, Carolyn. "Toronto Stock Exchange computers go berserk, floor closed for four hours. Breakdown bolsters opposition to computerized trading." *Toronto Globe and Mail,* March 4, 1992, p. B1.

18 Goldberg, Adele. "The Economics of Software Reuse." Talk at Tektronix, Inc., Portland, OR, Jan. 20, 1992.

19 This particular variant is from Roger S. Pressman and S. Russell Herron, *Software Shock: The Danger and the Opportunity*. New York: Dorset House Publishing, 1991, p. 18.

20 *vi*, *troff*, and MM or MS macros on a UNIX mainframe, for enquiring minds who want to know. Nowadays we have our choice of several WYSIWYG systems. In terms of functionality, it isn't pure improvement.

21 Corbató, Fernando J. "On Building Systems That Will Fail." *Communications of the ACM*, 34:9, Sept., 1991, p. 75.

22 See, for example, Dijkstra, Edsger W. "On the Cruelty of Really Teaching Computer Science," and the ensuing discussion among seven leading computer science professionals, in *Communications of the ACM*, 32:12, Dec., 1989, pp. 1398–1414. The March and June 1990 issues of *Communications of the ACM* continue the lively discussion in the letters column "Forum" (33:3, pp. 264–271; 33:6, pp. 628–633). For another modest proposal, see Parnas, David L. "Education for Computing Professionals," in IEEE *Computer*, Jan. 1990, pp. 17–22.

23 Cusumano, Michael. *Japan's Software Factories: A Challenge to U.S. Management*. New York: Oxford University Press, 1991.

24 Costello, Scott H. "Software Engineering Under Deadline Pressure," ACM SIGSOFT *Software Engineering Notes*, 9:5, Oct. 1984, pp. 15–19.

25 Samuelson, Pamela. "Digital Media and the Law." *Communications of the ACM*, 34:10, Oct., 1991, pp. 23–28. The quotes are from p. 24.

26 Weinberg, Gerald. *op. cit.*, p. 108.

27 Paté-Cornell, M. Elisabeth. "Organizational Aspects of Engineering System Safety: The Case of Offshore Platforms." *Science*, Nov. 30, 1991, pp. 1210–1217.

28 Paté-Cornell, *op.cit.*, p. 1213. For another paper that makes essentially the same argument with specific regard to software development, see Costello, "Software Engineering Under Deadline Pressure," cited above.

29 Weinberg, *op. cit.*, p. 103.

30 Corbató, *op. cit.*, p. 79.

31 Weinberg, Gerald. *op. cit.* See pages 100–102 on measuring performance.

32 This situation is typical of many large engineering projects. It describes SDI, the space station, *Mercury, Gemini, Apollo* and the Space Shuttle Programs, the B2 "stealth" bomber, satellite communication systems, and a wide variety of other taxpayer-funded projects.

33 Lee, Leonard. *The Day the Phones Stopped*. New York: Donald I. Fine, Inc., 1991, pp. 111–12.

34 *comp.risks*, 13:30, Mar. 23, 1992, item contributed by Peter G. Neumann from an article by William B. Crawford, Jr., in the *Chicago Tribune*, March 5, 1992.

35 Kidder, Tracy. *The Soul of a New Machine*. New York: Avon, 1981, p. 71.

36 I am collapsing two separate stages here—the requirements document and the system specification. Technically, *requirements* are what the system is required to do. The *specification* specifies how the requirements will be met. Large, complex projects sometimes produce two distinct documents. Smaller, simpler projects often don't. For the purposes of this discussion, the distinction is unnecessary.

37 Wiener, Lauren. "A Trip Report on SIGSOFT '91." ACM *Software Engineering Notes*, 17:2, April, 1992, pp. 23–38. The quote is from p. 30. Actually, the Boeing 777 flight controls include a limited number of envelope protection features, but these have been designed in from the start. The problem isn't with envelope protection *per se*; it's adding new features willy-nilly.

38 Neumann, Peter G. "Expecting the Unexpected Mayday!" Inside Risks column, *Communications of the ACM*, 34:5, May, 1991, p. 128.

39 Neumann, Peter G. "Flaws in Specifications and What to Do About Them." Proceedings of the Fifth International Workshop on Software Specification and Design, ACM *Software Engineering Notes,* 14:3, May 1989, pp. xi–xv. The quote is from p. xiv.

40 Don't let me give you the impression I'm a programmer. I'm not. A few measly programs doth not a programmer make.

41 *Fortune,* March, 1967, p. 140. Help wanted ads illustrate the beginning of the article by Gene Bylinsky cited earlier. Look at the top of the page for the ad quoted.

42 This is formally known as Conway's Law: "Organizations which design systems are constrained to produce systems which are copies of the communication structures of these organizations." Conway, M.E. "How Do Committees Invent?" *Datamation,* 14:4, April 1968, pp. 28–31. This is another reason why hierarchies are seldom a good organizational structure for software development projects.

43 Baker, F. T., and Harlan D. Mills. "Chief Programmer Teams." *Classics in Software Engineering.* New York: Yourdon Press, 1979, pp. 195–206.

44 Brooks. *The Mythical Man-Month,* pp. 29–40.

45 Brooks. *The Mythical Man-Month,* pp. 14–16.

46 Augustine, Norman R. *op. cit.,* p. 204.

47 Carroll, Paul B. "Painful Birth: Creating New Software Was Agonizing Task for Mitch Kapor Firm." *The Wall Street Journal,* May 11, 1990, p. A5.

48 Brooks. *The Mythical Man-Month,* p. 25.

49 For example, encapsulation, information-hiding, standardized and documented module interfaces, object-oriented programming.

50 Paté-Cornell, *op. cit.,* p. 1212.

51 Boehm, Barry W. *Software Engineering Economics.* Englewood Cliffs: Prentice-Hall, 1981.

52 Brooks. *The Mythical Man-Month,* p. 116: ". . . plan to throw one away; you will anyhow."

53 For a radical proposal to replace the typical software life-cycle (as discussed here) entirely with software and hardware prototyping, see Gladden, G.R. "Stop the Life Cycle, I Want to Get Off." ACM SIGSOFT *Software Engineering Notes,* 7:2, April 1982, pp. 35–39.

54 Carroll, *op. cit.* p. A5.

55 Weinberg, *op. cit.,* p. 165. Compare Costello, Scott H. "Software Engineering Under Deadline Pressure," ACM SIGSOFT *Software Engineering Notes,* 9:5, Oct. 1984, pp. 15–19.

56 Butler, Ricky W., and George B. Finelli. "The Infeasibility of Experimental Quantification of Life-Critical Software Reliability." ACM SIGSOFT *Software Engineering Notes,* 16:5, Dec. 1991, pp. 66–76.

57 Adams, E. N. "Optimizing preventive service of software products," *IBM Research Journal,* 28:1, pp. 2–14. You can get numbers such as "5000 years" because so many copies of the system are in use.

58 Andrews, Edmund L. "String of Phone Failures Perplexes Companies and U.S. Investigators," *New York Times,* July 3, 1991, pp. A1, A7.

59 Alford, Mack. "SREM at the Age of Eight: The Distributed Computing Design System." IEEE *Computer,* April 1985, pp. 36–46.

60 Andrews, Edmund L. "Computer Maker Says Flaw in Software Caused Phone Disruptions," *New York Times,* July 10, 1991, p. A10.

61 In fairness to DSC Communications, a company I find refreshingly forthright and honest in acknowledging the problem and taking responsibility, I must point out that there is no guarantee that the full thirteen weeks of testing would have found the problem, either. Moreover, given the present unwillingness to pay for software, if software developers have to run weeks of tests for every little change, it is quite possible

that some companies simply cannot afford to remain in business. What price reliability? What price jobs?

62 Goodwins, Rupert. *comp.risks*, 11:55, Apr. 29, 1991.

63 For example, see Gleick, James. "Chasing Bugs in the Electronic Village." *New York Times Magazine,* June 14, 1992, pp. 38–42.

64 Shub, Charles, posted in *comp.risks*, 11:15, Feb. 21, 1991.

65 Rettig, Marc. "ACM Forum," *Communications of the ACM,* 34:10, Oct. 1991, p. 14. The quote is in response to a letter which is in turn a response to Mr. Rettig's column in the May 1991 *Communications of the ACM,* "Testing Made Palatable," pp. 25–29.

66 Actually, when I solicited examples of useless comments from programmers, by far the most common response I received could be summed up as "Comments? Who has any comments? Not us!"

67 This one is from a language called LISP, noted for its profligate use of parentheses.

68 Hungarian is named after the nationality of its developer, Charles Simonyi.

69 Hencke, D. *op. cit.*

70 Peter Mellor, posted in *comp.risks*, 11:30, March 19, 1991.

71 *comp.risks*, 11:29, March 15, 1991. Item contributed by Jerry Bakin in reference to an article on the X-31 in the March 31, 1991 issue of *Aviation Week and Space Technology.*

72 *comp.risks*, 12:3, July 9, 1991. Item contributed by Martin Minow, who found the bug.

73 Wiener, Lauren. *op. cit,* p. 33.

74 Carlyle, Ralph Emmett. "Fighting Corporate Amnesia." *Datamation,* Feb. 1, 1989, pp. 41–44.

75 Leitch, Carolyn. *op. cit.*

76 Dijkstra, Edsger W. "On the Cruelty of Really Teaching Computer Science." *Communications of the ACM,* 32:12, Dec., 1989, p. 1401: ". . . if we wish to count lines of code, we should not regard them as 'lines produced' but as 'lines spent.'"

77 Pietrasanta, Alfred M. "Implementing Software Engineering in IBM." Keynote address, *Pacific Northwest Software Quality Conference,* Oct. 7, 1991, Portland, OR.

78 Neumann, Peter G. "Inside Risks: Are Dependable Systems Feasible?" *Communications of the ACM,* Vol. 36:2, Feb. 1993, p. 146.

79 Covault, Craig. "Mission Control Saved Intelsat Rescue From Software, Checklist Problems." *Aviation Week and Space Technology,* May 25, 1992, pp. 78–9.

80 Personal communication with Alan C. (Kit) Bradley, Canyon Crest Technologies, one of three Software Excellence Committee members, Oct. 7, 1991.

CHAPTER 4

# EXTRAORDINARY
# MEASURES

On
Dec. 3, 1985,
Solomon J. Buchsbaum,
Executive Vice President of Customer
Systems for AT&T Bell Laboratories, testified as follows before the United
States Congress on the subject of software for the Strategic Defense Initiative:

> *Some critics have specifically questioned if it is possible to generate great
> quantities of error-free software for the system, and to ensure that it is,
> indeed, error-free software.*
>
> *This is the wrong question. . . . Software is always part of a larger sys-
> tem that includes hardware, communications, data, procedures, and
> people.*
>
> *The right question . . . is the broader one of whether the total BM/C3
> [battle management/command, control, and communication] system can
> be designed to be robust and resilient in a changing and error-prone envi-
> ronment. The key, then, is not whether the software contains errors, but
> how the whole system compensates for such errors. . . .*
>
> *Can such a large, robust, resilient system be designed—and not only de-
> signed, but built, tested, deployed, operated, and further evolved and im-
> proved? I believe the answer is yes. I seem confident of this answer
> because most if not all of the essential attributes of the BM/C3 system
> have, I believe, been demonstrated in comparable terrestrial systems.*
>
> *The system most applicable is the U.S. public telecommunications net-
> work. . . .* [1]

Four years and a few weeks later, the system Mr. Buchsbaum held up
as an example for SDI was telling half its clients, "I'm sorry, all circuits
are busy. Please try again later." Fortunately, its clients were merely frustrated long-distance callers, not incoming nuclear missiles.

Mr. Buchsbaum is right to be proud of the U.S. public telecommunications network. The events of January 15, 1990 notwithstanding, it is an

enormously robust and reliable system. If his comparison is inappropriate, it is not because his pride is misplaced, but because he has failed to distinguish between a mission-critical and a safety-critical system. He seemingly did not ask himself what was at risk if the system failed.

*Mission-critical* software is often financially disastrous when it fails: programs for electronic funds transfer, stock exchange transactions, or telephone switching, for example. The information system with which corporate management makes its decisions is certainly mission-critical for the corporation in question, if not for the rest of us. Too many bankruptcies, however, can affect the economy of a nation and create a difficult situation for everyone.

*Safety-critical* software, on the other hand, can kill when it fails. Real-time process control systems are often safety-critical: programs for the daily operation of chemical or nuclear plants, their emergency shutdown procedures, air traffic control, digital flight control, or railroad switching systems. Health-related software is often safety-critical by its nature: the software in a radiation therapy machine (such as the Therac-25), a patient monitoring system for a hospital, or even a pharmacist's database can all cause serious problems.

The truly critical aspects of a situation, however, are not always apparent. A computer-aided design tool may not ordinarily be critical, but what if it's being used to design a stadium whose collapse could kill thousands? Or the cooling system for a nuclear power plant? In the 1970s, certain nuclear power plants in the United States were declared able to withstand earthquakes and built on that basis. Then a bug was discovered in the program used to calculate stresses on the pipes necessary for the cooling system. A sign in one instruction was reversed, leading stresses to be subtracted rather than added. In 1979 the U.S. Nuclear Regulatory Commission temporarily shut down five nuclear power plants until they could prove that, using the corrected calculations, they could still withstand an earthquake. Ultimately, they did, but they are presumably operating within a smaller margin of safety now.[2]

As the previous chapters have shown, software rarely works correctly the first time it is used. It achieves reliability only after a long period of service, if at all. But for critical systems, this haphazard performance is simply not good enough. Mission-critical or safety-critical software must work correctly as soon as it is put into service. To help increase the chances that it will, certain extraordinary measures can be taken to increase system reliability. By definition, extraordinary measures are not ordinarily taken because they are expensive, difficult, and time-consuming. But for critical software systems, such measures are essential.

Some of these measures are part of the overall software engineering process. The previous chapter discussed certain software engineering activities: writing a spec, testing the program, documenting it. For critical systems, we must take even greater pains to increase our confidence: specifying the system formally, verifying the program mathematically, and paying more attention to software standards, software development standards, and personnel issues.

Additional activities are outside the software engineering process, but are concerned with how the software fits into the overall system—part of a discipline known as *systems engineering*. Systems engineering integrates the software with the rest of the system. Systems engineers manage the physical interfaces—they keep rain out of the box, ensure that the power supply is not interrupted, ensure that the signals reach the actuators. They also manage the logical interfaces—the connection to a network, for example.

Enormous, costly, and complicated megaprojects can soak up virtually endless effort. If we are willing to spend what it takes—and if we are smart enough—we may increase the reliability of digital systems. But can we increase it enough? That depends. How much effort are we willing to budget for? What are we willing to risk?

## SOFTWARE ENGINEERING

We know a number of ways to improve the software development process itself. Specifications can be written in formal mathematical languages. Design and coding can proceed in accordance with mandated standards. Quality assurance can be improved by the use of mathematical logic to verify that the software will perform its function correctly. Those responsible for software development can pay more attention to personnel issues. None of these improvements is foolproof, but each can contribute toward improving the final product.

### Specifying the System Formally

Natural language is a supple and wondrous instrument. It allows us to say things like: "Do you feel more like you do now than when you came in?" or: "'Twas brillig, and the slithy toves/did gyre and gimble in the wabe" or even (a sentence I heard first in October 1971, and that still confuses me): "Portland doesn't have anything that San Francisco doesn't have." In other words, just because you can express something in a human language doesn't mean it's logical. Mathematics is logical. Natural language is not.

Specs written in a natural language such as English have been known to show a variety of logical flaws. Internal contradictions and tangled threads of execution are hard to catch when reading static prose descriptions of behavior. After all, the spec is not chopped liver—it goes on for hundreds of pages. It is entirely possible, even likely, that one requirement contradicts another. Obvious contradictions are spotted early, of course, but many are far from obvious. Sometimes the contradictions only emerge after the programmers have started to implement the system: a given processor may simply be unable to respond as quickly as required to the number of messages it is getting, for example. This is the computational equivalent of the instruction to the grocery checkout clerk to "put it all in one bag, but don't make it too heavy."

So people have tried to express the spec in such a way that contradictions become obvious. To harness the power of mathematical logic, a fair bit of energy has been spent developing specialized notations for expressing system requirements. Such notations are called *specification languages.* They aren't languages, though, in the sense of a human language. They look much more like symbolic logic, and working with them requires many of the same skills. Using them, internal inconsistencies and logical errors become apparent and can be corrected.

Writing a formal spec in a specification language may be a useful exercise, but it is difficult and time-consuming. Therefore, large, complex, and critical systems are virtually the only systems for which anyone takes the trouble. Like any approach, it has drawbacks. Some of the computer types may be able to read the spec, but customers or users or domain experts are unlikely to make head or tail of it unless they feel at home in the realm of mathematical logic.

Telectronics Pacing Systems, a manufacturer of implantable defibrillators, develops software that could someday run inside your chest to keep your heart beating properly. Keenly aware of the safety-critical nature of the problem, the company determined to write the spec in a formal specification language. But the cardiac experts were unable to participate in the process as they had before. They could not tell if the spec was accurate or fatally flawed, because they couldn't understand it.

"So we rewrote it in English for them," said the head of instruments software, a bit sheepishly. "But nevertheless, it was a useful exercise, and we caught a few things we wouldn't have caught any other way."

This relatively happy ending is satisfying but uncommon. Because the process is so difficult and time-consuming, few specs are written formally. Huge and complex though it be, Boeing has written the spec for its 777 flight control system in English.[3]

### Standard Practice

As we saw in the previous chapter, both designing and coding a program can be done in an infinite number of ways, and no two people will do them alike. No cut-and-dried method exists that can guarantee to improve either of these processes. Recommendations and standards exist anyway.

It goes without saying that both design and code should be clear, comprehensible, and documented. We know that the initial programming effort represents only a fraction of the cost of the software. Bugs will have to be fixed, new features added, new hardware accommodated. These are facts of life: the software must be understood by people other than its developers. But these facts suggest goals, not practices.

To the extent that software engineering can offer anything akin to "standard practice," as the phrase is understood in medicine or civil engineering, it is codified in software standards. Certain software tends to be regulated by the agencies within the relevant domain. In the United States, for example, medical software is regulated by the Federal Drug Administration and aviation software is regulated by the Federal Aviation Administration. Software written for the U.S. government must be written using a certain process. Military software must always comply with a bewildering welter of regulations, wherever you are. But a lot of software does not have to comply with any standards at all.

It may be just as well. Those who write the standards do not have any clearer idea than anyone else how to produce safe and reliable software. Indeed, standards efforts usually brew considerable controversy as they attempt to determine whether to mandate the process, the result, or both. If they choose to mandate the process, which process? If the result, how do they assess it? No experimental evidence demonstrates that complying with any particular software standard reduces errors.

Clearly, someone should attempt to gather evidence one way or the other, but the software engineering community has little idea how to conduct such research. As David Parnas recently summed up a software standards panel for a gathering of critical systems experts: "I looked for examples of systems that met certain standards, to determine if the standards were good—but I couldn't find any examples!"[4]

Indeed, evidence exists that some standards, at least, do harm. A 1989 congressional report makes the point:

*Government policies on everything from budgeting to intellectual property rights have congealed over time in a manner almost perfectly designed to thwart the development of quality software.*[5]

And an article in *Science* baldly states: ". . . the federal procurement system effectively demands that contractors write the software using bad methodology."[6] Clearly, we need to codify standard practices for software engineering—just as soon as we discover what they should be. Regulations uninformed by evidence, however, can make matters worse.

### Verifying Programs Mathematically

By contrast, quality assurance is an area in which we know how to improve. A lot of research has been done on better methods for testing software. Organizations that produce critical systems often take a more professional attitude toward testing than their commercial counterparts, testing more rigorously, thoroughly, and systematically. But no one can test a program exhaustively. Instead, software's nature as a structure of logic suggests an entirely different approach to the problem of determining whether the program functions correctly. If we can reduce a program to its logical essence, perhaps we can prove that it is *correct*—that is, that it will function as specified.

How can you prove a program is correct? Imagine a program to control the traffic lights at a four-way intersection. Suppose you know that, in order to ensure a safe system, the north light and the east light must never be green at the same time. You express this as a statement in formal logic. Then you determine the logical effect each line of the program will have on this formal statement. If you know that it is always true when the program starts (*asserting a precondition,* in the jargon), you can try to prove that, after each line executes, it is still true (*asserting a postcondition*). If it is false, you have found some unsafe code. You can fix it and start the process over again.

Proving correctness is not an exercise in absolutes. You can only prove that something is correct with respect to something else. For example, you can prove that a given program correctly implements a spec. If the spec had an error, however, all you have proven is that you have cor-

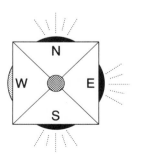

**Figure 4-1.**
A Four-way Traffic Light
With North, South,
and East on Green
—an Unsafe State

rectly implemented the wrong thing. As John Rushby, a researcher in the field, puts it:

> . . . we cannot equate formal verification with unequivocal correctness. This is because correctness is a property of the real system and of real-world expectations, whereas formal verification is concerned with mathematical models of the system and of its requirements.[7]

In order to prove something correct, you write the spec in a formal specification language, and write (or rewrite) the program in a language that allows it to be proved with respect to the spec. Then the two can be compared, usually using some formal verification tool that can automate some of the tedious and overwhelming detail.

A variety of verification tools have been proposed. Some have been designed. A few have even been implemented. Some of the simplest are compilers that include a feature known as assertion-checking. If the programmer asserts pre- and postconditions within the program, the compiler will check the assertions and report any errors.

A few verification tools are considerably more elaborate. They can include such exotica as specification languages (described above), theorem-provers, and a usable user interface.[8] Such tools are not in wide use.

Formal verification can increase confidence, but it has limitations. First of all, any scheme that depends on software to debug software has an obvious problem: someone has to write and debug the software that does the debugging. How can you ensure that it is any more reliable than the stuff you are using it to check?

Another limitation comes into play if the verification tool requires its input in a form other than the programming language of the final product. Two independent versions of the software open the door to bugs.[9] Even if you make no mistake during the translation, translating a program (from, say, C to PL/I) can cause different behavior if the compilers handle such things as loops or concurrency differently.

Nor can formal methods protect against ultimate typographical errors, such as typing a "6" instead of a "D."

Logical deduction is arduous, tedious, and wearying. Symbolic logic is a skill that few are good at; fewer still can continue such work for hours on end. David Gries, a well-known proponent of formal methods, concedes as much in his textbook, when he writes:

> . . . be assured that complete attention to formalism is neither necessary nor desirable. Formality alone is inadequate, because it leads to incomprehensible detail; common sense and intuition alone—the programmer's

*main tools till now—are inadequate, because they allow too many errors
and bad designs.*

*What is needed is a fine balance between the two.*[10]

Symbolic logic follows strict rules, but people must apply these rules,
and people are not machines in this respect any more than they are in
any other.[11] Logic rules must be applied with the same ingenuity and insight that mark any other creative human endeavor. A landmark paper
on the subject points out that: ". . . mathematicians' errors are corrected, not by formal symbolic logic, but by other mathematicians."[12] A
mathematician, it says, responds to a proof of a theorem not by being
certain of its truth, but by seeking someone to tell it to. The mathematician seeks a listener because the proof itself means nothing unless it con-
vinces others. It has happened that two groups of mathematicians have
discovered contradictory proofs about the same mathematical object, and
neither group was able to disprove the others' work.

Mathematicians gleefully find flaws in each other's proofs. But no
promise of glee can motivate a programmer to look through a colleague's program verification, because a program verification, unlike a
good mathematical proof, is a long, complex, and stultifying series of
shallow logical statements cranked out by mechanically applying alge-
braic substitution rules for each program statement. "Verifications cannot really be read; a reader can flay himself through one of the shorter
ones by dint of heroic effort, but that's not reading" comments the paper.[13] John Rushby, a proponent of formal verification methods, agrees:
"No one reads this stuff with a lot of care—it's too boring."[14]

In practice, therefore, only relatively small software systems can be formally verified. A group at the National Institute of Standards and Technology reported on formally verifying a system that used smart cards to
control access to a computer network. The system consisted of 2600
lines of C code, which, as commercial software goes, is tiny. The formal
verification process concentrated only on security aspects of the system.
It took three people about two and a half weeks, representing 6 percent
of the system's cost. The modest investment was worth it: they found
two significant errors in the code, and a major flaw in the spec—an unstated requirement.[15]

By contrast, verification of the emergency shutdown system for the
Darlington nuclear power plant is about as ambitious a project as formal
verification has yet attempted.[16] Darlington nuclear power plant is located on the shore of Lake Ontario, slightly over 40 miles outside of
Toronto, Canada. The plant, like other nuclear power plants built in

Europe and North America, has two independent dedicated systems to shut it down in the event of an emergency. One system is intended to serve as backup in case the other fails. Ontario Hydro, the utility that built the plant, decided to implement both systems in software instead of the hardware systems of switches and relays and analogue meters that constituted their previous shutdown systems. They decided to migrate from hardware to software for several reasons:

- They thought the system would be safer. The software would allow the operators to discriminate more precisely among different conditions, thereby providing better information.

- They thought it would save them money. They would no longer have to buy hardware parts costing about $1 million.

- They thought it would be easier to maintain. Eventually, they feared, it would no longer be possible to buy replacement parts for the old analogue machinery.

- They thought it would allow them to claim higher system availability[17] to the Atomic Energy Control Board, the Canadian institution charged with regulating the nuclear power industry.

Wisely, the Atomic Energy Control Board was not so sanguine about computer-based emergency shutdown systems. They insisted that the software be rigorously examined and verified, and hired David Parnas to advise them.

Each emergency shutdown system consisted of about ten thousand lines of code. That's still pretty small—a commercial word processing system could easily be ten times as large—but it considerably strains the state of the art for formal verification.

The Ontario Hydro engineers were divided into four teams. One team converted the programs into tables that mathematically described the function of each piece of the program. Another team converted the spec into similar tables. A third team compared the tables, noting any discrepancies between the two. A fourth team checked the work of the third.

Most people could tolerate this tedious and laborious process for about six weeks at a time. They were then rotated out to be replaced by fresh fodder. Including planning, the effort took over two years and cost between $2 and 4 million. It resulted in about one hundred changes to the system, all relatively minor. No show-stopping bugs were found.

Other problems delayed the plant's opening by about eighteen months, but Ontario Hydro ended up waiting about six months for the verification process to be completed. Since the plant cost its investors $20 million for each month it sat idle, the digital emergency shutdown systems weren't quite as economical as Ontario Hydro had hoped: 6 months @ $20 million per month = $120 million plus $2 million for software verification minus $1 million for unpurchased hardware parts = $121 million. Oh, well.

Formal methods are extremely time-consuming and expensive. At present they are cost-effective only for the most critical systems. They may not find errors in the specification. There are some kinds of errors in the code—typos, for example—they may not be able to find, either. They may use software tools that themselves may have bugs. Formal methods of program verification can increase your confidence in the system, but they are not an ironclad assurance.

However, the strengths and weaknesses of testing and formal verification are complementary. A well-conceived testing program is an effective reality check on the spec. It also catches small oversights such as typos. By contrast, formally verifying program correctness can provide you with confidence in the soundness of the program's logic that decades of testing cannot provide. If we really wish to be assured of a critical system's reliability, therefore, we cannot afford to neglect either approach. The result may still have bugs in it; absolute certainty is not to be had on this earth. But a thorough job with both methods allows you as generous a measure of confidence as you're going to get.

### Personnel, Round Two: Certifying Software Engineers

In the end, it comes down to the confidence that society places in the judgment of the people who build critical systems.[18] So how much confidence can we have in the judgment of those who build or operate critical systems? Who are they? Consider the advertisement from a Sunday *Oregonian* Help Wanted section shown in Figure 4-2.

---

#### Elections Programmer–Auditor

The Auditor's Office is seeking an individual with solid personal computer network and trouble-shooting experience to work with the election/voter registration computer system. This individual will be required to maintain present computerized system and assist with the election tabulation process.

*Qualifications:* A Bachelor's degree in data processing or closely related field and two years data processing experience in an elections department; or, any combination of training and/or experience in an elections department; or, any combination of training and/or experience that provides the required knowledge and abilities.

---

**Figure 4-2.** A Sad Ad

I would classify elections software as mission-critical. Enough people are already cynical about voting without undermining confidence that their votes will be counted faithfully. An incompetent, negligent, mercenary, or malicious person could do serious damage in this job. Ample evidence exists of computer-assisted electoral mayhem.[19] But I search this ad in vain for a sign that its writers are aware of this. They do not ask for a candidate who is mature, responsible, principled, or schooled in techniques for maintaining critical software. Probably the job itself does not pay very much.

The ad shown in Figure 4-3 appeared on an on-line computer bulletin board for job seekers. I have changed the name of the company and deleted irrelevant information to maintain their anonymity. I have deleted nothing germane to the safety considerations.

---

XYZ Information Systems, Inc., a medical software company, is looking for software developers to join a small group involved in the development of a new clinical information system for hospital intensive care units.

<A paragraph about the software tools the developers will be using >

### Development positions

1. Communications interface development. Position will be responsible for development of communications software for transferring data between systems . . . in large hospitals.

2. Bedside device interfacing. Position will be responsible for development of communications software for collecting data from bedside devices such as Vital Signs Monitors and IV pumps.

Desired skills include significant work experience in one of the areas described plus significant work experience with the development tools listed. Medical software development experience would be a plus.

### Minimum requirements

- Proficiency in C and UNIX
- At least a good working knowledge of C++ and object-oriented techniques
- A BS or MS in computer science or applicable experience
- Good communication skills with the ability and desire to learn quickly

---

**Figure 4-3.**  Sad Ad Too

This software is safety-critical; some bugs could cause a patient's death. But the ad shows a single-minded concentration on technical issues. It specifies the programming language, the operating system, and the development tools; it includes not a word about design skills, documentation, formal verification, hazard analysis, or any other technique to enhance the safety of the product. Perhaps the company is using all of these and more. But they're certainly not asking for someone who's been exposed to any of these methods. To be fair, if they insisted on it, they might not get many applicants.

The software community knows it should be doing these things. But too few know how, and even fewer want to pay for it.

Civil engineers must be registered before they assume responsibility for designing bridges or other structures whose failure can kill. A lax attitude toward personnel issues has prompted many to call for software professionals to be similarly certified. The issue has been discussed somewhat in the popular press and extensively among software professionals themselves.[20] In 1991, the New Jersey State Legislature even attempted to enact a bill requiring such certification.[21] The proposal to certify software professionals usually meets with considerable resistance from software developers; significantly, this bill was resisted not just by the rank-and-file, but by mighty AT&T itself, which contended that implementing the proposal would cost them far too much.

There is sense on both sides of this debate. Proponents of certification point out that software engineering cannot really be said to be a professional discipline while the present free-for-all atmosphere holds. No civil engineering firm would dream of putting an unregistered twenty-six-year-old in charge of building a stadium, for example, although exactly such a person might be in charge of developing the software used to design it. Those in favor of certifying programmers believe that the process may serve to concentrate some minds.

Certifying software engineers might also clarify issues of legal liability. It might be simpler to tell who is at fault in the wake of failure. It would add new evidence to such disputes, in any case.

On the other hand, the process of setting up certification boards is certain to be highly political. Once in place, these boards may serve as guilds have always done, to limit the supply of professionals and thereby increase the price of their services.[22] It will cost something.

More to the point is the real risk of enacting the wrong process. Just as wrong standards can harm the process of software development, so can they harm the quality of software professionals. No consensus exists in the software community as to the core competencies of software engineering. Even among proponents of certification, the discussion is wide-ranging and contentious. Yet there is nothing to be gained by enshrining the wrong set of competencies and standards. In the absence of any agreement, legislators would be wise to resist the temptation to mandate *something* to score political points in the wake of some future phone outage or airline disaster.

Whether software professionals are ultimately certified or not, let's be clear about the problem certification does *not* solve: software will still have bugs. Perhaps it will have fewer, but the nature and complexity of digital systems guarantees that failure will occur. Even the best people following the most careful process can't think of everything.

The software that IBM wrote for the space shuttle flight control system, for example, is supposed to be just about as good as it gets. (The program was written by the sole organization to earn a grade of 5 from the Software Engineering Institute.) That software cost about $1000 per line, while the industry average is between $25 and $100.[23] But it's not perfect, either; based on bugs found in previous versions, IBM itself estimates that the released software contains about fifty bugs.[24] There's no way anyone can know for certain, of course, any more than anyone can tell which bug might cause a significant failure under the wrong circumstances. However, failures there have been—on several occasions. In addition to the synchronization problem that delayed the first launch, several other bugs have caused problems.[25] For example, Space Shuttle Mission 49 went up and attempted three times to capture Intelsat, a communications satellite, to put it into an orbit in which it could be useful. The third time was successful, but only just—the onboard shuttle computer refused to compute the final maneuvering vector and velocity change Instead, it issued alarms. The requisite data could be supplied by NASA's computer on the ground—and they were—but the alarms called into question the entire shuttle guidance and control software. The event gave the astronauts a bad hour or so wondering what else was wrong. The problem turned out to be caused by prelaunch changes that IBM had made, with NASA's permission, to the rendezvous software. "It didn't work exactly the way we thought it would work," said the flight director.[26]

If software failure is inevitable, therefore, we had better plan for it. We need techniques for determining which failures may occur and how likely they are. We need to understand what is at risk. And finally, we need strategies for coping with the results. The techniques by which we accomplish this are part of a discipline known as systems engineering.

## SYSTEMS ENGINEERING

*DRAMATIS PERSONÆ*

*TESTING specialist, planning how the system is to be tested, and amassing the resources necessary.*

*RELIABILITY specialist, worrying about how reliable each part of the system is, and the reliability of the system as a whole.*

*MANUFACTURING specialist, contemplating how the system is going to be manufactured.*

*HUMAN FACTORS specialist, cajoling the rest of the team to design a system that ordinary mortals can learn and use.*

*LOGISTICS specialist, trying to figure out how the system is to be maintained, what will break, and how it's going to be fixed.*

*SAFETY specialist, imagining hazards, failures, mishaps, accidents, and catastrophes—impersonating Stephen King.*

THE SCENE: *We know that even if we could guarantee that the software would function correctly, the system that it is part of might not. Therefore, as the software engineers go through their efforts, some folks are worrying about how the software and all the other miscellaneous pieces will integrate to make the whole system.*

The curtain rises. *Safety emerges (or fails to) as a property of the system as a whole. A bunch of unsafe components can make a safe system if they mask each other's failures. Conversely, a bunch of safe components, functioning as specified, can nevertheless make an unsafe system. Therefore it is crucial that some people approach the problem from the standpoint of the whole system. Those are the Dramatis Personae above.*

The following discussion peeks over the shoulders, as it were, of the reliability, human factors, and safety specialists (the folks in the second column), as they engage in various arcane rites that go under the heading of risk analysis.

### Analyzing Risk

Risk analysis is a formal attempt to answer the questions: what can go wrong? how likely is it? what are the consequences if it does? how can we avoid or mitigate them?[27]

Risk analysts distinguish between a hazard, a failure, a risk, and an accident. A *hazard* is a condition that can cause an accident, if other events also occur. A *failure* is the inability of some part of the system to perform its intended function. *Risk* is the probability of a failure combined with its consequences. An *accident* is the event that causes harm, injury, or damage. It is possible to have a failure without hazard, risk, or accident: a traffic light that experiences an electrical problem can default to flashing red in all directions, converting an intersection into a four-way stop.

Similarly, risk analysts distinguish between reliability and safety. *Reliability* is the probability that the system (or some part of it) will perform its function for a specified period of time. *Safety,* on the other hand, is the probability that hazards will not occur. It is possible for a reliable system nevertheless to be unsafe. An example is the following tale of a computer-controlled chemical reactor whose designers failed to take a whole-system approach, with unfortunate consequences.[28]

The reactor's designers did not really understand what the computer did, or how. They told the software developers that, if something went wrong, the computer should behave like an inept babysitter: leave everything just the way it is and call us (sound an alarm). The software developers, for their part, failed to educate the systems people or understand how their software fit into the larger system. They did as the systems people told them without further inquiry.

One day the computer received a signal indicating that a gearbox needed oil. (The signal turned out, in the end, to be spurious.) The computer performed exactly as specified: it changed nothing and sounded the alarm. However, by sheer bad luck, a catalyst had just been added to the reactor to increase the speed at which the reaction was taking place. The faster reaction generated more heat. Normally, the computer would have been increasing the flow of cooling water at this time to compensate for the increased heat. It had just started to do that when it received the spurious low-oil signal; but now it was supposed to leave everything just the way it was. So it kept the flow of cooling water at too low a level; the reactor overheated and vented its contents into the surrounding air.

To prevent this kind of thing is an arduous undertaking, requiring people of imagination, experience, and talent who can concentrate while awash in a storm of technical detail. A certain amount of luck is not amiss, either, to help choose precisely the right detail out of the thousands vying for attention. Serious risk analysis is not trivial. It involves some of the following activities:

- *A preliminary hazard analysis* tries to identify hazards as early as possible.

- *Hazard and operability studies* may follow, to identify further hazards when more is known about how human beings will operate the system.

- An *event-tree analysis* starts with some untoward event, such as equipment failure or human error, and imagines all the consequences that could result.

- By contrast, a *fault-tree analysis* starts backwards, imagining a specific system failure and trying to think of all the ways that failure might have come about.

- A *failure modes and effects analysis* (known by its acronym, FMEA) attempts to identify every possible way each component (or each interface between components) could fail—that is, each *failure mode*. It then goes on to consider the effect each failure mode will have on the system.

- *Human reliability analysis* tries to identify how people interacting with the system might cause it to fail.

- Most difficult of all, *common-mode failure analysis* attempts to determine in what way a single event can cause more than one of several supposedly independent components to fail.[29]

Common-mode failures are difficult to anticipate because they require the analyst to consider unintended connections, unplanned interactions. For example, when United Airlines Flight 232 suffered engine failure on July 18, 1989, the resulting explosion disabled all three hydraulic systems. This tale includes no digital technology, for once, but the system—a jet—is sufficiently complicated for a common-mode failure to go undetected. Designers of the jet provided three hydraulic systems because hydraulics are critical to modern jets—without them, the enormous machines are all but uncontrollable. Three systems are supposed to ensure that, no matter what happens, at least one will be available to control the airplane. However, lines for all three hydraulic systems converged in one small area near the tail. When something exploded near that critical site, the pilot had a common-mode failure on his hands—the unanticipated failure of all three hydraulic systems. The FAA and airplane manufacturers had been so sure that such a thing could never happen that they had no emergency procedures for the occasion. In retrospect, this may seem amazing, but when the airplane was being designed, I guarantee you that a number of competent, experienced, and diligent people missed it *not* for lack of trying, but because of all the other things they caught instead. However, the incident has added to their experience. Wiring for the digital flight control system of the 777, for example, is routed all over the airplane, so that no single local explosion can disable it.[30]

Common-mode failures are a worst case, but multiple failures—a bad day—are what cause most serious accidents.[31] In theory, FMEAs, for example, are supposed to cope with multiple failures. One first identifies all the single failures that can take place, and what their effects on the system could be. Then one considers what would happen if any two of those failures occur at the same time. Then three simultaneous failures are considered, and so on. Mathematically inclined readers doubtless see the combinatorial explosion rearing its head again—the number of possible situations proliferates and overwhelms us. But multiple failures can be critical where a single failure is tolerable, such as when the low oil pressure light on your dashboard burns out shortly before the oil pan is breached.

I once met a fellow whose previous job had been to conduct FMEAs for certain aircraft subsystems. Curious, I asked him how the combinatorial explosion of multiple failures was handled for real projects. His answer was frank, disheartening, and what I'd come to expect: "I know we were supposed to consider multiple failures," he said, "but in practice, we barely had time to identify and cope with all the single failures." We were flying, at that moment, in an airplane whose takeoff had been delayed due to a faulty altimeter, so I changed the subject.

### Failure Strategies

If we know that failures must occur, it is wise to consider strategies for coping with them. Strategy #1 we might call the country-and-western strategy:

*I Fall to Pieces.* Sometimes total failure is a valid option. For example, although video game makers undeniably labor hard to give their customers a good time for their money, if the system crashes for some reason—well, it was only a quarter, after all. Likewise, if a business spreadsheet program crashes, it may infuriate its user, but what's one spreadsheet in the cosmic scheme of things? Systems for which total failure is an option are not critical, by definition.

But it's not always clear what's critical and what isn't. For example, the project leader for Symphony, a well-known commercial spreadsheet, tells of a phone call from a surgeon who was using the spreadsheet to analyze data from a patient during open-heart surgery. He described the phone call as "sobering."[32]

One can hardly hold the software company responsible, in such a case, for not foreseeing this use of its product, labeling its spreadsheet "safety-critical," and going through the enormous expense of validating the product for such a use. For one thing, no one would buy the spreadsheet at the resulting price. But if that surgeon were operating on me, I would want to discuss backup plans in case the software crashed during surgery.

Strange to say, total failure isn't always evident, either. Consider the information tool that blandly delivers the wrong information without a hint of any kind that anything is wrong. A database query language might answer a question put to it by the VP of Marketing with a plausible but utterly erroneous set of figures. A simulation may confidently predict a certain outcome based on overly simple input or an inaccurate algorithm. An expert system might lead a repair technician astray because the original pool of experts was thin in one area. Bargain Harold's, a discount retail chain in Canada, filed for bankruptcy as a result of such undetected bugs in its new management information system:

> *Apparently this system was incorrectly predicting gross margin on sales and profits. Based on this incorrect information management built up excessive inventories and were unable to reliably predict the company's annual profit. A profit estimate of $500,000 on Oct. 2 [1991] was changed the next day to an estimated loss of $3–4 million.*[33]

Systems that are supposed to turn data into information deliver correct or erroneous results in the same flat, uninflected manner. The critical component of the system is our awareness of its limitations. Our own credulity is the factor we should monitor most closely. Such systems need a reality check.

Information tools are often used when a political decision must be made. Someone who favors a course of action is happy to point to a computer study that applies a patina of objectivity to the position. But inputs to models, simulations, and other information tools are not objective; they represent someone's best guess as to which facts matter, and how much. The operations used to process the inputs are not the result of an analytical "discovery" either: they represent someone's best guess or fond wish about how the world behaves. The result is mechanically arrived at by cranking the inputs through the modeled process. You could do this on paper, and people used to. The computer's contribution is that it can handle more inputs and process them in more complex and subtle ways. With sufficient attention to the inputs, proponents of any course of action can have the satisfaction of a computer study to point to. But we act as if the computer knows something. Worse, we act as if its lack of emotional stake in the outcome were a strength instead of a weakness.

**Do Something Different.** A system can respond to some conditions, such as an overload, by functioning more slowly, doing fewer things, or servicing fewer users. These are common strategies when computational resources are stretched to the limits. They can be viewed as methods to bring about partial or "safe" failure in order to avoid total or hazardous failure.

You may have experienced using a time-shared computer running under a heavy load. The processor devotes more of its time to other things and less to you. This neglect turns the inside of your machine to electronic molasses: the cursor sticks where you last put it; you watch the menus paint themselves. You and the computer are trapped inside a Valium nightmare.

Uncomfortable as it can be for users, this strategy is nevertheless an option for interactive software, because people can exercise judgment and respond flexibly. This strategy is not, however, an option for software that must operate in real time, because real-time software must respond to physical, real-world events on the schedule dictated by those events, such as the air traffic control software that is controlling airplanes hurtling through the air and consuming fuel at rates dictated by the physics of the situation. Manufacturing and chemical process control, automotive systems such as fuel injection and antiskid brakes, the emergency shutdown system for a nuclear power plant—even spreadsheets used for data analysis during surgery—must operate in real-time.

Doing fewer things might be an option for some overloaded process-control software, since this allows a stressed system to meet at least some of its requirements. The AT&T phone system uses this approach. A degradation scheme uses simpler features, handles less capacity, or permits less flexible 800 calls during times of peak demand.[34] The phone system may also take longer to give you a dial tone or establish the connection.

If it is possible to specify only a subset of system functions as "safety-critical," even safety-critical systems can use this strategy. Failures affecting other functions can be engineered so that they leave the system up and performing its core functions (as defined by the safety analysis) until the full set can somehow be restored. Commercial air traffic control in the United States uses such a strategy—in this case, a four-tiered approach to keeping the system going under failure conditions. In 1987, the FAA was planning a system with a backup mode, and an emergency backup mode for the backup mode. Each backup mode provides progressively fewer services.[35]

The problem is that it is often difficult to determine which parts of the system really are safety-critical. For example, the *Patriot* missile failed to shoot down the *Scud* as it headed for the barracks in Dhahran because of an error in its tracking equation. The tracking equation error had been identified early in the war; the software had been upgraded since. But the upgrade (Version 34) had not fixed the tracking equation error because it had not been seen as critical until after the Dhahran fatalities demonstrated otherwise.[36]

Serving fewer users is a related failure strategy, particularly for distributed systems, many of which are distributed precisely so they can serve many people at a time. It is often a good strategy. For example, if an ATM breaks here or there, the rest go right on functioning. Ideally, you get back into your car and head down the road to the next one.

Still, when resources are scattered thinly or when a large area is struck by the failure, the failure represents a total system collapse for those users with no other options. The seriousness of the consequences then depends entirely on who those users are and what they are trying to do.

So far, even during the worst telephone system failures we have experienced, most people on earth with access to telephones could still call each other. A failure in one part of the network hasn't brought the whole network down—yet. But some experts are now warning that the global phone network is becoming so highly connected that it will lose its present ability to respond to failure with only a partial loss of service. John C. MacDonald, head of a 1989 National Research Council study of the telephone system, is worried that the system has already reached that point. In a newspaper account, he is reported to have said that "the entire system interlocks in such a way that failure anywhere potentially could shut down the entire network."[37] In order to avoid the possibility of a global telephone network collapse, he advocates yet another strategy for coping with failure—building a whole extra telephone network.

***99 Bottles of Beer on the Wall.*** The use of redundant components to ensure system reliability is familiar to anyone who has ever gotten a flat tire and used the spare. You can increase system reliability by adding spare components. The argument goes like this:

A system (a machine, for example) is made up of $n$ components. We want to find out how reliable each component is, so we test it to see how often it fails. For example, perhaps we know the light bulbs will last for ten thousand hours. The engine can operate for eight thousand hours. The tires can go forty thousand miles. And so on.

Assuming that all components are necessary, and that the failure of any component is independent of the failure of any other, then, armed with this data the reliability specialist calculates the probability of failure for each component during, say, a ten-hour or a one-year mission. If a component has a 1 in 20 chance of failing during the mission (5 percent), then it is considered 95 percent reliable. To determine the reliability of the system as a whole for that mission, the engineer multiplies the reliability percentages for all of the system components. For example, a machine built of ten components, each of which is 95 percent reliable, has an overall reliability of slightly under 60 percent.[38] If a spare light bulb decreases the chances of failure for its component from 1 in 20 to 1 in 40, you can multiply by 97.5 percent and get a better answer.

For example, to improve availability, the AT&T long-distance network has a backup switch for each primary switch. If a failure occurs in a primary switch due to a hardware fault, the backup switch can take over. But the two sets of switches use the same software, and therefore do not always fail independently of each other. When faulty software caused the primary switches to fail on January 15, 1990, the backup switches came into play, and the same bug had the opportunity to corrupt memory in both sets of switches. Down went the network.[39]

Redundancy can often be counted on for hardware components, which are made of materials that wear out according to physical processes we understand, and which can often be tested exhaustively. When software was still a relatively new component in large critical systems, reliability specialists sometimes treated it in the same manner. It is now clearer, however, that it is difficult, if not impossible, to test software exhaustively. Software is prone to failure due to errors we can neither predict nor eliminate. Including software in a system, therefore, means that the customary formula for component reliability will not be useful for at least one component.

But if the software is going to fail, can we at least apply the strategy of redundant components to mitigate the effects of that failure? Can we, for example, include several versions of the same program, in the hopes that at least one will always be running?

This is the strategy NASA adopted with the Space Shuttle flight control software. As mentioned earlier, the space shuttle has four identical computers running identical software and a fifth, ultimate backup running completely different software. The idea is that independently developed software will have independent bugs, and the two systems will not crash for the same reason at the same time.

The approach sounds plausible, and for a while it was the hope of those who wished to include large, complex software programs in large, complex, critical systems. Ultimately, however, leading software safety specialist Dr. Nancy Leveson and a colleague attempted to validate this approach experimentally. They discovered that the results did not bear out the assumption of increased reliability. Students at different graduate schools wrote many versions of the same program, and each version was tested extensively. The same inputs caused different programs to fail.[40] It turns out that the hard parts are hard no matter who writes the program. People tend to make the same mistakes for the same reasons. Software is a product of human minds; its failure is mental, not physical. Unfortunately, you can't count on redundant software components to increase system reliability the way spare hardware can.

*Help! I Need Somebody.* When an error appears on your telephone bill, you can call the number provided and speak to a human being able to correct it. The phone company pays people to answer that phone number, and gives them the authority to change the situation, because they know that people can be the ultimate reliable, robust, and user-friendly components in a system. Unlike the computer, people can recognize when a situation is plausible or absurd. They also understand the value of long-term customer goodwill.

Similarly, people can prevent catastrophe by a timely action, but only if the system is monitored so that humans know when their intervention is needed. Monitoring is a function that computers do very well, since they don't get bored, hungry, sleepy or restless. Humans, on the other hand, do it poorly. People need to be involved in an activity or their attention will wander. They need to be committed to some action—*doing something.* Eventually, if the system does not require anything of them, they will commit themselves to another activity (eating, chatting, daydreaming), and thus will be unavailable, distracted, or slow to respond when needed. A system design requiring continuous human attention to many unchanging details for long periods is inhuman.[41]

If a system requires people to intervene for a safety-critical function, then good design requires them to be actively involved throughout the process. The final level of emergency backup for air traffic control, for example, consists of very busy, dedicated human beings working frantically to contain the current situation, decrease the short-term need for the system's services as much as they can, and restore the system to its normal state as soon as possible. In between failures, the controllers are far from passive monitors. They actively direct the traffic within their air space, using the computers to enhance the amount and type of data available, and to make it more manageable.

The tension between continuous passive monitoring versus active involvement is presently a source of controversy for the digital flight control systems being designed for the newest commercial jets. Pilots complain that the systems reduce them to passive monitors. If their involvement is suddenly required, they are likely to be less alert.

Another concern is that the system will not give them the authority to perform the required actions in any case. Recall the envelope protection functions in digital flight control systems—functions made possible for the first time by software. Envelope protection ensures that the pilot cannot make maneuvers with the aircraft that will exceed its structural integrity.

On the face of it, this seems reasonable. If the airframe specifications state that the wings can withstand only so much torque before they tear off the fuselage, then why not have the flight control system compute the forces on the airframe from the acceleration and other factors, and ensure that the aircraft turns safely? The answer lies in how much we think we need pilots.

Unlike the flight control system programmers, pilots are on the scene and can assess how appropriate a drastic measure might be. If the result of a safe, shallow turn is crashing into a mountainside, why not test the limits? Pilots can take action when there is nothing more to lose. Better, they can exercise initiative and creativity, coming up with a solution that the computer is simply not equipped to think of.

For this reason, designers of commercial aircraft have pretty much backed off from some initial, extreme positions in which the software had ultimate authority (which many pilots hated).[42] Boeing, for example, will allow pilots to override protection functions on its new 777 by exerting extra force on the controls. The system requires the extra force as a way of telling the pilot that the maneuver being attempted could be dangerous to the airframe.[43]

Completely automated systems—those with no human beings involved in their operation—are referred to as *autonomous systems.* Few systems are truly autonomous—it's just not practical at this point. That's just as well. Autonomous systems will fail like any others. That can be a pain, such as a vending machine that takes your money and delivers no product. But safety-critical autonomous systems pose a sobering ethical question: given the state of the art for digital systems, is it moral to put life-and-death decisions into the "hands" (as it were) of software?

Airline pilots are expensive, and completely fly-by-wire airplanes exist. Why don't airlines simply get rid of pilots? Is it possible they believe that the public would not feel safer flying in an airplane piloted by a computer? Similarly, chemical and nuclear reactors are extensively computerized. Why not get rid of the operators, who make union wages and require expensive benefits? Why not install an expert system to manage the plant? Is it possible that corporations believe their profits would go down, not up, if they did not pay people to handle problems?

The present status of digital technology can be summed up thus: no one even dreams of running a computer-controlled system responsible for a critical mission without also employing people to monitor the system and intervene when necessary. No one, that is, except the military, wielders of the most lethal technology on earth. Yet military systems have hardly been immune to failure.

A variety of proposals in both the United States and the former Soviet Union have advocated that nuclear weapons be launched just as soon as one side receives warning of an impending attack. These launch-on-warning proposals (of which SDI was, in some incarnations, a variant) make demands on computer-controlled systems that are not warranted by what we know of their reliability and their performance to date. An article published in a leading software journal lists actual false reports of a nuclear attack on the United States. The false alarms were caused by a faulty integrated circuit, a bad system design, a testing tape, the rising moon, a flock of swans. In each case, the report notes, "human judgment played an essential role" in determining that the end of the world was *not* nigh, and in preventing serious mistakes.[44]

Indeed, one computer professional grew so concerned that he sued the U.S. government, contending that a launch-on-warning policy "unconstitutionally usurps the power of Congress to declare war, and unlawfully delegates presidential powers to subordinates, since the very short times involved would not allow time for a decision by the president." Regardless of the constitutional issues involved, it is irresponsible and immoral madness to adopt policies that presume complex digital systems will function reliably when the future of life on earth, or most of it, hangs on this presumption.

***Walking and Falling at the Same Time.***  The point of all these strategies for coping with failures is to produce a system that recovers so quickly and transparently that its users never even know it has failed. It is sometimes possible, depending upon how much slack is available from other factors, to design a system that can catch itself before you know it stumbled. David Parnas identifies four factors that allow a system to *failsoft:*[45]

- The kinds of failures likely to occur can be predicted on the basis of what has happened before.

- Individual components are, on the whole, reliable; and the failure of one will not cause others to fail.

- The system has extra capacity and is unlikely to be running under a heavy load most of the time.

- If the system misses a deadline, no great harm will be done in the long run.

If the world is forgiving enough in some of these ways, you can design a system whose failures are invisible to its users. For example, if the bank's mainframe computer is down, the ATM machine may accept your deposit anyway. All it needs is memory to store the interim transactions, and instructions to keep trying until it can reach the mainframe. It can then send all the transactions it stored.

Production pressures being what they are, systems designed with extra capacity tend to be used more and more heavily until they are pushed to their limits. A system may start out able to fail soft, but become increasingly bogged down as more and more of its resources are called upon for everyday operation.

Still, it's worth a shot. Or is it?

### The Danger of Safety

Safety features are useful, often essential. But they undeniably add complexity, introducing new failure modes and causing headaches of their own. The January 15, 1990, AT&T long-distance telephone network slowdown, for instance, turned out to be a problem with the part of the software that *recovers* from errors, an irony almost too common to be noticed anymore. The bug that kept the first space shuttle flight from launching on schedule would never have occurred if not for redundancy. Two independent systems needed to be synchronized, or the backup system would not have been able to take over instantly if needed. But they needed the two independent systems in the first place in case one of the systems failed. The result was a synchronization bug. The program alarms that nearly aborted the first moon landing during its final seconds were, after all, incorporated in the program as debugging aids. They were supposed to help catch problems, not cause them.

The phenomenon of safety devices that pose hazards of their own is not limited to the digital realm, of course. A fully loaded logging truck once hit a toll booth on the Astoria Bridge (over the Columbia River between Astoria, Oregon, and Ilwaco, Washington). The truck knocked the booth off its foundation, and the toll collector inside was hurt by a falling first-aid kit.[46] Evidently, it can happen to anyone. But complexity is software's nemesis, and adding safety features adds complexity. Ultimately, special safety features give the system more ways to fail.

### What Are We Risking?

So far we've discussed only part of the risk equation—exploring, maybe controlling, the probability of failure. But we also need to understand its consequences. Not all accidents are equally serious. What is at risk? How serious is that risk? We need to gauge the effects of system failure and factor it in as part of the system costs. We can then decide *before* we commit our precious resources whether a proposed system is worth it.

The nightly news totes up disasters in terms of the number of injuries, the number of fatalities, and how many dollars' worth of damage was caused. We feel that a disaster in which five thousand people are harmed should be considered worse than an accident with fifty victims, and one with fifty worse than one with five. Perhaps such numeric assessments seem cold-blooded, but the large, complex, expensive systems we build are prone to failure, and we need *some* framework within which to discuss the consequences. Before we sink mountains of precious resources into building these systems, we should at least have a clear understanding of what we are risking. We need some way to ask and answer these questions: What are the consequences of system failure? What is at risk?[47]

Several categories might be considered:

• Loss of, or damage to, money, property, data or information

• Injury or fatalities to plants or animals

• Injuries to owners, operators, users, passersby, or future generations

• Fatalities to owners, operators, users, passersby, or future generations

• Injury to the life-sustaining qualities of the earth

You may be wondering about some of these categories.

Data and information are certainly valuable, but society has not yet clearly established their value, nor even precisely whom they belong to. We have some indicators: the Bank of New York demonstrated that ninety minutes of securities transactions are worth over $5 million, and if your credit history becomes polluted, you'll find out how much it costs to clean it up.

The environment involves two different kinds of problems: harm to particular species, and harm that endangers the system that sustains life for us all. Harm to particular plants and animals does not always count for much. A lot of loggers in the U. S. Pacific Northwest, for example, are presently making it known that the continued existence of spotted owls does not mean a great deal to them, compared to being able to live their lives as they have always done. But I don't think anyone, loggers included, wants to share the world only with rats, cockroaches, and crabgrass. The nonhuman world is necessary for us, and we are stressing it considerably these days. We have to factor in such damage somehow, or we risk bringing the entire intricate ecosystem to its knees.

Nor is all harm to people considered equal. If the flight control system for a new jet fighter turns out to be faulty, killing the test pilot, we mourn, but we seldom sue. Test pilots sign up for their risky job. If a chemical reactor explodes, injuring dozens of workers, we perceive the situation differently than if it had injured dozens of uninvolved passersby. The workers may have understood the risk; they may have agreed to it in exchange for higher pay; they may even have had some control over it. The passersby, on the other hand, had no choice about what happened to them—they are in the position the residents of Lockerbie, Scotland were in when a jet came crashing down on their heads. They did not even have the level of involvement of the jet passengers, who at least knew that they were taking a risk, however slight.

We feel differently about victims who have some control over their fates, or who may have hoped to benefit from the risk they took. Many of us want a world with commercial airline travel and the products of chemical plants and perhaps even the electricity from nuclear power plants. But future generations are the ultimate innocent victims. There is no sense in which they can be said to have participated in the decisions to, say, poison portions of Nevada, the South Pacific, and the Ukraine with radioactivity.

Building a digital system will probably not be cheap. We should ask ourselves: do we really want to spend these resources and accept this level of risk? Sometimes we gain very little when we computerize. When Washington State Ferries decided that pneumatic control systems were adequate to accomplish its mission, it recognized that it is possible to overautomate. Washington State Ferries had to learn this the hard way, after building electronic control systems that proved too prone to failure. But at least they learned. Too often, we fail to ask the key question: Is this the right system to build, after all?

## FORESTALLING DISASTER

The following is another story that is not about software:

On Friday, May 12, 1989, a runaway freight train derailed in a poor neighborhood of a small California town, killing four people and destroying or seriously damaging eleven houses. The clean-up and rescue operation that followed was efficient and extensive. When it was over, thirteen days later, a fourteen-inch pipeline running through the same neighborhood ruptured. The pipeline, damaged by the derailment, released

300,000 gallons of high-octane gasoline which ignited, destroying eleven more houses and killing two more people.

George Trow described the sequence of accidents in a gripping article for the *New Yorker*. Reflecting on these events, he wrote:

> *The railroad system in this country is huge. The National Transportation Safety Board is tiny. The system of hazardous-liquid pipelines in this country is huge. The Office of Pipeline Safety is tiny.*
>
> *I learned quite a bit about the scale of things in America while I was reporting this story. We are set up to build. And we are set up to respond to disaster. What we are willing to do to forestall disaster is: very little.*[48]

This chapter has been filled with various methods available to software engineers and systems engineers to forestall disaster. These methods are arduous, time-consuming, and expensive, so we are seldom willing to use them as extensively as we should. Even when we use them, however, matters may not improve that much. You can take great pains and spend significant amounts of time and money without ensuring comparable increases in the safety and reliability of digital systems. Even when we bend over backward, digital disasters occur.

You would think that would give us pause, as we consider the future and dream of the systems we would like to build. But, as the next chapter shows, the systems we are proposing, planning, and have started to develop pose even greater risks than many of those whose failures now disturb us. Many of these systems represent genuine social and technological experiments. But public discussion of these proposals has been disappointingly sparse. We have not really been participating in the decisions to implement the experiments for which we serve as guinea pigs. Often, we hear nothing of a system until its benefits are described in a rosy glow by those who will profit from it. No disinterested voice describes the risks. Yet the risks are usually shared more equally than the profits.

## NOTES

1 *Hearings before the Subcommittee on Strategic and Theater Nuclear Forces of the Committee on Armed Services of the United States Senate*, 99th Congress, First Session, Dec. 3, 1985 (Superintendent of Documents number Y4.Ar 5/3:S.hrg. 99–933). Solomon J. Buchsbaum, Statement, pp. 273–280; answers to questions, pp. 322–328.

2 Petroski, Henry. *To Engineer is Human: The Role of Failure in Successful Design*. New York: St. Martin's Press, 1985, pp.197–200. Also discussed in Waldrop, M. Mitchell. "Congress Finds Bugs in the Software." *Science*, Nov. 10, 1989, p. 753.

3 Wiener, Lauren. "A Trip Report on SIGSOFT '91." *ACM Software Engineering Notes,* 17:2, April, 1992, pp. 23–38. See p. 32.

4 Wiener, Lauren. *op. cit.,* p. 35

5 Paul, James. "Bugs in the system: Problems in federal government computer software development and regulation." Subcommittee on Investigations and Oversight of the House Committee on Science, Space, and Technology, U.S. Government Printing Office, Washington, D.C., U.S.A., Sept., 1989.

6 Waldrop, M. Mitchell. "Congress Finds Bugs in the Software." *Science,* Nov. 10, 1989, p. 753.

7 Rushby, John. "Formal Specification and Verification for Critical Systems: Tools, Achievements, and Prospects." Paper presented at the Electric Power Research Institute Workshop on Methodologies for Cost-effective, Reliable Software Verification and Validation, Chicago, IL, Aug. 7–9, 1991. The quote is from p. 2.

8 Rushby, John and Friedrich von Henke. "Formal Verification of Algorithms for Critical Systems." ACM SIGSOFT *Software Engineering Notes,* 16:5, Dec. 1991, pp. 1–15.

9 The problem, roughly known as version control, is practically a cottage industry for computer-aided software engineering tools.

10 Gries, David. *The Science of Programming.* New York: Springer-Verlag, 1981, p. 164.

11 DeMillo, Lipton, and Perlis, "Proof as a Social Process." *Communications of the ACM,* 22:5, May 1979. The ideas presented in this discussion draw heavily on this paper, which I found readable and thought-provoking.

12 *ibid,* p. 272.

13 *ibid,* p. 275.

14 Rushby, John, in his oral presentation of the paper, "Formal Verification of Algorithms for Critical Systems," by John Rushby and Friedrich von Henke, in *Proceedings of the ACM SIGSOFT Conference on Software for Critical Systems, ACM Software Engineering Notes,* 16:5, Dec. 1991, pp. 1–15.

15 Cherniavsky, John C., D. Richard Kuhn, and Dolores R. Wallace. "High Integrity Software Standards Activities at NIST." *Proceedings of the Pacific Northwest Software Quality Conference,* Oct. 7–8, 1991, pp. 48–61.

16 My sources for this story are: Parnas, David L. Personal communication, Dec. 5, 1991. Joannou, Paul K. Supervising Design Engineer, Ontario Hydro. Personal communication, Dec. 6, 1991. Peterson, Ivars. "Finding Fault: The formidable task of eradicating software bugs." *Science News,* vol. 139, Feb. 16, 1991, pp. 104–106.

17 *System availability* is a magic number. The notion is that the key property of an emergency backup system is that it must be instantly available when called on. Otherwise, what good is it? So system availability is the proportion of the time that the plant is operating during which the emergency backup system is available—an important number to report to the AECB. Here's how it's determined:

An analogue hardware backup system is tested once per shift. If it passes this test, fine—it is available. If it fails, when did it stop being available? You cannot say for sure, so the rules of the game specify that you have to assume it broke immediately after the start of the shift, say, at 9:01 A.M. The availability number goes down, perhaps more than necessary.

A software system, on the other hand, can report when it experiences a failure. If it reports a failure at 4:41 P.M., you can assume it was available up to that point, leading to a better availability number for the AECB. If it experiences a failure in its reporting system, it's still tested once per shift—if that test fails, the old rules apply.

18 For a discussion of engineering judgment and related matters, see Henry Petroski, *To Engineer is Human: The Role of Failure in Successful Design,* cited above.

19 See, for example, Dugger, Ronnie. "Annals of Democracy: Counting Votes." *New Yorker*, Nov. 7, 1988, pp. 40ff. Also see Mercuri, Rebecca. "Inside Risks: Voting Machine Risks." *Communications of the ACM*, 35:11, Nov. 1992, p. 138.

20 Popular press: For example, Rogers, Michael, et al. "Can We Trust Our Software?" *Newsweek*, Jan. 29, 1990, pp. 70–73. Computer science professionals: Software certification has been extensively discussed in the on-line forum *comp.risks*—see, for example, 10:37, 38, and especially 41 and 43 (Sept. 13–22, 1990).

21 The text of the proposed legislation can be found in *comp.risks*, 12:9, July 25, 1991. Ensuing discussion in issues 10 and 11 (July 29 and 30) is also interesting.

22 See Young, S. David. *The Rule of Experts: Occupational Licensing in America*. Cato Institute, 1987.

23 Pressman, Roger S., and S. Russell Herron. *Software Shock: The Danger and the Opportunity*. New York: Dorset House, 1991. See p. 77.

24 Joyce, Edward J. "Is error-free software achievable?" *Datamation*, Feb. 15, 1989, p. 53ff.

25 Neumann, Peter G. "Inside Risks: Are Dependable Systems Feasible?" *Communications of the ACM*, Feb. 1993, 36:2, p. 146.

26 Covault, Craig. "Mission Control Saved Intelsat Rescue From Software, Checklist Problems." *Aviation Week and Space Technology*, May 25, 1992, pp. 78–9.

27 For this discussion, I am indebted to: Bell, Trudy E. "Managing Murphy's law: engineering a minimum-risk system." IEEE *Spectrum*, June 1989, pp. 24–27.

28 Leveson, Nancy G. "Software Safety: What, Why, and How." *Computing Surveys*, 18:2, June 1986, pp. 125–163. The story is on p. 133.

29 Bell, Trudy E., *op. cit.*

30 Wiener, *op. cit.* p. 31.

31 Perrow, Charles. *Normal Accidents: Living with High-risk Technologies*. New York: Basic Books, 1984. See especially pp. 3–14.

32 Lammers, Susan. *Programmers at Work: Interviews*. Redmond, WA.: Microsoft Press, 1986, p. 188.

33 *comp.risks*, 13:26, March 6, 1992. Item contributed by David Wortman.

34 Wiener, Lauren. *op. cit.* p. 33.

35 Avizienis, Algirdas, and Danforth E. Ball. "On the Achievement of a Highly Dependable and Fault-Tolerant Air Traffic Control System." IEEE *Computer*, February 1987, pp. 84–90.

36 Hughes, David. "Tracking Software Error Likely Reason Patriot Battery Failed to Engage Scud." *Aviation Week and Space Technology*, June 10, 1991, pp. 25–6.

37 Ramirez, Anthony. "Global Phone Systems Act to Avoid Failures." *New York Times*, Oct. 12, 1991, p. 25. Also, Robert Rankin, "Telephone Failures Alarming," *Oregonian*, July 11, 1991, p. A13.

38 $.95 \times .95 \times .95 \times .95 \times .95 \times .95 \times .95 \times .95 \times .95 \times .95 = .5987$, or 59.87%. An item in Harper's Index (*What Counts: The Complete Harper's Index*, Charis Conn and Ilena Silverman, eds. New York: Henry Holt & Co., Inc., 1991, p. 136) illustrates how quickly reliability can degrade for complex systems: "Chances that a space shuttle will crash within the next four years, assuming all systems are 98% reliable, according to NASA: 1 in 2." In this formulation, each "component" is actually a system made up of many components, each of which has to do a lot better than 98% to achieve that overall reliability. The space shuttle has *a lot* of systems. Presumably, NASA is going for better than 98%.

39 Mason, C., and D. Bushaus. "Software problem cripples AT&T long distance network." *Telephony*, Jan. 22, 1990, pp. 10–11. Rogers, Michael, et al. "Can We Trust Our

Software?" *Newsweek*, Jan. 29, 1990, pp. 70–73. Also, *comp.risks*, 9:62, 64, 66, and others.

40 Knight, John C., and Nancy G. Leveson. "An experimental evaluation of the assumption of independence in multiversion programming." IEEE *Transactions on Software Engineering*, SE-12:1, Jan. 1986, pp. 96–109.

41 Donald Norman has written extensively on this topic. See, for example, *The Design of Everyday Things* (a previous edition was titled *The Psychology of Everyday Things*). New York: Doubleday, 1988.

42 For a concise and thoughtful discussion of this controversy in the context of the crash of an Airbus A320 (whose flight control system is entirely digital, and of a revolutionary design), see "Who's flying the plane?" *The Economist*, Jan. 25, 1992, pp. 88–9.

43 Wiener, Lauren. *op. cit.* p. 31.

44 Borning, Alan. "Computer System Reliability and Nuclear War." *Communications of the ACM*, 30:2, Feb. 1987, pp. 112–131. The first quote is from p. 114. The second quote is from p. 118. The discussion of launch-on-warning can be found on pages 116–18. The entire article is a detailed and concerned discussion of the issues raised by the use of unreliable technology to control an unprecedentedly lethal technology. For a discussion of SDI in particular with regards to this issue, see "Autonomous Systems: the Case of 'Star Wars,'" the appendix to Forester, Tom, and Perry Morrison, *Computer Ethics: Cautionary Tales and Ethical Dilemmas in Computing*. Cambridge, MA: MIT Press, 1990, pp. 173–181.

45 Parnas, David L. "Software Aspects of Strategic Defense Systems," in *American Scientist*, vol. 43, Sept./Oct. 1985, pp. 432–40, reprinted by permission in *Communications of the ACM*, 28:12, December, 1985, pp. 1326–35. See p. 434.

46 Watson, M. Colleen. "Memory Span." Sunday *Oregonian, Northwest Magazine*, Sept. 16, 1990, p. 8.

47 The following discussion owes a great deal to Charles Perrow, *op. cit.* See pp. 66–70 and pp. 324–28.

48 Trow, George W. S. "A Reporter at Large: Devastation." *New Yorker*, Oct. 22, 1990, pp. 54–79. The quotes are from pages 67 and 68.

# CHAPTER 5

# BIG PLANS

*Hey, pal,*
*how do I get to town from here?*
*And he said—*
*Well, just take a right where they're gonna build that new shopping mall,*
*go straight past where they're gonna put in the freeway,*
*and take a left at what's gonna be the new sports center,*
*and keep going till you hit the place where they're thinking of building*
*that drive-in bank—*
*—you can't miss it.*
*And I said, this must be the place.*[1]

Like Laurie Anderson's protagonist in "Big Science," we are so obsessed by our big plans for the future that we can hardly communicate in terms of the present. We are fascinated with digital technology. Imagine—a machine can be made to do almost anything! The systems we can build with this! A hardware engineer now graduating from college may *never* build a machine without a microprocessor in it. We are ambitious.

But projects absorb more resources than expected, and the systems we build will not always work. Sometimes a lot is at stake when they don't.

Introducing new systems introduces social risks, even if the technology does its job with well-oiled precision, as the expression used to go in a mechanical world. New technologies do not spring fully formed into a vacuum. Every system we propose will change aspects of society we have taken for granted for centuries. We might want to stop and think about this first:

- Seeing may mean believing even less than it does now. Digital video means that videotape will be easy to fake, for example. How much further can we undermine direct experience before we drive ourselves nuts?

- We are already losing our private lives. Our whereabouts, our habits, our pleasures and our problems are increasingly matters of public record. How far do we want this to go?

- Society may fragment further: human contact may no longer be needed to satisfy an increasing number of human needs. We will all have different experiences. We will be able to assume little common knowledge.

- Computers may be delegated some seriously inappropriate jobs: standing vigil over prisoners, caring for the old and sick, making life-and-death decisions in hospitals. Do we really want to end our days being tended by a program in an understaffed nursing home?

- Mechanisms by which we have for years regulated ownership and copyright will have to undergo significant changes. No one is quite sure how to set up a system of incentives that will sustain the production of new books, programs, or even works of art.

And that's if things go the way they should. But accidents will happen, and then we face graver risks. The failure of some of these systems could have serious consequences. What if a robot surgeon slices someone in the wrong place before a human surgeon can stop it? When cars on a rush-hour freeway are under central computer control, a computer failure could wipe out as many people in a freeway accident as might ordinarily die in a jet crash. With commercial air traffic likewise under central computer control, the failure of an air traffic control computer could involve as many jets as a freeway accident involves cars. Companies could go bankrupt because of the silent failure of information management systems. We could watch the disappearance of coastal lands all over the world because an overly simplified computer model led to a disastrous decision about permissible atmospheric carbon dioxide levels.

We really ought to discuss all of this first. Trouble is, events move at incredible speed in this field, and it's hard to pin down a moving target. But we may as well try.

We hear a lot about the benefits of proposed systems, and many of them are beneficial, certainly. But we seldom hear what we are risking or get an accurate picture of the cost. Public discussion tends to be sparse and one-sided, often dominated by those thrilled to breathlessness by the thought of building these systems or collecting the profits from them. They tend to describe benefits in glowing, unrealistic terms.

Some of these systems will indeed bring benefits—digital technology has some impressive strengths. But some of these systems are not worth building. They will be ruinously expensive and the risks will outweigh the benefits.

This chapter surveys a variety of proposals for the use of computers and software that have been put forward in recent years. The number and variety of proposals you are about to encounter is stunning, but society's resources are finite. Under the circumstances, let's evaluate them first, instead of committing resources haphazardly or on the basis of who is waving the best flags. We can't build them all.

You may wish to read the following discussion in the spirit of a game called Find That Risk.[2] I hope you don't find this game too unrelievedly gloomy. It is intended as a counterbalance to the all-too-pervasive "gee-whiz" tone of most other published discussions, technical and popular. A number of the more ambitious systems are unwise; unfortunately, work on some has already started anyway. I'll tell you why I think they are too risky, and you might disagree with me; perhaps vehemently, and probably more than once. That is to be expected, but it is beside the point.

At bottom, it doesn't matter if I fear an outcome you consider you could live with, or if you see a risk that I missed. What matters is that we think about what we are doing and reach an intelligent consensus about how we spend our finite resources. The cutting edge of technology cuts both ways.

### WARNING

*Engineers love acronyms. TLAs[3] and ETLAs[4] abound in this chapter. The acronym-sensitive are advised to don protective gear before continuing.*

## INFORMATION IN DIGITAL FORM

When we put a microprocessor into a machine, we have decided to digitize the information that machine deals with. What are the consequences of this decision?

No matter what it represents, all digital information has certain characteristics in common. It is all equivalent and interchangeable zeroes and ones as far as the machines are concerned. This can be handy or amusing or a pain. Interchangeability fosters integration of systems: a number of different microprocessor-based machines can be connected into one big integrated system. Integrated systems have artistic, psychological, and social ramifications that have as yet to be appreciated.

Digital information is easy to spread, copy, and change. Computers connected in a network can exchange information constantly. A modem opens the network to other modems. It is easy to access information and hard to restrict such access. This can be good or bad, depending on the situation. A ride-sharing bulletin board, traffic information system, or on-line professional discussion benefits from the nearly effortless and instantaneous way digital information can spread. Other applications present problems for privacy, individuality, copyright, and ownership.

Digital information is nearly as easy to modify as it is to copy. Anyone knows this who has spent hours tinkering with a report or spreadsheet or picture. It is hard to detect traces of the modifications, though—which can have psychological or legal consequences.

### Easy to Access: Disseminating Information

As faxes and e-mail have shown, one of the things that computers do best is disseminate information quickly. This isn't always a good thing, but often it is. For example, sometimes information disseminated in traditional ways travels too slowly; a research report that might save lives can take up to a year to make it into a medical journal. So we now have "The Online Journal of Current Clinical Trials," jointly published by the American Association for the Advancement of Science and the Online Computer Library Center. The first medical journal in electronic form uses computers, modems, and phone lines to send information about cancer, heart disease, and AIDS research to subscribers all over the world. Information will arrive months sooner than it used to—a clear boon.[5]

Spreading traffic information has clear benefits, too. If drivers can get frequent, updated traffic reports, they can then plan their trips to avoid the congestion. Such negative feedback introduced into the system stabilizes it. Broadcasting such information is cheap, so why not? Sensors built into the roads themselves allow such systems to be automated: the city of Chicago broadcasts automated traffic reports on AM radio based on information received from sensors beneath the asphalt. The traffic reports are updated every ten minutes, interspersed with a tape recording detailing construction projects or other events that affect traffic flow.[6]

This relatively simple system has one fascinating characteristic: it fails utterly at the worst possible time, and it is still better to have it than not. When traffic is at an absolute standstill, no cars travel over the sensors. The computer detects nothing and reports no traffic. But the worst case doesn't occur very often, and when it does, common sense might tell those familiar with this quirk that the main expressway out of town is unlikely to be empty at 5:00 P.M. on a Friday before a holiday weekend. The Chicago traffic information system practically defines a benign system: its worst failure has no consequences worse than its absence.

Traffic information systems are being developed or deployed in many cities that experience chronic traffic jams. In London a driver can subscribe to a system called Trafficmaster. For about $33 a month, the system displays traffic snarls on an electronic map. A network of radio transmitters is being expanded in Berlin to provide a similar function.[7] And traffic information systems are part of a comprehensive solution proposed for the Los Angeles area.[8]

Traffic will continue to be a problem, however, as long as everyone insists on driving him- or herself everywhere. Systems that might get some cars off the road might be more helpful. In recognition of this, a network for spur-of-the-moment ride-sharing has also been planned for the Los Angeles area. It's supposed to decrease the number of cars in the downtown area. A network of terminals linked to a central computer can pair drivers and riders at a moment's notice, providing an incentive for people to leave their cars home, where they needn't pay for parking. The trip-planning computer would allow a carless individual to dial up and get the bus schedule or request a ride from a driver going in the same direction. Such a system might decrease traffic congestion and promote social cohesion in many cities, but I find it an odd system for Los Angeles. I suspect it would work better somewhere with a higher level of trust and a lower level of private gun ownership than the Los Angeles area has at present.

Anyway, a high-tech approach to ride-sharing is unnecessary. For example, in the San Francisco area, a lot of commuters are to be found at the east end of the Oakland Bay Bridge every morning, where they catch rides with drivers wishing to travel in the faster, carpool-only lanes into the city. In the evening, they are at the west end, helping drivers leave faster. The hitchhikers improve their chances by placing themselves near the incentive—the carpool-only lane—and also by allowing themselves to be looked at, thus allowing drivers to make their own risk assessments.

### Easy to Copy: Some Thoughts on Handwriting

In spite of all the recent hype about multimedia (using voice recordings to annotate documents, playing video and music in windows, and such stuff), text and numbers are still the main reasons we use personal computers. They're still the main problems as well. A lot of people don't like typing; some of us like to write with a pen. Pen-based computing is on its way; close to a dozen different companies have announced offerings. Personal computing may now become accessible to the keyboard-averse.

To use a pen-based computer, you hold an input device made to feel and act like a pen. You place the pen against the screen (the "paper") and write. Your writing appears on the screen. The result of this used to be just a pattern of pixels, meaningless to the computer, but pen-based computers will be able to interpret your loop-and-stick as the letter d and your loop-and-curve as the letter g. They will convert handwriting to ASCII,[9] the representation of text that most computers use today. This will be handy.

Even without a pen-based computer, you can design a typeface that looks just like your handwriting and use it on your present PC. For about a hundred dollars, you can pay someone else to do it.[10] However, digitizing your handwriting exposes you to fraud. You are giving anyone who can use your computer the ability to print out documents that look as if you wrote them. That may be fine. Then again, it may not—digitizing your signature makes it easy for others to get, keep, and use. What can a fax with your signature commit you to?

You don't even have to own a computer to get into this kind of trouble. If you've received a package lately from the United Parcel Service, you probably signed your name with a computer "pen" on a liquid-crystal display. A digitized copy of your signature now reposes in the UPS database forevermore, available to anyone who wants it badly enough to break into their system.

Soon signatures will no longer mean what for centuries we have assumed that they mean. How are we going to replace them? There are other ways to indicate consent to a contract. The Japanese use *hanko*, for example. Due to the characteristics of their writing system, Japanese signatures are not necessarily idiosyncratic. So they buy specially made stamps showing the Chinese ideographs of a name carved in a unique way. *Hanko* can be forged or stolen, and might not work well for us. What would?

### Easy to Modify: Undermining Direct Experience

In popular parlance, trusting your senses is tantamount to sanity. Our senses evolved to enable us to perceive the world, and the effects of millennia of evolution are powerful—people are swayed by the evidence of their senses. We used to be able to believe what we saw, but photography, film, and especially television have undermined our faith in direct experience. The consequences for our hearts and minds have yet to be appreciated.[11] To this modern problem, digital technology adds a whole new dimension—digital media is easy to alter convincingly.[12] Once photographs, documents, or videotape are commonly kept in digital form, the ease with which they can be altered is likely to further undermine direct experience.

The plasticity of digital media is terrific for artists. Ted Turner's portrait on the cover of *Time* (he was *Time*'s "Man of the Year" for 1991,

his head surrounded by a globe made up of television images) consisted
of forty-four exposures combined with a computer.[13] The photographer,
Greg Heisler, handed an electronic cassette to his client, not a print or a
slide.[14] Computer imaging has a lot to offer professional photographers,
and they are aware of both the potential and the risks. One photo lab
that produces images using digital technology clearly labels them: "Electronic image manipulation by Meteor Photo."[15] That's laudable and
good for business, too, but not everyone is going to be so scrupulous.

Altering data can be done without leaving a trace. It can be just like
telling a lie, only harder to detect. A child who was never in Ohio can
be placed there in a picture, with the rich October evening light falling
on her just as it falls on the others. Or a man who *was* there can be deleted, and the pattern of the chairs or the leaves or the sky in the background can be filled in just as the camera would have recorded it in his
absence. Film or video can be modified in the same manner; it just takes
longer and costs more. Pretty soon, a videotape such as the one showing
the Los Angeles police beating Rodney King will no longer be admissible
as evidence in a courtroom. It will be too easy to fake, and too hard to
detect the fraud. In a few short years, videotapes may go from being the
most persuasive possible evidence to the least persuasive, as access to
digital video editing equipment spreads.

Sounds, too, can be snatched, stored, sliced, replayed. Timbre can be
altered, an ordinary voice can sound spacey or spooky, speech rhythms
can be changed, an everyday phrase can be made to sound ominous. It
is easy to produce a tape recording of your voice saying something you
never said.

If Stalin had commanded this technology, what couldn't he have done
with it?

### Easy to Access, Copy, and Modify: Copyright Problems

So far, it isn't falsification that's caused legal trouble, though—it's art.
Digital sampling has already prompted one copyright infringement case.
Snatches of previously recorded music can easily be woven into new music using digital sampling technology. The music thus produced is like a
collage containing snippets of photographs, such as the *Time* cover discussed above. This is just the sort of thing that artists love to play with,
but rap artist Biz Markie had to go to court for it. His album *I Need a
Haircut* was pulled from stores after a judge ruled he should not have
sampled a snippet from Gilbert O'Sullivan's 1972 paean to self-pity,
"Alone Again (Naturally)."[16]

This ruling is easier to enforce than the license to use only one copy
of a software program: organizations such as EMI Music Publishing now

pay people to listen to records and detect samples so that clearance is paid for. For the moment, therefore, the ruling has had an inhibiting effect on digital sampling in music.

It's too bad. Michael Green's quirky book *Zen & the Art of the Macintosh* shows that a more open attitude is possible. The book is about Michael Green, a graphic designer who falls in love with his computer while producing the book. The pages get wilder and wilder. Each is beautiful. At the back of the book, Green talks about the hardware and software and techniques he used to do it. Then he writes "On the philosophy of Digitizing:"

> *Digitizing captures an* idea. *And when you finish playing around with it, what you have (if it's still recognizable) is an* homage *rather than a rip-off. In keeping with this, let me go on record as saying* anyone who wishes to digitize any of the images in this book is welcome to do so. *May a hundred flowers bloom! [emphasis his]*[17]

Data in digital form has real advantages. You can hunt for phrases, jumping around with more freedom than is provided by a table of contents or index. These advantages lead people to proclaim that some day, all the world's data will be stored on compact disc. But how will it get there? Who is going to volunteer to type in the Library of Congress?

As it happens, some people are signing up to do it, one book at a time. Michael Hart, a systems analyst and zealot in Urbana, Illinois, has been typing since 1971. About forty volunteers have been helping him for a while now. The goal of Project Gutenberg, as he has dubbed the enterprise, is ten thousand books in digital form by the year 2001. What Mr. Hart yearns for is a world in which you enter the library with a blank diskette and leave with a diskette containing the books that you want. You would not have to return anything. You might not even have to go anywhere; the "library" could be a computer that you dial up with a modem.[18]

Project Gutenberg avoids the difficult issue of copyright by scrupulously typing in only books in the public domain. Heaven knows those are many, but it's only a matter of time before the issue has to be faced. If you can go to the library and walk off with a book on a diskette that you will never have to return, then who will buy a book at a bookstore? And if no one buys books anymore, what incentives will authors and publishers have to produce new ones?

Digital media thus has the potential to break the economic mechanism that produces books. The music industry has been facing this problem since it went digital: technology enables anyone to make a perfect, crystalline copy of a digitally recorded compact disc. Musicians, music publishers, and record labels have fought for laws to keep digital cassette tape recorders out of people's homes, fearing the economic effects of widespread, perfect, homemade copies. The advantages of the technology for recording were undeniable. So the music industry identified a choke point—the easy availability of digital tape recorders to home consumers. It halted production of the machines until an economic remedy and a technological fix could be introduced into the system: royalty fees were built into the cost of the machines and their tapes, and the machines themselves will be artificially limited to produce only first-generation copies.[19] The music industry picked the right moment to fight the technology. After the machines became commonly available to consumers, the music business would never have been the same. Print publishers will be facing this issue soon, and it is unclear what approach will best serve everyone's needs.[20]

Because information in digital form is easy to alter as well as to copy, other problems crop up—problems similar to those that software developers must grapple with. When programmers write software, they use a word processor to write lines of instruction in a programming language such as C or FORTRAN or BASIC. The file they create this way is called *source code*. They take the source code file and run it through a compiler, and the compiler spits out a file called an *executable file* (because the processor executes it). Most software is sold as executable files. Programmers do not like to sell source code because it can be read and modified, albeit with difficulty. This puts the vendor in an impossible position. If a bug is found, whose bug is it? Who should be responsible for fixing it? What happens if the vendor releases an update with new features, and one of the new features collides with one of the custom modifications? It opens the door to endless problems, which most vendors avoid by selling only executable files.

A book is both source and executable; it is source when it sits on the shelf, and it is "executed" when you read it, and the author's mind speaks to yours. If books are distributed on digital media, we risk breaking the link between the mind of the author and the reader. What is to prevent someone from giving *King Lear* a happy ending, or slipping a pornographic passage into the *Book of Mormon*? Forty subtly different versions of *Moby Dick* will circulate. How are we going to tell which is the original? Will we support a bureaucracy to certify books?

### Interchangeable: The StereoVideoFaxPhonePC and HouseController

As a child, I went to the 1964 New York World's Fair and stood in a long, long line to use the world's first picture phone. I had plenty of time to consider that the neighbors I was calling did not also have a picture phone, but it didn't occur to me. I was disappointed to sit in the futuristic, egg-shaped booth and only hear voices, just as always. Soon after, AT&T put the picture phone on the shelf: it was difficult to install and cost $9 per minute in 1964 dollars.[21]

It's now the early 1990s, and the long-awaited picture phone is here at last. The interchangeability of digital data means you can send pictures down the telephone wires along with sound. You can also send video or weather maps or medical X-rays; it's all just ones and zeroes to the computer. You can put a little television tube into the phone. You can put a computer in there, too. You can put a computer in the television. (A television is already part of the computer—it's the screen.) Some computers have built-in modems. Some modems have built-in fax machines. Why have separate machines? Why not just have one ultimate all-purpose machine to do it all?[22]

With this mythological computer, you could send a fax, talk to a friend, do your word processing, listen to music, watch television, look at the pictures you took of last year's summer vacation, and record any of it. Consumer electronics are going to change.[23, 24]

And grow. We can take the all-in-one computer and tie it to every appliance with a microprocessor. Then you can teach your house to run itself; a few prototypes have already been built.[25] A so-called "smart" house (I think we should ban this use of the word "smart" before we're sorry) could save energy and keep down utility bills. It could wake you up if it detected smoke, intruders, or a noise in the baby's room. No harm in this when it works, unless you count as "harm" becoming too lazy to turn off the lights when leaving a room.

Science fiction stories about smart houses have often focused, for some Freudian reason, on the problem of a house that is too motherly or overbearing. The scenario usually goes something like this:

HOUSE: You'd better wear your boots, it's raining outside.
GROWN MAN: Open the door, I'm in a hurry.
HOUSE: Not until you put on your boots.
MAN: Grrrr!

If you take those scenarios seriously, you might ensure that your integrated house control system has no voice. A more likely problem, though, is a flaw in the house controller that causes bizarre interactions between various subsystems. Integrated systems can be quite complex, because many different kinds of interactions among the components are possible. The bugs could be interesting: using the garage-door opener might turn the dishwasher off. Clever software might allow a broken house controller to call a repair technician. What if it called spuriously? What if it dialed the wrong number? Repeatedly? Integrated systems are complex; they can be challenging to troubleshoot. Repair technicians will need quite an education. Their services will probably not come any cheaper.

But suppose it all works just as it should. Cocooning goes electronic. We watch movies at home with the VCR, we use the home shopping network, we pay bills by phone, we work from home with our modems, we satisfy our needs for companionship with computer bulletin boards. Want interaction? Thanks to any of several proposed technologies, you will soon be able to interact with your television set. Play along with the game show. Request the special $2-off pizza coupon (probably in exchange for having your name and address enter yet another database under the labels "pizza-eater" and "Friday-night-TV-watcher"). Live like Vashti, the heroine of E.M. Forster's story "The Machine Stops," cozy in a little cell, horrified at the thought of actual face-to-face contact. That's one way to cope with urban overcrowding.

Okay, I'll lighten up. Data interchangeability also opens the door to new art forms. Imagine dialing up the library, downloading Shakespeare's sonnets, and reading the resulting file into a program that generates music. The program takes the ASCII character codes for the text and interprets them as musical notes instead, thus creating a "melody" (it is sure to sound weird, especially at first) to go along with the poetry. The human talent for perceiving patterns being what it is, at least one of those sonnets will end up with a song that some critic will describe as "haunting and fraught with significance."[26] Then someone will take a video recording of a conversation with Aunt Maeve and run the audio through the music program and the video through a color graphics program, and the fun will really begin.

### An Unexpected Bonus: Digital X-rays

Sometimes the effect of digitizing information can be hard to predict, because the particular characteristics of the system using it can make a big difference. For instance, digital technology improves dental X-rays. Dentists can place an electronic sensor inside your mouth and see the resulting image only seconds later on a video screen. The images are detailed and magnified, enhancing the dentist's diagnostic abilities. Your exposure to radiation is reduced by 90 percent.[27]

And the bill goes up: the new technology costs about five times as much as the old. There's no such thing as a free lunch.

## MOVING LOTS OF INFORMATION FAST

These consumer electronics toys presume the ability to move a lot of information—voice, pictures, books, shows, music, and more—all over the world, very fast. Conventional copper-based telephone cable is not up to the job. *That* will require fiber optic cable, which can carry a vastly greater amount of information. In the United States, plans for the Integrated Service Digital Network (ISDN) call for building the data equivalent of the interstate freeway system. After the telephone companies, cable companies, utilities, and government finish squabbling over who gets to build this fiber optic network, homes and businesses will be linked in an ambitious communications infrastructure that makes what cable companies have done to connect city-dwellers look paltry by comparison.[28] Our present system trickles data to us, and ISDN will be a firehose.

But as we've seen before, advantages and weaknesses go together. When ISDN is a boon to every household, *a lot* of services will be disrupted when one backhoe operator has a bad day.

The ability to send huge amounts of data quickly over the phone lines allows new sorts of information to be sent, such as X-rays or other medical images (those taken with magnetic resonance imaging technology, for example).[29] It is undeniably safer to move the image than the patient under certain circumstances. If we grow to depend on this technology, will we concentrate the required facilities into fewer and fewer big-city hospitals? When the phone lines go down again, what then? Like so many other things, it's a tradeoff. Which risk is worse?

A subtler risk is the possibility of missing some critical detail in the process of digitizing the image. Unlike analogue images, which consist of details smoothly shading into each other, digital images are of a finite resolution—the picture, like a newspaper photograph, consists of only so many tiny dots per millimeter. What if, in the process of turning the data into these dots, a tiny but critical detail happens to fall into the cracks between dots, and is thus not visible in the digitized image?

Compressing digitized data poses another risk. Compressed data can be transmitted faster. Using compression schemes, telephone companies now bundle many telephone conversations and send them across the country together. If the compression scheme used causes a small problem here and there, it's no big deal: human language is so redundant that speakers are likely never to notice.[30] Compressing and decompress-ing medical images, however, could be riskier, as altering even the small-est detail could affect diagnosis and treatment.

ISDN's huge increase in capacity erases the distinction between broad-cast and cablecast television.[31] Instead of watching or taping shows when they're broadcast, you will be able to choose from a menu of offerings at any time. Dial up a film library and download the movie you want to watch. Get a news broadcast tailored to your own local area—this may encourage people to learn more about local problems on which they could actually have an impact. Tailor the news to suit yourself. Get a deeper look at a story that interests you. But don't take it for granted that you and your neighbors share much common knowledge when you tackle those local problems you are now eager to solve.

Interactive television news permits people to retain pristine ignorance about any aspect of the world they decide not to care about. Sports junk-ies can forget that international politics exists until a war converts their country into a team they can root for. Bigots can choose to ignore all news coming from communities they disapprove of. Will this augment the already frightening fragmentation of society?

Utility companies are developing meters that send information on util-ity usage from the consumer's home or business to the utility company's computers. This information can be used to decrease the need for new power plants by allowing more sensitive projections of demand. Of course, the same lines that send information out can send it back. For a small rebate on your electric bill, would you sign up for a service that would turn off your hot water heater at times of peak power demand? Would you pay for a service that would turn off all but essential appli-ances when you were gone on vacation?

This has privacy ramifications as well:[32]

> *Once an intelligent meter is linked via sensors to home appliances, "we're going to know every time someone in the house turns on a toaster or an egg-beater," Mr. Weinberg [manager of research and development at Pacific Gas & Electric Co. in San Francisco] says. "Market-research guys would love that information. We have to be very careful or we'll look like Big Brother."*

### INFOMARKET

The champion Orwellian technology, though, is the information market. It's no longer news that, as we go through life using credit cards and ATM machines and checks and medical insurance and car insurance and driver's licenses and marriage licenses and mortgages and mail-order catalogues and airline reservations and rental cars and even supermarket coupons, we leave a trail of electronic bread crumbs for credit agencies and direct-mail marketing organizations. Our electronic personae grow more well-rounded daily. Given the extensive amount of data that is available electronically about each of us, some people fear we will lose our privacy, or have already done so.[33]

### Data as a Commodity

Some data is collected for us for purposes we choose. Our names are in the database of the Department of Motor Vehicles because we want to own a car and drive. If we take a class, our academic transcripts are kept to determine our eligibility for a degree. In order to care for us properly, health care providers keep records of our medical histories, and pharmacists keep records of our prescriptions.

This system has been in place for decades, originating in a time of paper records. The responsibilities of each party are clearly defined: the data subject wishes to purchase a service (electricity, vehicle ownership); the agency declares a need for certain of the subject's data; the subject provides the data. Both parties need accurate data and assume certain responsibilities for maintaining its accuracy: the subject provides updates as necessary, and the agency acts on those updates. It is not a bad model; so far, it has worked for us.

Incentives and capabilities are distributed in quite another way with agencies, such as credit-reporting and direct-marketing organizations, that collect data on us for their own purposes. Data as a commodity is a relatively new phenomenon, and it's unique: the producer does not own it; the collector—the agency—does. Yet errors in the data do not reduce the value of the commodity, nor otherwise harm the owner, because they are so difficult to detect. Instead, they harm the producer, the data subject. Correcting errors, however, benefits the data subject and costs the owner. The owner has little incentive to correct errors, and the data subject has little power to do so. As the residents of Norwich, Vermont, found out, it is not an ideal arrangement.

So far the data agencies have had it all their own way. Any information they could wheedle or trick people into revealing was fair game. UPC bar codes, for example, can be used to determine your buying habits.[34] In one instance, a television commercial for an allergy-relief medication advertised a toll-free number that allergy sufferers could call for "a pollen count in your area." When called, the number used the newly implemented Caller ID feature of the phone system to capture the phone numbers of the callers. Various directories allowed the marketing organization that dreamed this up to get names and addresses from the phone numbers, thus obtaining a nice list of people who had telephones, televisions, and allergies.[35]

Scams like the allergy ad described above are not transactions that both parties agree to. They are not even transactions that both parties are aware of. The data subject is duped into giving something valuable away for next to nothing, and on top of that, allowing it to be used for purposes he or she may find objectionable.

Data collectors use, sell, or trade data like baseball cards. Data collecting agencies proliferate, and so do exchanges between the computers on which the databases reside. But these agencies have not been forward about assuming responsibility for the accuracy of their data. Inaccurate data can cause serious damage; people have been thrown in jail—and kept there—because keepers of databases have been unresponsive about correcting data they knew to be erroneous.[36] If data agencies cannot be trusted to use their property responsibly, people may soon demand to own their data themselves. It won't be easy to figure out how to structure such a system.

### Risks to Privacy: Medical Records and DNA on File

Medical records are a special kind of data. They are kept for us and we pay for the service. They can be quite complex and heterogeneous— words, images, and probably audio and video someday soon. Most important, their privacy is privileged; they are nobody's business but our own and that of the professionals concerned.

At the moment, most medical records exist on paper, with the consequent problems of bulk, inconsistency, and unavailability familiar to almost anyone who has worked with vast quantities of information on paper. In response, the inevitable solution has been proposed: on-line medical records.[37] The chief obstacle to this proposal may be doctors themselves: they reportedly hate typing, and it is difficult to tell them what to do. In health maintenance organizations, doctors are mere employees, so a few health maintenance organizations are now trying online medical records.

The system is touted as solving a number of problems that it actually does not solve: the problem of missing information, for example. Yes, doctors sometimes forget to record the patient's age or chief complaint, or for that matter, their diagnosis. They can be just as forgetful with a computer as with pen and paper; whether they are or not depends on factors only marginally related to the media.

Information can be lost or unavailable because another specialist has
the paper records, because someone mislaid them—or because the computer is down. Maybe the network is flaky. Maybe an upgrade scrambled
the database. A well-designed on-line system might improve matters; it
could certainly cut down on bulk. But it might not cut down on waste
paper: if it is easy to push a button and print the patient's entire file,
that is what people will do.

If the system turns out to be reliable and available, it may enhance
communication between various specialists, several of whom may wish
to view the same record while they discuss it over the phone. It could
help patients who move and want doctors in their new towns to have
immediate access to their records. But on-line systems pose problems for
privacy and confidentiality. Computer systems are notoriously insecure
and vulnerable to break-in. Sufficiently motivated, anyone will be able to
read your medical files without the risk of physically breaking into your
psychiatrist's office.

Your prescription records, in fact, have most likely already been scrutinized by a total stranger. Most doctors may not keep their records on-
line yet, but many pharmacists do.[38] Pharmaceutical companies provide
them with state-of-the-art computers and software to do so at nominal
cost. The drug manufacturers are not exactly altruists; the systems include a modem and software for them to upload prescription records. In
this way, drug companies learn which doctors prescribe their products
and which prescribe their competitor's. They claim they delete patient
names, but who is able to check? "In fact," says an article describing the
situation, "certain data-collectors that pledge total confidentiality sell
drug companies the age, sex—and an ID number—for individual patients." Other companies include patients' social security numbers.

Once again, the incentives seem distributed to ensure an unresponsive
system. If your privacy has been breached, what can you do about it? If
you sue, the whole world gets to hear your private concern.

Some proposed databases pose serious risks even without security
breaches. Imagine a database holding your genetic information. Its mere
existence changes the rules.[39]

Imagine the uses to which such data could be put. Health insurance
companies could require screening for genetic diseases or predispositions
to certain conditions before agreeing to insure you. *Everyone* has such
genes. It would open the door to arbitrary decisions for which some
might have no recourse. So far, U. S. health insurance companies have
given us little reason to think they will be generous about extending
benefits to the "unfit."[40]

DNA samples allow biologists to infer paternity. Under some circumstances, this is useful; under others, it can be disruptive. Lives of relative peace and contentment are not to be destroyed lightly. Who will decide when a paternity search is to be made? Who will have the power to block it?

How might this technology change the process of applying for a marriage license? Will both partners have to undergo a routine genetic screening? If both carry the same potentially lethal recessive gene, will their license be refused? Will it be granted only under the condition that one partner be sterilized? What if the gene isn't lethal, just undesirable?

The proposal for the DNA database comes from the United States Army, which wants to keep a database of genetic information on its soldiers in order to identify battle casualties. If you're geared for wholesale slaughter anyway, I suppose it's practical and humane to identify casualties quickly and surely. But what mechanisms can ensure against misusing this data? Let's think this through carefully before we pull the cork on this technology. This genie will be tough to rebottle.

### Risks of Connectivity: BigBrotherNet

In July 1990, Thailand inaugurated a giant central database for the government to keep tabs on all 55 million Thai citizens, and the Smithsonian Institution gave them an award for it. No kidding. Each person receives a PIN and a computer-readable card. "The system will store date of birth, ancestral history, and family make-up and was designed to track voting patterns, domestic and foreign travel, and social welfare. Eventually 12,000 users, including law enforcement, will have access by network terminals."[41] For some reason, an official body of the U. S. government thinks this system is just great.

At almost the same time Thailand was implementing its National Big Brother Network, a debt collector in Australia proposed a functionally similar system:

> *"Tomorrow's credit grantor will be extending credit in a perfect market with total knowledge of the debtor," Mr Owens [former president of the Institute of Mercantile Agents and head of a debt-collecting agency] asserted. "The credit grantor in the future will have access to all the debtor information. This will be made available through linked data bases in the manner of George Orwell's 1984."*[42]

And Singapore seems to have adopted the master database as a national mascot. Everything in the country is going on-line, from building blueprints to property surveys to records on every citizen.[43] It's a trend, so no one should be surprised that some folks in the United States are also hearing the siren song of perfect information. Also in July 1990 (the summer of 1990 is beginning to sound dire), the U. S. Justice Department proposed spending $60 million to create a national drug intelligence center.[44] Although the attorney general attempted to calm the fears of such groups as the ACLU and Computer Professionals for Social Responsibility, saying "It's not 'Big Brother'" (a mandatory allusion for these discussions, I guess), he also mentioned that cooperating agencies would include the Customs Service, the Coast Guard, the Immigration and Naturalization Service, the FBI, and possibly the Defense Department. Sounds like quite a database.

The problem with such databases is not the information they store. All the information is already stored elsewhere, as proponents will point out. In fact, our present data system has some of the characteristics of a hologram: because it has so much redundancy, any small local failure allows virtually all data to be reconstructed—in theory. But in practice it requires effort and purpose to do so. Putting it all together changes the system characteristics; connectivity makes the system as a whole different from its parts. Having all the data about you in one place eliminates the effort needed to collect it. It's so easy, the system creates its own purposes. It allows a nimble human mind to notice patterns, infer, conjecture, extrapolate. So much information about an individual in one easily accessible place paints a detailed, comprehensive picture.

Proponents of such systems often argue: if you are doing nothing wrong, what do you have to fear? This puts the onus on individuals to explain why such data should *not* be kept. That is not where it belongs. Proponents need to explain to the rest of us why the data *should* be kept. No one wishes to live under scrutiny. Criminality is not the issue: the distinction between our private lives and our public personae is crucial for our sanity. Our privacy is as vital—and as fragile—as the fuzz on the wings of a butterfly.

## MODELING THE WORLD IN BITS

Anyone using a spreadsheet can now become an instant statistician. In its popular Excel spreadsheet program, Microsoft has included a facility it touts as "the ability to forecast trends."[45] The spreadsheet uses a specific sequence of instructions to make its forecast. Are these the instructions you would have used if you had done it by hand? Is the spreadsheet answering the question you are asking? How can you tell for sure? If the simple spreadsheet is going to get sophisticated, we had better be equally sophisticated in the way we interpret its results. Statistics can be dangerous in the wrong hands.

When statistics are incorporated into spreadsheets, the spreadsheet becomes a kind of computer model of some aspect of the world. Computer modeling takes myriad forms—for example, expert systems, simulations, database query systems, or virtual reality. All are a game of "what if." Users supply initial data, which is transformed according to the rules programmed. When NASA measured ozone levels in the 1970s and 1980s, for example, they measured them with software programmed to reject readings below a certain level. So the computer, unable to tell us what we wanted to hear, threw out the results and told us nothing. Computer models seem to show you something objective, but all the while you are looking in the mirror, your biases and preconceptions coloring the questions you ask and the way you perceive the answers. In order to use models intelligently, we have to understand this.

Computer models are necessarily limited. As digitized information, they require a finite resolution. Only so many characteristics can be considered, only so many details factored in, the result carried to only so many decimal places. Models may be crude or subtle but they are always cruder than infinitely complex reality, in which each detail enfolds seven or seventeen others, no matter how closely you look. When you model a phenomenon, you can only hope you have abstracted the essential information you need for a meaningful result. You won't always be right. And you won't always know if you were right or not.

It is pitiful when you hear of a company going bankrupt because its managers took the reports they were getting from their information systems as oracular pronouncements. Did they understand what their programmers were doing when they coded the system? Did they try to get any information from another source to see if the results reflected what was actually going on? Did they ask themselves if common sense supported the answers they were getting?

The computer is *not* an oracle; it doesn't know anything that we don't. Its value lies in being able to apply rules quickly and consistently to far more data than any human would have the patience for. If the results are going to be of any use, you must first ask, "How can I tell if I ought to believe this?" Depending on what you are modeling, the question can have economic, legal, political, psychological, or ethical ramifications.

### Ethics of Expert Systems in Medicine

Expert systems represent an attempt to use a computer to store and apply the knowledge of an expert. They have been tried extensively in medicine, especially for diagnosis and prognosis. Expert systems for physicians have been developed to aid diagnoses of skin disease, blood disease,[46] bacterial infections,[47] and some forms of cancer. The tools can be useful, but they have glaring drawbacks. For one, they are constrained to view the world in terms of the narrow niche they know about. In the PBS special "The Thinking Machine," for example, artificial intelligence researcher Doug Lenat tells of describing his rusting 1980 Chevy to a skin disease diagnostic system for a lark. It concluded that the patient had measles,[48] and it hardly seems fair to laugh at the poor thing.

Such systems can also be difficult to maintain. To incorporate new knowledge about the causes or symptoms of a disease may require extensive rewriting and retesting—almost a brand new development effort each time.[49]

Medical personnel may find the tools useful anyway. Simple diagnostic systems have even been made available to patients directly.[50] In Bedford, Massachusetts, an experiment has put terminals in the homes of 150 health plan members with either chronic illnesses or young children. Patients dial up the database and type in symptoms. The system responds with questions; depending on the answers, the system either recommends a treatment or an appointment with the doctor. Reportedly, patients love it, and it is certainly easy to see the appeal to the health maintenance organization, which receives the same monthly fees whether doctors' time has been used or not. The wrong recommendation could lead to a lawsuit, of course. I suppose the issue can ultimately be dealt with—if we decide such a system is worth it, we just have to agree ahead of time to settle disputes another way.

Systems for prognosis are more problematic. Such systems draw on an extensive database to project the likelihood that a given treatment will help a patient, or they state the statistical probability (carried somehow to two decimal places) that a patient arriving in an intensive care unit will die. Tools such as these are helping doctors decide what treatment to offer or whether to withhold treatment. An editorial in the *Washington Post* focused on a system called APACHE used at a hospital in Michigan.[51]

Statistics, as we ought to know by now, are extremely easy to misunderstand and misuse.[52] As the editorial points out, "a person with a 95 percent chance of dying under a procedure is not the same thing as a person whom that procedure cannot help, or a person from whom care can be withheld with no compunctions."[53] Indeed, as one contributor to *comp.risks* has pointed out: "Even if [the] data is 100% correct, it still leads to positive feedback which will further skew the output data."[54] That is, if a system advises a doctor to withhold treatment on the basis that a patient is unlikely to survive, the patient goes untreated and is therefore even less likely to survive. The system adds one more case with a negative outcome to its database and produces an even gloomier assessment next time.

Still other prognosis tools are used by governmental agencies who wish to measure the quality of care provided by specific hospitals. Hospital administrators now fear that bureaucrats will use the resulting information to pressure hospitals to "restructure" their care. In 1991, an article and accompanying editorial appeared in the *Journal of the American Medical Association* to assess the technology and discuss the associated problems.[55]

A fundamental problem with prognostic systems is that, as far as users are concerned, their pronouncements are opaque and mysterious. Many systems are proprietary, so users cannot know what operations are performed on the data they supply. Yet even small omissions or errors can have large repercussions for patients. The system examined in the JAMA article, for example, was found to have significant statistical biases in the one area the doctor was able to research thoroughly.

Even if the source code for the system is open to inspection, to assess such systems requires significant knowledge of complex statistical formulas. No standards require that such systems be safe and effective, as the magic FDA incantation has it, and it is practically impossible to test them rigorously and thoroughly. They are difficult to refine if they prove to be inaccurate, or when understanding of their domain deepens. And they could alter medical practice, just as schools sometimes react to standardized tests by altering the curriculum to "teach to the test." But a better score on such a system may bear only a vague relation, if any, to better care as perceived by doctors, patients, or patients' families. Computer-assisted triage may not be our best response to rising health-care costs.

### Politics of Environmental Simulations

The scientific method is supposed to proceed by carefully comparing the results of controlled experiments. But sometimes it is impossible to perform a controlled experiment. In the absence of a duplicate planet, how can we understand the effects of humanity and its activities upon the earth? How can we untangle the factors that affect the atmosphere, its ozone layer and greenhouse gases, oceans, weather, and climate? Simulations offer the only way to experiment in these arenas.

We must research the questions, for we need the answers. But we don't have them yet. Climatologists cannot even get their models to predict what we know has already occurred. This understandably causes skepticism about predictions of the effect of greenhouse gases on global warming, a skepticism only exacerbated by the numbers of different predictions those models have so far produced.[56] At present, computer models provide a shaky basis for public policy, as little progress has been made on environmental questions.

Perhaps we are asking the wrong question. Perhaps we should take the hint and, for the moment at least, ask a humbler question: Given our ignorance, our present circumstances, and the high stakes, what is a prudent holding position?

### Psychology of Simulations in Court

A report full of numbers is easier to view dispassionately than a video clip showing a car accident. Using computer graphics and animation, you can simulate accidents or other events and create cartoonlike videos to show juries during trials.[57] Computer animation is so expensive that it is used only in cases in which a lot of money is at stake. Truly lifelike computer animation is even more expensive, so simulations still look relatively crude. It will get cheaper, though. Before it does, let's consider the comparative effects on a jury of a page of numbers, a one-minute cartoon, and a five-minute re-creation of an accident complete with facial expressions and bright red blood.

In a news report on courtroom simulations, lawyers seemed embarrassingly frank about the benefits of entertaining the jury.[58] Said one, "75–80 percent of all the information people get is through television." Why buck a trend? Simulations can be valuable to a jury trying to understand a lot of complex material, but only if they are understood for what they are. They should be presented along with the assumptions that went into them and the rules used to transform those assumptions into the information shown. If this cannot be done clearly, they should be viewed with skepticism; without additional evidence, they are just another TV show.

### Virtual Reality

Computers show us alternate worlds. They can show you what you'd look like with lilac hair, or what the kitchen would look like with a lilac breakfast nook, or what the bathroom would look like with lilac wallpaper, or what your yard would look like with lilac bushes.

Virtual reality is the most extreme form of the what-if game. As presently envisioned, *virtual reality* is a technology by which the user can enter the world the computer creates. Put on special glasses, and the computer projects its display in front of your eyes. Put on a special helmet, and the computer adjusts its display when you've turned your head. Earphones built into the helmet play sounds. A special glove permits the computer to distinguish your gestures. The computer can respond by moving you or some other object in the simulated environment. Eventually, a full body suit may allow you to move through a simulation normally; it could even include full sensory feedback (though I'm hard pressed to imagine the olfactory interface). This will require many more computations per second than we can presently achieve, but computations per second is one of those numbers that have been rising swiftly and steadily since the computer was invented.

Full virtual reality isn't always necessary, though. It might be nice to walk through your imaginary landscaped yard, but seeing it on a screen can give you a pretty good idea.[59]

Chemists and drug researchers need more than a two-dimensional picture of a molecule. To guess how it might interact with other molecules, they need to understand its three-dimensional structure. Remember those 3D movies in which you wore special glasses to see monsters floating out of the screen at you? A similar principle allows three-dimensional displays for computer-aided chemistry. The molecules appear to pop out of the screen; they can be rotated and made to interact with other molecules.[60] Virtual reality adds to this process, and researchers are presently using it to help them learn about new molecules and design new drugs. They claim the process is "revolutionary."[61]

Using virtual reality to help design buildings seems like another great idea. Before the building is built, you can walk through it, see what it will look like, feel how it will feel.[62] As long as the new technology is not used as a substitute for rigorous engineering analysis, it seems bound to save money and produce pleasanter buildings. In Tokyo, a showroom allows people to remodel their kitchens in virtual reality. Reportedly, this sells more kitchen renovations than traditional methods.[63] Maybe virtual reality is persuasive. Maybe clients have already invested a nontrivial sum just to get the demo. Maybe they design a kitchen they really want.

VPL Research, pioneers of virtual reality technology, have been exploring its uses in surgery, structural inspections, and financial analysis, too. Using virtual reality in surgery is particularly intriguing. With the aid of a virtual reality computer system, a surgeon in, say, Toronto might perform an operation on a patient in the remote Northwest Territories.

Obviously, this is going to be a safety-critical application; a bug could kill the patient. But what if the patient could not survive without the operation, nor could be physically moved to Toronto? What if the medical personnel at hand cannot save him or her unaided? Why not take the chance? What have we got to lose? Well, for one thing, the system is bound to be extremely costly, both to develop and to operate. Will it be available to the ordinary patient or to millionaires only? Is it reasonable to spend enormous sums on exotic technologies while millions lack access to basic medical care? Would it be cheaper to provide financial incentives for doctors to serve in remote areas instead?

The most accessible virtual reality applications so far, though, are just exciting, expensive shoot-'em-up games. Two video-arcade games are already on the market (at prices considerably steeper than a quarter), and more will follow soon.[64]

Where violence is, can sex be far behind? People have naturally been speculating about virtual pornography. With more computational power and a full body suit, high-tech masturbation may enable those who can afford it to hoist anchor and sail away forever from the frightening and forbidding Dark Continent of the opposite gender.

## TRACKING AND MONITORING

*Business travel is a pain, but sometimes it must be done. Armed with my key, I headed out to the car rental parking lot. The car was programmed to respond to the key—the display lit up with a map of the airport area. "Your motel reservation has been entered into my database," said the car. "Would you like to check in now?" For some reason, it spoke with a strange Scandinavian accent.*

*"Later," I said, and told it my client's address.*

*The map zoomed out over the greater metropolitan area, panned north-northeast over the landscape, and zoomed in a bit to show the airport and my destination in one tightly framed rectangle. A red arrow painted itself along the route, scrupulously pausing at traffic lights. "Proceed to the exit and turn left," said the car. As I drove, the prepainted route faded to pink. I shifted my gaze between the road and the display, watching the red arrow which was now replaying the route for me in real time. I hate traveling on business, but at least I wasn't going to get lost.*

### Navigation

Okay, I freely admit the above is a fantasy—I'd get lost anyway. But maybe you wouldn't, and a navigation system in your car could come in handy, especially in a strange town.

If you lived in Japan, you might already have a car navigation system—over 400,000 people do.[65] The 1991 Mitsubishi Diamante sold in Japan, for example, included a television set mounted on what used to be called the dashboard. It shows broadcast television programs when the car isn't moving. When the car is moving, it has "a compass display and a CD-ROM-based navigational system that shows vehicle position against a road map." The Mitsubishi system uses a compass and the vehicle's odometer. The compact disc contains the addresses and telephone numbers of about 20,000 service stations, golf courses, hotels, department stores, art galleries, and amusement parks.[66]

The Mitsubishi Diamante proves that the odometer, a built-in compass, and a compact disc are enough to know where you are. Nevertheless, others are designing systems that will use U. S. military satellites—the Global Positioning System (GPS). GPS technology was developed to help the military know exactly where all its soldiers are, and to make sure that they get where they're supposed to be, even when crossing hundreds of square miles of trackless desert.

If you know your location with respect to three reference points, you know where on earth you are. To supply the required reference points, a receiver containing the ubiquitous microprocessor receives signals from GPS satellites 11,000 miles above the earth. These satellites have incredibly accurate clocks. They send their identification and precise time codes to GPS receivers that remember where each satellite was before. The receiver actually requires signals from four satellites to figure out where it is—the redundant fourth signal helps check for errors. The GPS system isn't complete yet; the twenty-fourth and final satellite is scheduled to be launched in 1993. When it is, any GPS receiver anywhere on earth will be within range of four satellite signals at all times. In theory, no one need ever be lost again.[67]

After they have all been built and launched, the satellites will require maintenance. Either commercial users will take over the expense of maintaining them, or they will have to depend on the military to keep them running.[68] There's a lot of commercial interest. GPS navigation systems are already in use in some airplanes and ships. Cities are using surveying equipment with GPS receivers. Trucking companies are considering combining GPS receivers with radio transmitters to track freight.[69] For about $1000, you can order your very own GPS personal navigator from a catalog. GM and Motorola are planning to spend $35 million to test a program called Advance that will equip 5000 cars near Chicago with navigation gear.[70]

In order to be useful, a car navigation system needs more than a GPS receiver. The system also needs maps, a communication interface, and some smarts about driving. Maps are required in digital form, with information about restaurants, motels, gas stations, and so on. Betting that advertisers will find digital maps an excellent medium, Rupert Murdoch, the publishing magnate, has bought Etak, Inc., a small maker of digital maps.[71]

A car navigation system also needs a way to accept input from its driver—and a keyboard just won't cut it. A system called TravTek that Avis is testing allows drivers to press menu items on a touch screen. In response, the system speaks in "a computerized male voice with a Scandinavian accent."[72] The technicians call it Sven. (You thought I was just kidding about the accent back there, didn't you?)

In addition to its maps and a database of travel information, the system also has to understand certain aspects of driving. As usual, this is trickier than it looks. In a test drive reported in *Business Week,* TravTek warned of an impending right turn with a mere ten yards to go. The driver was in heavy traffic in the wrong lane. This mishap is the result of an unstated requirement in the spec, or more likely, several. As usual, the activity being modeled—driving, in this case—is more complicated than anyone thought it was at first. You can't think of everything, can you?

TravTek has been installed in seventy-five cars in Orlando, Florida for a year-long test. It uses GPS satellites, sensors buried beneath intersections, and video cameras. It is supposed to navigate, warn of traffic congestion, and provide information in case of emergency. But the test drive turned out to be disappointing; in addition to issuing directions with too little warning, its database was incorrect.

### Tracking

Knowing where you are is handy; having everyone else know might not be. There's no denying that tracking, either using GPS or other systems, could be a boon to spies and police departments. Various antitheft devices have been proposed. Location data can be commercially useful for tracking stolen items such as cars, so we may soon be tracked whether we like it or not. Already an insurance company has refused to insure a car for more than half its value unless its owner installed a tracking device—a device reportedly so accurate that it can determine driving speed.[73] I cannot believe an insurance company has the right to demand this. How else will this information be used? What privacy protection does the driver have?

Foiling car thieves can be done another way. A company in the United Kingdom has announced it will market a system of owner-encoded microprocessors, small chips that you can hide inside your car, motorcycle, or other items of value. The system, call Datatag, requires registering your chips with the police, who will have special equipment to read the chips. The police can then check the registration database to determine if an item is stolen.[74] A similar system called TeleTrace has also been proposed in the United States. Such systems aren't foolproof either—thieves can still dismantle the car and sell its parts, often a more profitable activity. But at least it doesn't track the driver all over the continent.

The concept of electronic tagging has been extended in a number of ways already, and almost certainly more will come. A 1991 advertisement by Samsung touts a computerized monitoring system to determine the location and direction of travel of victims of Alzheimer's disease. Presumably, tracking devices could also be used for potential kidnap victims, pets, or mountain climbers.[75]

The telephone system provides other opportunities for paranoia about tracking. When they enter a new cell, cellular phone users are greeted with a phone call welcoming them to the new area and informing them of available services.[76] The data gathered from tracking cellular phones can be accurate to within an area of about a square mile (a "sector"). A court order is required to tap someone's phone or use the results of such a tap. It is not clear whether data gathered from cellular telephone tracking is afforded the same civil protection. If cellular phone users truly wish their whereabouts to remain private, they may have to turn off the phone.

Soon you won't need a cellular phone to face this issue. AT&T has announced that a phone number (prefix 700) can now be yours for life. Using a 4-digit PIN, you call your personal phone number and specify the regular phone number to which your calls should be forwarded. Naturally, the record of which calls were forwarded to you at which numbers and at what times constitutes a record of your whereabouts—perhaps a very detailed record. The phone company will have to keep these records for billing. What happens to them? What is their legal status? Can the police review them simply by asking the phone company, or will they need a search warrant? What about people who break into the phone company's computers?[77]

### Automated Billing

A transponder in your car provides yet another way to track you. Some agencies are pushing to install transponders in cars in order to ease traffic congestion. The California Department of Transportation (Cal-Trans) wants Automatic Vehicle Identification (AVI) transponders to automate the process of collecting tolls. Roadside transmitters will send a signal to the cars driving by, whose AVI boxes will respond with a coded number. In theory, fewer toll booths will allow more traffic to flow unimpeded, while drivers are billed for the highways and bridges they used.[78]

Initial plans call for the system to be implemented in a manner allowing individual motorists to remain anonymous, but it looks as if there will be no legal way to turn the transponders off.[79] Ominously, a relatively late version of the CalTrans spec left the door open to further uses later. One possibility mentioned was tracking individuals by the Drug Enforcement Administration or the Immigration and Naturalization Service,[80] prompting one concerned software professional to write:

> *"We ought to stop now and think. Do we want to set up a bureaucratic mechanism that can turn out automatic tracking schemes on an assembly-line basis, hoping that we can hold the line on privacy and other civil liberties by keeping careful enough track of this process? Or should we . . . get this entire process to be suspended long enough for a proper public debate?"*[81]

### Monitoring

Some jobs are so distasteful we want to automate them. At first blush, they seem good candidates for automation. Computers can serve as nurse-maids, for example. A system for monitoring Alzheimer's victims is being developed in Sweden, where a computer watches over Gunnar, a 77-year-old man suffering from senile dementia.[82] The computer is programmed to play prerecorded voice messages if it senses certain situations. At night, it tells him to go to bed; if it detects smoke, to leave the building. The man does not understand that he is a guinea pig in this technical and social experiment.

There have been a few technical glitches: after the system had been in place for some time, it was discovered that in the event of a fire at night, the computer would have told Gunnar to go to bed. But I find the social problems more troubling yet. Do *you* want to end up being tended by a computer?

Nursemaid isn't the only distasteful job being handed over to computers. Jailors, too, wish to distance themselves from their charges. Prisons in the United States are becoming quite overcrowded, and one response has been to place certain categories of offenders under house arrest. Various schemes use some combination of computerized polling, telephone calls, voice recognition, Caller ID, and electronic anklets to attempt to ensure that the detainee remains at home. Results so far are mixed.

Voice recognition technologies are slowly coming into their own, and at present, systems are available that take dictation, fill out forms, control PCs, and deal with people over the telephone, such as AT&T's automated long-distance operator service.[83] These systems can cause economic dislocation—AT&T caused some fuss when it announced the number of operators it was going to lay off, for instance. However, the best of these systems can provide a flexible and natural interface to a computer, enhancing the machine's utility.

When you use voice-recognition technology to monitor people under house arrest, though, the system has a different and more difficult job. Users are not trying to help the system, but to foil it.

House arrest schemes are apparently cheaper than prison—about $13/day versus $67/day, according to one source.[84] Sending people to overcrowded prisons does not seem like a good idea, nor does releasing them early. People don't want to pay for building more prisons. Why not house arrest?

Security is a difficult requirement. Voice recognition, electronic anklets—whatever you use, there will be holes that prisoners can exploit, and they have. Existing systems have so far seen two escapes. One fellow escaped repeatedly to rob gas stations on weekends when he learned that the system's monitors worked an ordinary forty-hour week. Another fellow committed murder because of an unstated requirement, a questionable design, and an odd user interface. He escaped by removing the rivets holding his electronic anklet together. The computer dutifully printed his name out with an asterisk next to it, on a display on which seven hundred names move constantly. No one noticed, because for some reason the real monitoring effort ran on another computer. The first computer placed the anklet on "tamper" status and called the computer that people were actually monitoring. It got a busy signal. Having marked the anklet as tampered with, and having called the other computer to say so, the first computer proceeded to drop the subject. Nobody said the phone call actually had to get through.[85]

The house arrest system that was so easily defeated was designed by Digital Products of Florida. In the wake of the murder, the New Jersey Senate Law and Public Safety Committee decided they ought to shop around and look at other systems. They will probably find a system that doesn't have these problems. If they decide to switch, they can learn about the problems of their new system, instead.

Security is indeed a tough problem. After a few postings describing house arrest systems and escaped prisoners, the software professionals who read the on-line news bulletin board *comp.risks* rose to the challenge. One brave soul described the best system he could design and asked if anyone could find a problem with it. In less than a week, experts in computer security matters found seven ways for the prisoner to escape from this theoretical system: six technical solutions and one psychological strategy.[86]

## VERB-BY-WIRE

Real-time process-control presents another set of tough requirements. Previous chapters discussed several examples, notably fly-by-wire systems wherein symbolic, electronic connections replace direct, mechanical connections between pilot's gestures and aircraft controls. The computer controls the process of flying the plane, responding quickly to pilot inputs. If the system responds in error, the airplane can crash. If the system responds correctly but too slowly, the airplane can likewise crash. Process control does not give you a second chance.

Not all real-time process-control software is safety-critical. Systems to muffle noise by canceling sound waves are usually not, for example. But many are, and such proposals are proliferating. Software to operate on you, sail supertankers, and drive your car are all examples of real-time process-control systems wherein safety is at risk. They may be asking too much of the technology.

### Hush-by-Wire

The electronic muffler is a relatively simple system: a microphone sends the sound waves to a microprocessor. The microprocessor directs a speaker to produce sound waves that mirror those it received. If the microprocessor works fast enough, the two sound waves cancel each other out, and the result is blissful silence. In addition to doing a better job reducing engine noise, electronic mufflers for cars are also supposed to increase horsepower and fuel efficiency, because no muffler chamber builds up exhaust to create back pressure on the engine.[87]

The worst failure mode one can imagine for such a system can be fixed with an OFF switch. If the microprocessor gets badly out of phase somehow, the system is noisier instead of quieter, since you now hear the speaker as well as the engine. In this case, turning the system off may not leave matters much worse than they were before. When it works, the increased fuel efficiency may even partially compensate for the power that the system will consume.

Noise canceling technology isn't limited to cars, of course. Right now, you can buy (expensive) headphones that do the same job. Operators of noisy machinery, such as helicopter pilots, can save their hearing by wearing them. Perhaps factories will use this technology to responsibly dispose of their noise pollution someday. (When the price of electricity goes way down, like they said it would back in the 1950s.)

### Cut-by-Wire

At least three groups are presently working on robots that can perform surgery: a group in Britain is developing robots for prostate surgery, a group in the United States for hip surgery, and a group in France for brain surgery. There are benefits: the quicker and more precise the cut, the more quickly the patient will heal, and a robot may be steadier and quicker than a human surgeon.

The risks are obvious; we all know enough to be chilled at the thought of a robot with a scalpel poised directly above our skins. So everyone's taking a lot of precautions: the robots are designed to be easy to interrupt, and a human surgeon is supposed to be there to finish the job if things go wrong.[88]

### Sail-by-Wire

Some folks in Japan are reportedly developing systems to automate the sailing of enormous unmanned supertankers that transport oil across oceans.[89] I hope that reports are wrong. What about the other, smaller ships and boats they meet? Will they be able to get out of the way in time? Will they expect to be able to communicate with a human captain? How will these unmanned tankers respond to another ship's distress signal?

Yes, accidents can happen—and have—because of the actions of human captains and crew. But to eliminate such accidents, you have to provide a system that human beings cannot override. Is this wise? The ocean has a lot of water, but there are limits to how much oil and filth it can absorb. The trickiest situations are apt to occur near coasts. We have seen how fragile are the complex and beautiful ecosystems found along coastlines. Is it really that much cheaper to dispense with supertanker crews? What are we risking here?

### Drive-by-Wire

The military pioneered fly-by-wire aircraft, and a couple of decades later commercial jets are plying the air with digital flight controls. They're easier and cheaper to manufacture, they weigh less, and, their designers feel, they can be made safer by building in such functions as envelope protection, functions that require software to implement.

For all the same reasons, the advent of drive-by-wire has been creeping up on us piecemeal for the past decade or so. As of the early 1990s, hardly an aspect of driving has not been under the control of a micro-processor. Some cars integrate several driving functions under the control of one microprocessor, and some cars have four or five microprocessors. We are within a gnat's eyelash of having all driving functions integrated in one master control program. The reasons given are all the same—the vehicle is easier and cheaper to manufacture, it weighs less, and it can include built-in safety functions.

Drive down the road. The fuel injection system determines the best time to squirt fuel, and how much. The ignition spark controller decides when to create the spark to ignite the fuel. If you hit a bump, the active suspension system reacts within milliseconds to firm the shock absorbers so you won't feel it. Your intelligent cruise control system adjusts your speed to that of the car ahead of you. Another car gets a bit too close, so your collision avoidance radar buzzes at you. As you accelerate around a curve, the transmission shifts to give you the extra power you require, while traction control ensures that you won't start to skid. The electronically controlled four-wheel steering responds to a tiny twitch of the joystick. If you start to drift over the center line, the heading control system nudges you gently back to the center of your lane. The antilock brakes ensure that you stop precisely and smoothly at your destination. The only parking spot you can find looks barely big enough, so you get out of the car and let it park itself.

So far, no car you can buy includes all these features, but you can buy many of them, and the rest are at least in the prototype stage. Fuel injection and "spark management" systems have been in use for years, as have antilock or antiskid braking systems. Cadillac, among others, has already sold cars (such as the Allanté) with active suspension systems. The Cadillac Allanté also includes an electronically controlled transmission that anticipates when the driver will require a gear shift—aggressive drivers will feel the Cadillac stay in gear a bit longer to maintain acceleration, while the car shifts earlier for sedate drivers in order to improve gas mileage.[90] City buses and school buses also have electronically controlled transmissions these days, to which manufacturers can add such safety features as routines that ensure the bus cannot shift into gear if the door is open. And the radar-based collision avoidance system is being installed in Greyhound buses to buzz at the driver in stressful moments, which will no doubt have a helpful, calming effect.[91]

Electronically controlled transmissions can be designed to save the engine, by reading wheel speed or engine rpm and shifting up if the vehicle is moving too quickly for the gear that the driver selected. Such a feature has been implicated in a school bus crash on July 31, 1991, outside of Palm Springs, California. The bus, which was carrying sixty Girl Scouts and their chaperones, was headed down a steep, winding road from the Palm Springs Aerial Tramway when the driver lost control. It slipped off the road and down an embankment, overturning as it fell. Seven people died, including the driver, and the rest were injured, some seriously. Like most accidents, this one had multiple causes—the brakes were later found to be bad, and the hapless driver (who is easy to blame, being dead) was at first accused of having selected the wrong gear for the steep descent. The California Highway Patrol examined the bus wreckage and found the bus to be in third gear, too high for compression braking. But the driver had a clean driving record and had been instructed on how to handle a bus going down mountain roads; his instructor had been pleased with his performance. His instructor did *not* tell him that the electronic transmission would upshift automatically, because the instructor himself was unaware of this feature. During the investigation that followed, "Stephen J. Bayt, a supervisor with Allison Transmission Co., which built the transmission, testified . . . that even if [the driver] had tried to shift to a lower gear, a mechanism designed to keep the engine from over-revving would have automatically shifted it back up into a higher gear."[92] And the bus transmission didn't even save the engine when it sacrificed the Girl Scouts.

Over-revving prevention doubtless seemed like a good idea at the time. Electronic control allows you to dream up skillions of ways to make the system "safer" under the circumstances you envision. Safer or not, though, the transmission has one clearly awful feature: it ignores or negates a direct driver action, apparently without giving the driver a clue that it has done so. This is not a well designed user interface.

Some of this stuff may be motivated by safety, but I can't help suspecting that some of it is there just for the whiz-bang-wow factor. To judge by the ads and the panting articles in car magazines, a lot of people get breathless over high-tech cars. "When three microprocessors talk to each other, what do they talk about?" asks an ad for a 1992 Lincoln Continental—a pointless question that contains the magical phrase "three microprocessors." According to the ad, the Lincoln includes an electronic engine controller that handles fuel injection, ignition timing, and coordinates with the electronic transmission; computerized suspension; antilock braking; and "computer-regulated speed-sensitive power steering."

The award for the most digital technology crammed into one presently available frame goes to the Mitsubishi Diamante.[93] In addition to digital engine and transmission control, active suspension, and antilock brakes, it includes the navigation system described earlier and an "intelligent cockpit" that puts the seat, steering wheel and mirrors into the positions you have specified when you unlock the car. This sounds handy, and I suppose it is when it works. When it doesn't, can you position things manually, or have they blithely discarded the backup system?

The Mitsubishi's real contribution to the technology race is its traction control system. It is really two systems, slip control and trace control, and each can be turned off independently. Slip control monitors wheel speed and steering-wheel angle; if the system senses a loss of traction it will ease off the throttle. Trace control is a nervous-passenger-in-a-box. The system has a table that relates vehicle speeds to steering wheel angles, and eases off the throttle if the driver exceeds the predetermined values. "The effect is uncanny," writes a test-driver. "You head into a tight turn with your foot planted and, next thing, the car loses power."[94] They want me to pay for this? What if the day comes when I prefer to drive into a ditch rather than hit the child on the bicycle?

Like Lake Wobegon's children, most of us think we are above average; we pride ourselves on our driving. I suspect that most drivers will react to trace control as did the test-driver quoted above: "Personally, I think I can live without trace control, but I'm willing to admit it might be a handy feature . . . for those occasions when the car is being driven by a valet parking attendant or by a friend or family member whose driving isn't entirely trustworthy."[95] Any bets on his Aunt Ethel's opinion of her own driving, and on how long it takes her to figure out how to turn off trace control? Technological breakthrough or not, trace control code may require little testing, simply because it may almost never be executed.

Saab has a traction control system, too, as you'd expect from a car designed by engineers who often drive on ice and snow. If you buy a Saab 9000 Turbo in Europe, you can include an optional "traction control system incorporating brake, ignition, and fuel injection controls, a virtual drive-by-wire system wherein the accelerator pedal is linked not just to the throttle of the fuel injection system, but also to a computer system. The computer decides how much spark advance, how much fuel, and how much brake application will achieve the best balance for maximum traction, even at full throttle on snow and ice."[96]

Since they're over halfway there already, it's no wonder that Saab has built its first steer-by-wire prototype. They don't expect to sell cars with steering joysticks for another twenty years or so, but they anticipate incorporating some digital steering technology into cars with conventional steering wheels much sooner.[97]

The heading control system mentioned above also comes from Europe. BMW has built a prototype that includes a camera peering ahead to track the lines painted on the center and side of the road. "If a driver gets too close to either marker, a small electric motor integrated into the steering system is activated to put things right. Later versions will gauge road conditions and differentiate between broken and solid lines, so the computer can tell such things as whether it's okay to pass. Drivers being corrected might feel a tug on the wheel. But they can easily override the computer . . ."[98] A number of questions spring to mind. How does the computer behave on roads with no lines painted on them, or nonstandard lines? How much will it cost to paint the required lines on all roads? Do I really want to feel a tug on the steering wheel just as I'm finally ready to pass that triple-trailer truck? Most important, if I can't steer the car, why am I driving?

When the first antilock braking systems came on the market, certain macho, competitive drivers took them to the limit, delighting in their new ability to "safely" scare the daylights out of those behind whom they stopped. The same sort of people will doubtless enjoy pushing the limits with traction control and "smart" steering systems as well. Safety features can make life safer, but they can also tempt people to abuse them. Such behavior not only negates any increase in safety the features may have achieved, it also heightens everyone's stress level.

The car that parks itself is presently a prototype built by Volkswagen of America. It has proximity detectors and can sense whether a parking spot is big enough. Then it can wedge itself into the spot with only a few inches on either side.[99] A lot of people hate parallel parking. If this application can somehow sense when a dog or cat or toddler is in the way, it could come in handy. But let's consider the larger system, including the environment in which it operates. Not everyone is going to have cars that squeeze themselves into parking spots with only inches of clearance, at least not at first. Suppose that you own a car with two-wheel drive and manual steering. You park downtown to see a movie. You return to find yourself wedged between two of these automated wonders. How are *you* supposed to get out?[100]

You can do wonderful things with digital technology. The Cadillac Allanté, for example, allows you to drive it for a limited distance with no water in the radiator.[101] That could be a life-saver in an emergency. But real-time safety-critical process-control systems are hard to design, develop, and verify. There have been bugs; there will be more. A 1982 Mercedes 500SE with an antiskid braking system somehow managed to leave 386-foot skid marks at the scene of an accident. Brake microprocessors have been recalled on El Dorados, and Lincoln Mark VIIs were recalled for problems with their computerized suspension systems.[102]

Microprocessor-based systems are vulnerable to EMI, for example. The environment in which cars travel is rich in electromagnetic radiation: police cars, ambulances, pizza delivery trucks and taxis all have radios; cellular phones, CB radios, broadcast towers and satellite dishes are everywhere. Because of the risk to the airplane's digital flight control system, some airlines have banned the use of personal computers with mice, because the mouse cables act as antenna and emit potentially disturbing radiation.[103] Is the shielding for automobile microprocessors really so much better? In 1990, certain cellular telephone manufacturers warned that their phones should not be used in cars with electronic antilock braking systems, because they might cause the system to malfunction.[104]

Yes, it's true that the old technology isn't completely safe, either. If the accelerator pedal isn't connected to a computer, it's connected to a spring that connects it to the throttle. The spring can break. But if it does, you might be able to reach down with your hand or your toes and physically pull the pedal back up in time to avoid the worst consequences. If the software has a bug, or if the microprocessor goes flooey when you get a call on your cellular phone, there is *nothing* you can do, short of shutting off the engine—and even that may not work out.

When we build a system, we should ask ourselves whether we will be worse off when it fails than we would have been if we hadn't built it. For example, many cars with computerized braking systems will leave you with a conventional braking system if the microprocessor shuts off for some reason. As long as you're not in mid-skid, or driving like the race-car driver from hell, you'll probably be fine. Electronic engine control, on the other hand, is not so benign. Although many cars with electronic engine control can limp home somehow if their microprocessor fails, their performance, gas mileage, and emissions will be atrocious. Other cars just lie down in the dust.

There's another risk in drive-by-wire technology, and folks involved in software development know all about this problem. You take your microprocessor-controlled car to the dealer for its regularly scheduled maintenance. You don't know it, but the dealer has just received a software upgrade from headquarters, which the mechanic obligingly loads into your car. You had better hope the new software has been developed carefully and tested thoroughly, because you can no longer count on your car behaving the way it used to. In some ways, it is now a completely different car—and there may be nothing you can do about it. Even if you hate its new behavior, you may never be able to return to its original software.

Furthermore, your entire driving history can be maintained in the microprocessor's memory and uploaded every time you take your car in for servicing. This is apparently already the case with 1992 Saturns, for example.[105] Is it cynical to guess that it is only a matter of time before information such as this is used to save the dealer money? "I'm sorry, sir," the service manager says. "Ordinarily, this repair would be covered, but according to your engine history, you have over-revved this engine three times. I'm afraid we'll have to void your warranty."

## VERB-BY-WIRE, MANY TIMES OVER, ALL AT ONCE

In this book, I've tried to avoid stacking up computer science buzzwords like so many cars in a rush-hour freeway accident, but here they come: this section is about distributed real-time process-control software. This verbal snarl is to the point: if real-time process-control systems are tough to design and develop, distributed systems are even more complex and fragile. Every one of the areas represented by a buzzword is a topic of research by some of the world's brightest people. Many problems have yet to be solved. Even the finest developers could not implement safe and reliable systems such as these, given present software and systems engineering techniques.

Drive-by-wire systems have built on and emulated fly-by-wire systems, and have been motivated by many of the same economic considerations. The resemblance between driving and aviation goes further. Traffic in many cities is now so bad that many of the same approaches are being proposed to control cars as we presently use for air traffic control.

Present air traffic control systems use computers to advise air traffic controllers on appropriate routes, altitudes, paths of ascent and descent. The air traffic controllers relay their instructions to pilots. If two airplanes get too close, one computer warns the air traffic controller and another computer warns the pilot. Either may observe the problem and take action without waiting for the computer.

In an effort to handle increasing levels of air traffic, the proposed air traffic control system abandons this paradigm. The computer assigns routes and altitudes, transmitting instructions directly to the computer flying the airplane. Pilots and air traffic controllers become monitors, able to override the system in emergencies.

Presently, computers control traffic lights and signs in a manner analogous to the instructions of air traffic controllers to airplanes. Drivers follow instructions according to the law, their own common sense, habit, present whim or pressing need. Various ways to expand these traffic control systems have been proposed, many representing distributed real-time process control. But these systems control only traffic lights and signs; they don't take over the vehicles for us.

A proposed vehicle control system will, however. The system takes the same approach as air traffic control: a central traffic control computer is supposed to drive your car for you, transmitting instructions directly to the appropriate microprocessor(s) in the vehicle. Research is ongoing.

In both these proposed systems, a central computer simultaneously controls a large number of processes distributed over a large area. Up to now, most distributed systems were concerned with information transfer—mission-critical they may have been, but nobody died when the network went down. That's just as well, since distributed systems add a significant new layer of complexity. Using computers to control many safety-critical processes simultaneously may *really* be asking too much.

### Traffic Control

Traffic control systems take an active role in managing traffic, adjusting traffic light timing or freeway signs. If traffic planners can get reliable, updated traffic information, they can sometimes improve a traffic jam. A fair number of such systems are already in place. Many cities have mounted video cameras at critical roads or intersections, allowing the traffic department to monitor flow and adjust the timing of traffic lights or the displays on traffic signs.[106]

More ambitious traffic systems are being planned. Not surprisingly, considering its traffic problems, the city of Los Angeles is in the forefront. For the 1984 Olympics, the city installed the Automated Traffic Surveillance and Control System, which uses cameras and sensors to monitor traffic on a lane-by-lane basis on certain highly traveled roads. The system acts on the information it receives, controlling traffic lights and freeway on-ramp meters. This system was the beginning of what its proponents are calling the Intelligent Vehicle and Highway System (IVHS), an overarching set of proposals to restructure the entire experience of driving from here to there.

IVHS planners want to take traffic control further in several directions: a more sophisticated, widespread traffic management system and some method of getting detailed traffic information to the individual motorist. If you had a car navigation system, wouldn't it be convenient to connect it to a traffic information service that could tell your car's computer where all the trouble spots were? The car could then route you around the congested areas. That is one kind of service IVHS planners visualize.[107]

The Chicago traffic system discussed at the beginning of this chapter automated the process of disseminating information. The Los Angeles system has automated the process of controlling traffic as well. They'd like to do it better, and are at work on an expert system that would capture the knowledge of the best traffic controllers. The knowledge of an expert in traffic control would be reduced to a few hundred rules and put to work everywhere one can bury sensors and communicate with a computer.

### Air Traffic Control: The Advanced Automation System
Digital flight control systems take the responsibility for action away from pilots. Automation is taking authority to make decisions away from air traffic controllers as well.

Air traffic control computers provide more information than controllers can get from staring out of windows or peering at radar screens. But so far, they do not issue instructions. The coming Advanced Automation System (AAS) will. Under development by IBM and the U. S. Federal Aviation Administration since the early 1980s, the AAS is a massive undertaking, incorporating about 150 large, complex, interdependent projects.[108] An ambitious integration of digital flight control, navigation, collision avoidance, ground proximity warning, communication, scheduling and routing, meteorology, and conventional air traffic control systems will computerize the air traffic flow of the United States daily. A network of computers will be responsible for maintaining aircraft separation. The flight control system and air traffic control computer will exchange data directly through the transponder. Pilots and air traffic controllers are supposed to be there to override the system if necessary—a human backup system.

The original schedule called for the system to be deployed in the late 1980s. That has slipped, of course, and no one will now say when the system will be placed in service. That's smart.

AAS is supposed not only to prevent midair collisions, but also to optimize traffic flow. At present, the air traffic control system is not as efficient as it could be, because each air traffic controller sees only the situation in his or her sector. No one views the air space over the entire continent for the whole day and determines the best way to route everyone. No one could. But AAS computers are expected to coordinate air traffic on a continent-wide basis, expediting flying time and saving money.

AAS is safety-critical, and the FAA has noticed. The overall reliability goal is ambitious: "safe, full-service operation within the required response times, 100 percent of the time." Nevertheless, the system's planners know that failures will occur, and that the system will not be able to recover from all of them quickly enough. The initial backup level oper-

ates with reduced capabilities, but includes all functions necessary for
safety. It may inconvenience pilots but is supposed to occur an average of
only 2.1 minutes per year. The next level of backup, emergency mode, includes only the most critical services; if maintained for any length of
time, emergency mode would delay a great many flights. But it is expected to be required an average of less than half a minute per year. The
final level of backup involves dedicated, sweating people shuffling pieces
of paper, doing the best they can; *that* is supposed to happen an average
of only 3 seconds per year.[109]

AAS will be phased in slowly, after many technical reviews, small-scale
tests, and larger-scale tests. It's needed; already, air traffic at the United
States's busiest airports strains and occasionally exceeds the capacity of
the present system. This can lead to incidents such as the busy day of October 14, 1989, at Dallas-Fort Worth. The computer, having more data to
process than memory to process it with, crashed and remained out of
service for *over 20 minutes.* Thanks to hard work, brains, and a measure
of luck, no planes crashed.[110]

Air traffic in the United States is presently increasing at the rate of 2 to
5 percent per year. We have a choice: we can upgrade the present system,
or we can scale back on commercial airline travel. We seem to have
made our choice. What is the best way to upgrade the system? Can we
do more of what we do now? Should we take this opportunity to examine the whole airspace-airplane-pilot system? Or shall we just hand decision-making to the computers? "AAS is the most complex civilian
undertaking since landing a man on the moon," says Jim Harris of Portland International Airport's Terminal Radar Control, and I suspect he is
not guilty of hyperbole. This system will not come cheap.

Donald Norman, author of *The Design of Everyday Things*[111] and an
authority on human factors in system design, has proposed scrapping the
entire system and redesigning it completely. He is studying aviation safety
under a NASA grant, and an article on the subject that appeared in *The
Economist*[112] moved him to respond with the following quick and informal comment on an electronic bulletin board:

> *The new addition of "datalink" to the cockpit will only create new prob-
> lems. Datalink is digital transmission of ATC [air traffic control] informa-
> tion to be received somewhere in the cockpit on a CRT display. This
> replaces some of the voice communication on the now overcrowded chan-
> nels. In principle it has merits, but it is yet another complex piece of
> equipment, yet another change in procedures, yet another Band-Aid and
> ill-considered addition to cockpit clutter. I used the word "somewhere" be-
> cause nobody yet knows quite where to fit the thing into the already
> crowded cockpit, and all the current suggestions seem to lead to foresee-*

*able future problems. The lack of positive confirmation from pilots will also lead to other (foreseeable) problems. Basically, one cannot fix a system problem by adding local patches. In fact, that tends to make things worse.*[113]

When do we listen to such voices? Before or after the money has been spent?

### The Advanced Vehicle Control System

My nomination for the wildest proposal goes to the Advanced Vehicle Control System, brainchild of the IVHS planners. Upon entering the freeway, cars equipped with microprocessors would place themselves under the control of a remote computer. The computer would control the throttles, steering, and brakes with radar signals sent out 55,000 times a second. These signals will then permit "platoons of cars, separated by only a few feet, to zoom along at 90 mph while their drivers read the newspaper."[114] Right.

Entering the Santa Monica Freeway, you surrender control of your car to a computer. It platoons you three feet from other cars at a speed you would not drive yourself. Suddenly, there's a glitch in the system. You must lift your head from your newspaper and instantly retake control of a car hurtling through space at 90 mph, surrounded by other drivers who have also been reading, or chatting, or drinking, or making love, for all you know, just in time for everyone to hear the collision avoidance buzzer. I don't think so.

A system such as this one radically changes the character of freeway accidents. When they happen, they'll be like airline crashes, both in terms of the number of casualties and the lack of control on the part of the victims. A systems safety expert working on the project says, "You'll be trading 100 accidents in which a total of 105 people get killed for 2 accidents in which a total of 30 people get killed."[115] This cold-blooded analysis is wrong on two counts.

*No* evidence exists to demonstrate that such a system would be safer in terms of the absolute number of people killed (or injured, or any other index of harm you'd care to use). Projections of the number of deaths or injuries are meaningless, based on unsubstantiated guesses and little evidence. Traveling 90 mph in platoons of vehicles with three feet of clearance between them could very well increase casualties, not decrease them. The above-quoted systems safety expert believes that the system will eliminate those accidents caused by human error. But again, that means the driver cannot override the system in any way. Given what we know of the likelihood of software bugs, the dangers of EMI or other inadvertent environmental inputs, and the staggering number of ways in which a complex system can fail, would you willingly climb into an automobile with no override capability?

But suppose that, somehow, traffic deaths go down, not up, after the system has been placed in service. Does that mean it's better? They may be wrong, but a lot of drivers like to think their superior skills will improve their chances in a bad situation. People want to control their destinies. When a synchronization glitch or a buffer overflow can be blamed for the deaths of thirty or sixty people all at once, their families will scream for someone's head. Lawyers are the only ones who will benefit.

Yet a more basic problem exists. As the city of Chicago so graphically demonstrated to us on April 13, 1992, the infrastructure of the United States is in bad shape. The tunnels underneath the city of Chicago were flooded, causing hundreds of millions of dollars of damage, because a $10,000 expenditure to repair a small leak was delayed.[116] As the "*CBS Evening News*" reported, highway bridges all over the United States are in bad condition.[117] City roads, state highways, and interstate freeways all suffer from potholes large enough to damage cars. Most water mains in the United States were laid at the turn of the century; many have not been repaired since. A nation whose entire southwest is dry loses an estimated 34 percent of its drinking water to leaks. And in fiscal 1991, the U.S. Federal Highway Administration spent $20 million on IVHS. In fiscal 1992, they are increasing this to $234 million.

Clearly, it's more fun to build than to maintain. It's more profitable, as well—for some. AT&T, Lockheed, Hughes Aircraft, General Motors, Westinghouse, TRW, Ford, Chrysler, Motorola, and Rockwell International all see the opportunity for big profits with IVHS. Money we spend on repairing the infrastructure goes to small community businesses instead. Those guys just don't pay lobbyists. But shouldn't we be taking care of the basics before adding all these frills? If traffic jams are such a terrible problem, why not build mass transit systems that run so often and go to so many places that they are actually convenient? We are going to feel awfully silly when those platoons of cars whizzing merrily down the freeway get to the place where the bridge has just collapsed. If the computer, having failed to update its model of the world recently, sends them plunging over the precipice, it will be the perfect illustration of our misplaced priorities.

## VIRTUAL DEMOCRACY

For a while now, software has been used during election campaigns to identify one's supporters for direct-mail appeals, or to comb databases for tidbits about one's opponent's heinous past. You can also use high-tech to vote, and some would like to. Schemes have been hatched to allow people to vote by interactive television, touch-tone telephone, fax machine—even computer network.

Proponents such as the Voting by Phone Foundation of Boulder, Colorado, envision voters picking up the phone, dialing a toll-free number, and interacting with a voice-response system similar to voice mail. "In the contest for Chief Dog-catcher," it might say, "press 1 to vote for Fido. Press 2 to vote for Dobbin." It's supposed to be more convenient than traveling to a polling place, and therefore to increase voter turnout. But as the voters of the Liberal Party in Nova Scotia found out, it's not necessarily that easy.

Nor is it clear why we need to vote by phone.[118] There is little doubt that voter turnout in the United States is dismal—in many elections, fewer than half of those eligible bother to vote. Is this because polling places are so difficult to get to, now that we have given up horse-drawn carriages for automobiles? Will voting by phone really bring about a groundswell of increased participation?

Is it really more convenient? People complain mightily about interacting with voice mail systems. And most of those interactions are undertaken to accomplish tasks simpler than voting in an election with national contests, state contests, local contests, and voter initiatives. The telephone interface is limited—twelve buttons and a voice. Unlike a paper ballot, a voice-mail system does not let you see what you have already done or what you have left to do. You cannot tell when you have made a mistake. You may not want an entire voter initiative read to you in tedious detail. You may wish to write in a candidate. You may even get a repeated busy signal: perhaps everyone waited until evening to perform this civic duty, perhaps an organized protest is tying up all the phone lines, or perhaps the system can't handle the load.

Assuming that we solve these problems, then what? A convenient and simple process is a good thing, but voters also need confidence that their votes will be registered as they intended and counted as registered. The voter's anonymity must be preserved. It must be difficult to alter the outcome of a contest by coercing or buying votes, using the votes of people who have not already voted, or altering or eliminating the votes of those who have. It must be possible to audit the process for reassurance and to conduct a recount in the event of a close race. How does voting by phone handle these requirements?

How can we ensure that the person voting is a registered voter who has not voted already? Voice recognition would require a database where every registered voter's voice is on file—and if you have laryngitis, you are disenfranchised. We could use PINs, as with automated teller machines, but PINs can be stolen or forgotten.

How can we simultaneously preserve the voter's privacy and archive votes in case a recount is needed? Those two requirements seem to be in direct conflict. What is to prevent an unscrupulous fanatic with computer expertise from breaking into the system at the last minute, determining who has not yet voted, and stuffing the electronic ballot box in the final moments?

Perhaps technical problems can be overcome, but what's the point? If we really want to increase voter turnout, it would be cheaper to make Election Day a national holiday, as it is in most European countries. Or we could hold elections over several days, including a Sunday. But most people who refrain from voting do so because they believe it makes no difference. This is a social problem, not a technological one. The real solution to increasing voter turnout is to change that belief.

The technology we use to vote is an obvious target for change. Less obvious, but more profound, is using the technology to change the basis upon which we organize representation. When the process of voting was set up, geography was the only reasonable basis for organizing large groups of people, so our representatives represent geographical communities. But this is no longer the case; nearly every day, for example, I log on to a computer and continue a discussion with a friend 3000 miles away, while in a year I've spoken to my next-door neighbor once. Computer networks allow us to consider alternatives to geographical representation. This aspect of digital technology could make democracy more representative or more chaotic, depending on your point of view.

Who but a network computing professional would suggest that we dispense with geography altogether as the basis for representation, and choose our representatives instead on the basis of ideology?[119] Instead of a U. S. Congress filled with similar politicians, this devotee of networking rightly foresees this vote-by-net scheme producing a Congress of extremists and one-issue zealots. For some reason, this prospect seems agreeable to him. "We've got the technology," he says, "why not see if we can use it?" Why not, indeed? Perhaps because the problems we face should drive the solutions we seek, not vice-versa.

Do we need the U. S. Congress at all if Americans can make their wills directly known on each of thousands of different issues as they come up? A nation can now be governed by referendum, with "electronic town meetings" as Ross Perot suggested.[120] The idea sounds appealing, but how it is going to be implemented? Public discussion of issues is necessary for democracy, and new forums for discussion are worth encouraging, certainly. But are these to be discussions? Or do we just listen to our leader's proposal and then press 1 for "yes," 2 for "no"? The ability to frame the terms of debate is a powerful position, easily abused. This system could be the triumph of demagoguery over democracy.

I have actually been to real town meetings—the nonelectronic kind. Every March in Vermont, the high school I attended trundled us onto various vehicles and sent us all over the southern part of the state to attend them. I watched neighbors stand up and discuss one proposal or another, often heatedly. The person with the gavel at the front of the room was not in a position to frame the terms of the discussion—sometimes, he or she could barely keep order. By and large, the whole town heard what various folks had to say. For those unwilling to stand up in front of everyone, remarks could be whispered in the aisles or in the halls. At midday, formal discussion ceased, but informal discussion proceeded apace over a potluck lunch with contributions from nearly everyone. Opportunity to air one's views or influence the discussion was ample. Opportunity to dominate the discussion was not.

On-line bulletin boards can approach this level of involvement among their participants, but I doubt that "town meetings" using telephone or television technology can. The channel is too limited and too expensive. The person or organization paying for it frames the discussion.

As it turned out, I also participated in one of Governor Barbara Roberts's "Conversations with Oregon" in the fall of 1991. In this, one of the first uses of interactive, closed-circuit television to gauge (and shape) public opinion, the governor discussed tax policy with several thousand citizens. During my session, she was on the screen more than 75 percent of the time the system was active. Although she clearly did not mean to, she spoke far more than she listened. It's hard to resist. She called all the shots, and she's only human. Technology can help us, but it isn't going to enable us to transcend our natures. Its entry into the political process should be managed carefully and with forethought.

### AND MORE . . .

Proposed uses for digital technology exhibit the fruitfulness of the human imagination. Funding continues for a space station, presumably to give the space shuttle somewhere to park. Manufacturers dream of integrating the design, inventory control, and the manufacture of their goods in one computer-integrated manufacturing system. Aviation authorities are putting TCAS, yet another collision-avoidance system, into airplane cockpits. People are planning or building systems to warn us of earthquakes, automate gas stations, sell us lottery tickets with Nintendo machines, put on-line help systems into airplane cockpits, lock doors, teach us to play the piano, monitor how often we open a pill bottle, arm or disarm nuclear weapons in midflight, modernize the U. S. Internal Revenue Service (that one sounds fun, huh?), automatically photograph any car traveling faster than the speed limit, refer you from a national toll-free number to the pizza parlor or burger joint nearest you, and search for evidence of fraud in securities transactions. While you read that sentence, someone had another idea.

Some of these systems will be useful—relatively cheap to implement, perhaps, and worth the risk, which may be small. Others will not be—the expense or risk or both will not be worth it, except perhaps to those few who make the profit. In any case, we cannot build them all. We simply do not have the resources to throw at any and every system someone proposes. In the final chapter, I would like to suggest criteria we might use to determine which systems are worth building and which are not.

### NOTES

1 "Big Science" by Laurie Anderson, 1982 Difficult Music (BMI).
2 Contributors to the on-line forum *comp.risks* will recognize the game. I would like to thank them all for their insights. They have been wonderful teachers.
3 Three-letter acronyms.
4 Extended three-letter acronyms.
5 Altman, Lawrence K. "Science Group Plans Electronic Medical Journal." *New York Times*, Sep. 25, 1991, p. A15.
6 *comp.risks*, 10:15, Jul. 26, 1990.
7 Schine, Eric, Mark Maremont and Christina Del Valle. "Here Comes the Thinking Car." *Business Week*, May 25, 1992, pp. 84–7.
8 Ferrell, J. E. "The Big Fix." *Los Angeles Times Magazine*, April 14, 1991, pp. 14, 16, 18 and 38–40. Taylor, Ronald B. "Street Smart: Testing High Tech on the Santa Monica Freeway." *Los Angeles Times Magazine*, April 14, 1991, pp. 16 and 38.
9 ASCII stands for American Standard Code for Information Interchange, and it is the basis of text representation in all computers but a few old or exotic ones. It assigns a number to each character on the keyboard. When the computer is told to interpret a string of numbers as text, it uses the code to read the numbers and determine which character to display.
10 "Your humble servant." *The Economist*, May 2, 1992, p. 78.
11 For a deeper exploration of these issues, see Mander, Jerry. *Four Arguments for the Elimination of Television*. New York: Morrow, 1978.
12 Hundertmark, Jane. "When Enhancement Is Deception." *Publish*, 6:10, Oct. 1991, pp. 50–55. Also, Durniak, John. "Camera." *New York Times*, Jan. 5, 1992, p. 19.
13 Cover of *Time*, Jan. 6, 1992.
14 Durniak, John, *op. cit.*
15 *ibid.*
16 Leland, John. "The Moper vs. the Rapper." *Newsweek*, Jan. 6, 1992, p. 55.

17 Green, Michael. *Zen & the Art of the Macintosh*. Philadelphia, PA: Running Press, 1986.
18 Graham, Ellen. "Plug In, Sign On, and Read Milton, an Electronic Classic: Project Gutenberg Is Sending Good Books to Computers Everywhere—For Free." *The Wall Street Journal*, Oct. 29, 1991, pp. A1, A9.
19 Reilly, Patrick M. "Electronics, Music Industries Set Pact On Digital Recording Use in the Home." *The Wall Street Journal*, July 12, 1991, p. B5.
20 Markoff, John. "Portable electronic newspaper gets closer." *Oregonian*, July 5, 1992, p. P1. Rogers, Michael. "The Literary Circuit-ry." *Newsweek*, June 29, 1992, pp. 66–7.
21 Langberg, Mike. "Putting a face with voice by telephone technology." *Oregonian*, Jan. 19, 1992, pp. D1, D3.
22 On April 8, 15, 22, 29, and May 4, 1992, PBS (the U.S. Public Broadcasting System) aired an excellent series of television shows about the computer, called "The Machine That Changed the World." The concept of the computer as an all-purpose machine was explored to great effect in that series, particularly in the first show.
23 Schwartz, John. "The Next Revolution." *Newsweek*, April 6, 1992, pp. 42–48.
24 Rogers, Michael. "Honey, I Shrunk the Disc." *Newsweek*, June 1, 1992, p. 64.
25 Sichelman, Lew. "Smart houses just around the corner." *Oregonian*, Sept. 8, 1991, p. H1.
26 Flowers, Bauvion. "Did Shakespeare Know ASCII?" *Mondo Modo*, July, 1999, pp. 13–15.
27 "Say aah: High-tech dental X-rays coming." *Oregonian*, Oct. 27, 1991, p. L12.
28 Schwartz, John. "The Highway to the Future." *Newsweek*, Jan. 13, 1992, pp. 56–7. Also, Schulberg, Pete. "Fiber optics: the future is now." *Oregonian*, Jan. 12, 1992, p. C10.
29 Ramirez, Anthony. "A.T. & T. Plans to Offer Faster Data Transfer." *New York Times*, Nov. 19, 1991, p. C2. Also: Dr. Robert Beck, Biomedical Instructional Computing Center, address to Software Association of Oregon, Beaverton, Oregon, June 28, 1991.
30 The redundancy of human language has allowed telephone technology to use a very limited bandwidth. The English sounds written as "s" and "f" differ only in their highest-frequency components. This high-frequency sound is not presently transmitted over telephone lines, but you are so good at understanding language that you may never notice in a lifetime of telephone use, until you get directions in an unfamiliar city, and can't tell whether your informant has named a street "Fable" or "Sable."
31 Schulberg, Pete. "Please Standby." *Oregonian*, Jan. 12, 1992, pp. C7–C10.
32 Zachary, G. Pascal. "Power Play: Utilities see the 'intelligent' meter as the hub of a new two-way communications network. No wonder some cable-TV companies aren't happy." *The Wall Street Journal*, April 6, 1992, p. R6.
33 Schwartz, John. "How Did They Get My Name?" *Newsweek*, June 3, 1991, pp. 40–42.
34 Rheingold, Howard. "Big Brother, the Grocery Clerk." *Publish*, Oct. 1991, pp. 40–42.
35 Reported by Jim Tuttle on *All About You*, television broadcast by Oregon Public Broadcasting on Oct. 2, 1991.
36 Neumann, Peter G. "What's in a Name? Inside Risks." *Communications of the ACM*, 35:1, Jan. 1992, p. 186.
37 Winslow, Ron. "Desktop Doctors." *The Wall Street Journal*, April 6, 1992, p. R14.
38 Miller, Michael W. "Patient's Records Are Treasure Trove for Budding Industry." *Wall Street Journal*, Feb. 27, 1992, p. A1.
39 *comp.risks*, 12:66, Nov. 26, 1991, and 13:8, Jan. 28, 1992. Item contributed by David States, member of the National Center for Biotechnology Information. Also see

"Genetic Records to Be Kept on Members of Military." *New York Times,* Jan. 12, 1992, p. 15

40  Quinn, Jane Bryant. "Insurance: The Death Spiral." *Newsweek,* Feb. 22, 1993, p. 47.

41  "True Colors." *Privacy Journal,* 16:9, July, 1990, p. 1. Quoted in *comp.risks,* 10:22, Aug. 22, 1990. Also see Mercuri, Rebecca. Trip report on Computers, Freedom, and Privacy Conference, March 26–28, 1991, in *comp.risks,* 11:39.

42  Owens, Norman. "Back to the Future for Commercial Agents." *The Mercantile Agent.* Quoted in "Sorry, you can't afford it." from the *Sydney* [Australia] *Morning Herald,* August 20, 1990. Which in turn is quoted in *comp.risks,* 10:22, Aug. 22, 1990.

43  "The World at Your Fingertips," Episode 5 of *The Machine That Changed the World,* broadcast on the Public Broadcasting System on May 4, 1992.

44  *comp.risks,* 10:16, July 31, 1990. From "Justice Proceeds to Create Its Drug Intelligence Center," *Government Computer News,* July 9, 1990, p. 8.

45  *comp.risks,* 13:45, April 28, 1992.

46  "The Thinking Machine," episode 4 of *The Machine That Changed the World,* PBS, aired April 27, 1992.

47  "Cogito, ergo something." *The Economist,* March 14, 1992, pp. 5–6 of "A Survey of Artificial Intelligence—Minds in the Making."

48  PBS, *op. cit.*

49  Lise Storc, developer. Personal communication, July 22, 1991.

50  Winslow, Ron. "Desktop Doctors." *Wall Street Journal,* April 6, 1992, p. R14.

51  "The Life-and-Death Computer." Editorial, *Washington Post,* Jan. 5, 1992, p. C6.

52  A classic book on this subject is Huff, Darrell. *How to Lie with Statistics.* New York: W. W. Norton and Co., 1954.

53  Washington Post, *op. cit.*

54  *comp.risks,* 13:2, Jan. 9, 1992, item contributed by Tom Perrine.

55  Blumberg, Mark S. "Biased Estimates of Expected Acute Myocardial Infarction Mortality Using MedisGroups Admission Severity Groups." *Journal of the American Medical Association,* 1991, 265:22, pp. 2965–2970. Iezzoni, Lisa I. "'Black Box' Medical Information Systems: A Technology Needing Assessment." *Journal of the American Medical Association,* 1991, 265:22, pp. 3006–7.

56  Easterbrook, Gregg. "A House of Cards." *Newsweek,* June 1, 1992, pp. 24–33.

57  "Computer Animations Aiding Lawyer's Cases." *Seattle Times,* July 23, 1990, p. E3.

58  Reported by Frank Currier on the "*CBS Evening News,*" May 4, 1992.

59  Bickford, George. "Computer landscaping simplifies garden plan." *Oregonian,* April 12, 1992, p. L24.

60  My thanks to Joe Hubert of CAChe Scientific, Inc. for the demonstration of the 3D computer-aided chemistry workstation.

61  Gupta, Udayan. "Designing Drugs." *Wall Street Journal,* April 6, 1992, p. R20.

62  "The Paperback Computer," episode 3 of *The Machine That Changed the World,* PBS, aired April 20, 1992, featured a thrilling segment in which we walk through a church before and after it was built.

63  Yamada, Ken. "Almost Like Being There." *Wall Street Journal,* April 6, 1992, p. R10.

64  Carroll, Paul B. "Let the Games Begin." *Wall Street Journal,* April 6, 1992, p. R10.

65  Schine, et al., *op. cit.*

66  Winfield, Barry. "Trace control: another step toward the foolproof vehicle." *Automobile Magazine,* Feb. 1991, pp. 41–44.

67  "Saying goodbye to 'Where am I?'" The Economist, Aug. 24, 1991, pp. 71–2.

68  When fully in place, GPS receivers should be able to calculate their positions to within 25 meters. But the U.S. military can degrade this accuracy when they deem it necessary, so that civilian receivers will be accurate only to within 100 meters. Per-

haps commercial users should instead take over deployment and maintenance of GLONAS, the former Soviet Union's version of GPS.

69 "Saying goodbye to 'Where am I?'" *The Economist, op. cit.*
70 Schine, et al., *op. cit.*
71 "4° East, 51° North, and a side order of 29." *The Economist,* Aug. 24, 1991, p. 72.
72 "Truett, Richard. "On the Road in Orlando: My Wild Ride with Sven." *Business Week,* May 25, 1992, p. 87.
73 *comp.risks,* 13:46, May 2, 1992.
74 Arlidge, John. "Firm Offers 'Foolproof' Car Security System." *The Independent,* quoted in *comp.risks,* 13:48, May 10, 1992.
75 Nicholas, Jonathan. "Some people still not getting the signal." *Oregonian,* May 24, 1992, p. L2.
76 *comp.risks,* 13:44, April 27, 1992 and ensuing discussion in nos. 45 and 46, April 28 and May 2.
77 Peter G. Neumann, *comp.risks,* 13:46, May 2, 1992.
78 *comp.risks,* 11:31, March 19, 1991.
79 *comp.risks,* 13:13, Feb. 8, 1992.
80 *comp.risks,* 13:09, Feb. 1, 1992.
81 Phil Agre, *comp.risks,* 13:09, Feb. 1, 1992.
82 *comp.risks,* 12:20, Aug. 30, 1991.
83 Keller, John J. "Computers Get Powerful 'Hearing' Aids: Improved Methods of Voice Recognition." *Wall Street Journal,* April 7, 1992, p. B1.
84 Schwaneberg, Robert. " 'Busy signal' aided an 'anklet' escapee." *Newark Star Ledger,* May 13, 1992, pp. 1 and 13.
85 Schwaneberg, *op. cit.*
86 *comp.risks,* 10:19, 20, 21, 22, 24, 25, 26, Aug. 10–29, 1990. It's a fascinating discussion. The subject is also discussed in 13:38, 40, 43, 49, April 10–May 16, 1992.
87 Hicks, Jonathan P. "Hushing an Engine, Electronically." *New York Times,* Oct. 2, 1991, p. C5.
88 "Robodoc." *The Economist.* March 14, 1992, p. 100–101.
89 *comp.risks,* 12:10, July 29, 1991.
90 Adler, Jerry and Myron Stokes. "A Cadillac With Smarts." *Newsweek,* May 4, 1992, p. 73.
91 Schine, et al., *op. cit.*
92 Malnic, Eric. "Causes of Fatal Girl Scout Bus Crash Detailed." *Los Angeles Times,* Nov. 1, 1991, p. B3. Other articles with relevant information: Warren, Jenifer. "Brakes Officially Blamed for Girl Scout Bus Crash." *Los Angeles Times,* Aug. 17, 1991, p. A24; and Malnic, Eric. "Girl Scout Driver Was Unaware of Gear Feature." *Los Angeles Times,* Nov. 2, 1991, p. B6. The original accident story was: Warren, Jenifer and Paul Feldman. "7 Die, 53 Hurt as Girl Scout Bus Overturns." *Los Angeles Times,* Aug. 1, 1991, pp. A1 and A24. My thanks to Mark Seecof of the *Los Angeles Times* for providing these and other references.
93 As of early 1992.
94 Winfield, *op. cit.,* p. 44.
95 Winfield, *op. cit.,* p. 44.
96 McCraw, Jim. "Wheels, Drives, and Dollars—The Cold Facts." *Popular Science,* Oct. 1991, p. 86.
97 Watts, Susan. "Computer Systems Developed for Aircraft Are Being Adapted for Use on the Road." *The Independent,* U.K. March 11, 1992.
98 Buderi, Robert, ed. "BMW Puts a Backseat Driver on a Chip." *Business Week,* July 30, 1990, p. 70.

99  *comp.risks*, 11:47, April 16, 1991.

100  *comp.risks*, 11:49, April 19, 1991.

101  Adler, *op. cit.*

102  *comp.risks*, 2:12, Feb. 18, 1986.

103  *comp.risks*, 13:26–8 and 30, March 6, 7, 16, and 23, 1992.

104  *comp.risks*, 10:15, July 26, 1990.

105  *comp.risks*, 13:57, June 10, 1992.

106  Mr. William C. Kloos, P.E., Signal Systems Manager, Bureau of Traffic Management for the City of Portland Office of Transportation. Personal communication, Aug. 22, 1991.

107  This entire section draws heavily on the following three articles: Taylor, Ronald B. "Street Smart: Testing High Tech on the Santa Monica Freeway." *Los Angeles Times Magazine*, April 14, 1991, pp. 16 and 38. Ferrell, J. E. "The Big Fix." *Los Angeles Times Magazine*, April 14, 1991, pp. 14, 16, 18 and 38–40. Schine, Eric, Mark Maremont, and Christina Del Valle. "Here Comes the Thinking Car." *Business Week*, May 25, 1992, pp. 84–7.

108  For much of this information, and a lot of background, I would like to express my thanks to Mr. Jim Harris, Assistant Air Traffic Control Manager, Portland TRACON, Federal Aviation Administration, personal communication, May 26, 1992.

109  "On the Achievement of a Highly Dependable and Fault-Tolerant Air Traffic Control System," Avizienis, Algirdas, and Danforth E. Ball, IEEE *Computer*, February, 1987, pp. 84–90. The quote is from p. 86.

110  Lee, Leonard. *The Day the Phones Stopped*. New York: Donald I. Fine, Inc., 1991.

111  Norman, Donald. *The Design of Everyday Things*. New York: Doubleday, 1988.

112  "Wings, prayers, and prudence." *The Economist*, Dec. 1, 1990, p. 104.

113  Norman, Donald. *comp.risks*, 10:67, Dec. 7, 1990.

114  Ferrell, *op. cit.*, p. 16.

115  Ferrell, *op. cit.*, p. 40.

116  Caldwell, Bruce, and Linda Perry. "Down and Out in Chicago." *Information Week*, April 20, 1992, pp. 12–3.

117  "*CBS* Evening News," May 21, 1992. Story reported by Frank Currier.

118  For this entire discussion of voting by telephone, I am indebted to Peter Neumann and the on-line *comp.risks* forum, especially 10:60, 61, 64, 67, 70, 72, 73, 78, 81, 83, and 11:1, covering the period from Nov. 14, 1990 to Feb. 4, 1991; and 11:75, 76, 77, 78, and 80, covering the period from May 29 to June 4, 1991.

119  Haight, Timothy. "Can network computing save the nation?" *Network Computing*, Feb., 1992, pp. 59–60. The quote is from p. 60.

120  Turque, Bill, Howard Fineman, and Clara Bingham. "Wiring Up the Age of Technopolitics." *Newsweek*, June 15, 1992, p. 25. Also: Stroud, Michael. "Perot's Bold Techno-Populism: Electronic Forums Could Be Abused, Critics Fear." *Investor's Business Daily*, June 11, 1992, pp. 1–2.

# CHAPTER 6

# THE WISE USE

## of

# SMART STUFF

Now that the
Software Crisis will
soon celebrate its silver anniversary,
it's time we recognized
that this is
not a crisis, it's a situation: software has bugs. It is in its nature to have bugs, and that fact is unlikely to change soon. Software products—even programs of modest size—are among the most complex artifacts that humans produce, and software development projects are among our most complex undertakings. They soak up however much time or money, however many people we throw at them.

The results are only modestly reliable. Even after the most thorough and rigorous testing, some bugs remain. We can never test all threads through the system with all possible inputs. Even if we could, the spec could have been in error in the first place, the requirements might have changed during development, or the system might be used in a manner that was never intended.

Nor can we know when a bug will occur. Software is not a "well-behaved" mechanical structure such as a bridge. As you put more and more weight on a bridge, it will start to show signs of stress—sagging, cracking, or buckling. Increasing the weight increases the stress until the bridge fails, and you can watch the process. But software can behave perfectly correctly until one bit, changing from a zero to a one, causes abrupt and total failure.

How many details and relationships can a human being track? If large, wealthy organizations bend over backward, expending huge amounts of resources, they can build larger and more complex systems, systems

**193**

that strain human limits. These systems are at best only somewhat more reliable.

Information in digital form shows the following characteristics:

- It is easy to change, but hard to foresee all the consequences of the change. As a result, software development is expensive—it takes smart people longer to get it right than the schedule ordinarily allows. Sequences can be complicated; when events occur in the wrong order, funny things can happen. So the software is prone to interactions neither planned, foreseen, nor possible to forestall.

- It is easy to copy and hard to keep the copies consistent. As a result, databases of constantly changing information are nearly always somewhat inaccurate.

- It is easy to spread and hard to restrict its spread. As a result, communication is easy but security is not.

- It is easy to modify and hard to detect modification. As a result, it's a wonderful medium for art but a terrible one for legal uses.

- And of course, all of the three previous characteristics combine to make it a nightmare to enforce copyright restrictions on digital media.

- It occupies memory, a finite resource, so infinitely rich real-world information must be squeezed through the sieve of a finite resolution. Only some details can be captured, and it's tough to tell which ones really matter. As a result, any computer model will be incomplete and inaccurate in some respects.

- It exists within a physical machine that sits in a wild and crazy world. Physical interfaces are vulnerable to interference or incorrect input. As a result, the unpredictable can happen.

- People operate it or monitor it or use it. People add an ability to recognize patterns, reach outside the situation, and appreciate what's at stake; they are necessary. But they can also be bored, distracted, sleepy, error-prone, unpredictable, or malicious.

As the previous chapter demonstrates, a lot of digital systems are being proposed. Our plate is full; indeed, I think our eyes are bigger than our stomachs. Some of these ideas are better than others; some ideas are very risky indeed. No system is risk-free, but we can try to assess the risks that each system entails before we commit the resources. We cannot build all of them. Which deserve our efforts? *How* do we want to use digital technology?

## SEVEN QUESTIONS

Our acceptance of technologies should not be unconditional: we should assess them before we embrace them. We don't have to passively accept anything that anyone chooses to build. As consumers and citizens, we have power.

As consumers, we can choose to buy simpler cars with fewer functions under software control. We can demand that data about us not be sold without our informed consent. We can insist on the power to correct erroneous information about us kept in computerized databases. We can write letters to corporations whose products we fear may harm us. Such a campaign has already had a demonstrable effect: when Lotus Corp. and Equifax, one of the three main credit-reporting agencies, teamed up to produce Lotus Marketplace, they were swamped by protest. The product, a CD-ROM containing personal financial data for thousands of U. S. households, was intended to be sold to direct marketing associations—people looking for mailing lists. Over 30,000 people wrote letters demanding to be removed from the database, or expressing concern over loss of privacy and control of personal data. Ultimately, Lotus and Equifax withdrew the product.[1]

Nor should we neglect our power as citizens. If corporations choose to throw away their research dollars developing "smart" freeways that can platoon cars under the control of a central computer, that's their privilege. But we can at least let the U. S. Federal Highway Administration know that we resent subsidizing this folly with our tax money. We don't have to consent. We can refuse to drive on the freeway. We can vote for people who favor developing pleasant and convenient mass transit systems instead.

Nor need we succumb to mindless appeals to patriotism or fear. We can listen to the arguments of those who oppose massive weapons systems and decide whether we believe their reasons that the systems won't work. Then we can let our elected leaders know how we feel.

We are not powerless when we choose not to be.

How should we assess proposals for digital systems? Without a Ph.D. in computer science, how can we tell a good idea from a bad one? What sorts of proposals should we view with skepticism? The following seven questions might be helpful to ask about any proposal to develop a digital system:

1. Is it the right system—will it solve the right problem? It is possible to overautomate: some systems simply don't justify their costs. And some

problems are just inappropriate. "People problems" do not need, and will not respond to, technological solutions.

2. What is at risk? Failures will happen. Systems for which one failure equals one disaster are a poor bet.

3. How big and complex will it have to be? Smaller and simpler systems cost less and stand a better chance of functioning properly.

4. How will it fit into the existing universe? Any system has to join what already exists, forming part of a larger system. Are the designers taking this into account? Are they designing the whole system, including the part they are not going to build?

5. What will the system require of its users and operators? People are good at some things; computers are good at others. Systems designed to maximize the strengths of both will cause fewer accidents.

6. Will it require extensive security? Information in digital form is easy to spread and hard to restrict. Access is cheap; security costs.

7. Will there be a backup? How to back up your work is the first thing you learn when you start using a personal computer. There's a good reason for this, and it applies to deploying new systems as much as to writing memos.

### 1. Is It the Right System?

Some systems just don't achieve anything. For instance, when Washington State Ferries decided on digital control systems for their new Issaquah-class ferries, it is not clear what goals they had, nor what benefits they thought they would reap. Whatever they were, they didn't make up for the flaky behavior that presumably cost them in dock repairs. They went back to the older pneumatic controls, which worked fine. I hope the experiment didn't cost them too much, but I give them credit for their ultimate good sense. If it ain't broke, why go broke fixing it?

It is tempting to throw technology at every possible problem, but some problems just can't be solved that way. People problems, for example, cannot be fixed with technology. Some onerous tasks cannot be escaped with automation.

For example, I'm glad the members of the Nova Scotia Liberal Party finally got to vote by phone, but access to a polling place is not the main problem with our political system. People don't care to vote, *not* because it's too hard to get to the polling place, but because they don't think their votes make any difference. Allowing people to vote from home by phone is not going to fix that. What *will* fix it is a profound change in the political system. This point was amply demonstrated by the 1992 U. S. presidential election, in which more eligible voters participated than in any election in decades, because people perceived that they had a real choice. Vote-by-phone schemes are a diversion.

To determine whether a system is the *right* system, you've got to define the problem the right way. When General Motors started losing business to Japanese competition, it proved willing to commit a fortune to recapture its lost market share. But a fortune can be spent in many ways. General Motors chose to spend it on robots, when it should have spent it on workers.[2]

General Motors faced the problem: how can we compete with the Japanese? It chose to define the Japanese as people who could command more technological wizardry than they. Perhaps so, but I doubt it. Prodigies of technical mastery occur the world around, but you cannot rely on prodigies to achieve the consistent results that the Japanese have achieved. Instead, they train their workers and commit to their long-term welfare. The workers, in turn, reflect this commitment with their own: they perform better.

After all, worrying about keeping your resumé polished can be distracting.

The entire domain of caring for people is one in which technological solutions are problematic. Caring for people—old people, sick people, children—is low-status work in our society. It is deemed nowhere near as worthy as making or selling things, so few want to do it.

We leave children to talking teddy bears. We puzzle ourselves to invent a computer system capable of caring for senile dementia patients. The time, effort, and money that goes into these tasks are a waste. Computers have neither initiative nor compassion. They cannot understand what it means to be human. Resources would be better spent actually caring for those who require it. The effort would teach us about our own vulnerability and capacity for compassion; it might even teach us to value this work.

Psychic care-taking is one of the more bizarre roles that computers have played. It was also one of the first—one of the earliest attempts at artificial intelligence was a computer program, now famous, named Eliza. Eliza was written by Joseph Weizenbaum at the Massachusetts Institute of Technology. The program mimicked Rogerian psychotherapy, which is relatively easy to mimic. Rogerian therapists turn their patients' statements into questions; it encourages their patients to elaborate on, and explore their feelings about, what they have said. In addition to the turn-a-statement-into-a-question algorithm, the program included some neutral prompting, such as: "How does that make you feel?" Keywords such as "mother" evoked canned responses such as "Tell me more about your family." By today's standards, the program is neither terribly long nor unduly sophisticated.

Nevertheless, Weizenbaum reports that Eliza proved to be powerfully compelling. His secretary watched him write the program over many months; she knew it was a man-made thing. Yet after interacting with it only briefly, she asked him to leave the room so she could tell it her innermost thoughts and feelings. Others in the technologically sophisticated MIT computer science community soon came to feel the same way.[3] At least, that's the story, but I'm dubious. I've played with several Eliza-type programs on different occasions, and it seems to me that nothing but a pathetic wish for a fairy godmother could make users believe they were getting understanding and guidance.

Children need to be cared for. Adults want to be cared for. It is natural to resist the realization that we have to care for ourselves. The computer is a blank screen on which to project the wisdom we do not possess, the certainty we crave. But we are fooling ourselves. The computer can't take care of itself, let alone anyone else. That work needs people.

### 2. What Is at Risk?

It is unrealistic to build a system of even modest complexity and assume that it will never fail. Common sense dictates that systems incorporating software must be designed so that a complete software failure does not cause a disaster. If a software failure leaves you worse off than you would have been, had you never built the system—don't build it. The role of software in safety-critical systems should always be a limited one.

When someone proposes incorporating software into a critical system, it is useful to ask the following questions:

• Are partial results better than nothing?

• Is occasional or intermittent operation better than nothing?

• Can the system be designed so that a subset of its full functionality is available in the event of a failure?

• Is this subset better than nothing?

If the answers are uncertain, so is the prognosis. Noncritical software comes much cheaper and can afford to be more ambitious than the critical stuff.

It's hard to make money on software, but Bill Gates has made billions of dollars on the stuff. It's instructive to look at how he managed it. Microsoft sells many copies of operating systems, spreadsheets, word processors, and related products for personal computers. The programs come relatively cheap. They're software—you might have trouble with them.[4] If so, you can call an army of technically knowledgeable product support folks. Microsoft pays their salaries. You pay for the phone call. Mr. Gates knows what he's doing—he knows there will be more of those phone calls than he wants to pay for.

The stuff isn't perfect, but it doesn't have to be. It is not designed for critical applications. If you choose to incorporate your spreadsheet into a real-time surgical patient monitoring system, it's your lookout. Prudent users take precautions: I save my files every time I stretch. I make backup disks the way some people take vitamins.[5]

Large, complex, exotic, and critical systems need expensive equipment and expensive research scientists. Research for such systems has been highly subsidized by the military, which is to say by all of us. Digital flight control systems, for example, would not have been cost-effective for commercial airplanes without all the years of military research that preceded their commercial use. They and other such systems have not had to hold their own in a competitive market. It's no accident that non-critical applications are the ones that have made someone a billionaire without government subsidy. PC products have paid their own way.

Critical systems have expensive requirements before they even start, as it were. Yet the most ambitious system ever proposed was supposed to hold the fate of the earth in its net: SDI, now mercifully almost defunct. At a time when President Ronald Reagan was promising the American public "a nuclear umbrella" to protect us from all enemy missiles, calculations in a professional journal suggested that a 90 percent interception rate for enemy warheads was optimistic. Further calculations using this optimistic assumption showed fourteen nuclear bombs reaching their targets.[6]

So the system works as well as it can, and fourteen nuclear bombs land on us, each a thousand times more powerful than Fat Man and Little Boy put together. Do you think the United States would continue to exist? What would this do to the world economy? What other worldwide suffering do you suppose would occur? How many bombs is too many, anyway? If the answer is a small positive integer, systems such as SDI won't cut it. This is *hubris*.

Even proposing such systems does harm: as of 1992, the United States had spent over $30 billion on SDI. We spent $5 billion a year at a time when we were told there was no money for improving education or health care.[7] Billions of dollars—and decades of the talents, skills, and energies of hundreds of our brightest scientists—are diverted from problems that can actually be solved.

### 3. How Big and Complex Will It Have to Be?

Software need not be huge and complex in order to be useful; a lot of handy work has been done by relatively small programs. Smaller, simpler software projects have distinct advantages over large, complex ones.

Smaller projects absorb fewer people for less time. Therefore, they cost less. A smaller program can be reasoned about more easily, perhaps even comprehended (mostly) by one mind. It can be tested more extensively. Smaller programs are especially apt for critical systems such as transportation or process control, or—if we must—control systems for nuclear power plants. Perhaps 12,000 lines of code can be formally verified, while 1,200,000 lines cannot.

Simpler projects have advantages without respect to size. They are less likely to founder for lack of communication; fewer people are involved, and the issues are easier to understand. They are easier to maintain for the same reasons.

Will a simpler system do the job? Well, it depends. How much advantage derives from digitizing this particular function, or that one? Must you completely integrate all functions? Which ones will benefit the most from integration? Systems usually have points of greatest leverage: points where a small effort yields a disproportionate reward. They're worth looking for, and the earlier the better.

Sometimes it's hard to see where the greatest advantage might come from. That's a good time to start looking at the system in context—as a component in a larger system. How does it fit into the world?

### 4. How Will It Fit into the Existing Universe?

When a new system is introduced, the universe has to shift around some to make room for it. The system forms relationships with other systems outside itself. It creates a larger system (or changes an existing one, depending on how you look at it). If the system is stable, it enhances the larger system's prospects for stability. By the same token, if the larger system is stable, it enhances the new system's chances for stability. The right feedback can help keep systems reliable, and the wrong feedback may precipitate failure.

When a system is proposed, therefore, we should ask ourselves how it will fit into the world. We should design the larger system that will include it. We should design the parts we don't build.

Taking a whole-systems approach, we can apply software with sensitivity, where it can do the most good and the least harm. Perhaps, instead of replacing an entire system with one massive software application, we might take a subtler approach. Which functions might best take advantage of the characteristics of digital systems? We could leave much of the system as it was, implementing smaller, simpler programs to replace only selected pieces of the system. We could save ourselves some grief.

This approach has other potential advantages. The nondigital portions of the system dwell in the real world, whose behavior is constrained by physical laws. Keeping much of the system nondigital may yield a more predictable system.

Likewise, this approach could minimize the number of interfaces between a digital system and its environment. Remember, each interface opens the door to environmental murphies: EMI, leafmeal, backhoes, tomato juice. The fewer interfaces there are, the fewer doors are available for the problems to enter.

It might be worth looking at the entire commercial air traffic situation in this light. In the past few decades, commercial air traffic has undergone all kinds of sweeping, rapid changes. Lots of new systems have been deployed, are about to be, or are being designed (in some cases, simultaneously). They are being debated in conferences and professional journals.

Cockpits are being intensively computerized. The pilot's job is changing, and there are lots of strong feelings on the subject. A new traffic alert and collision avoidance system—TCAS—is being implemented by the FAA to keep airplanes from midair collisions. It is a box that runs software and sits in the cockpit of commercial airliners, responding to the transponders of other aircraft in the vicinity. It is supposed to warn the pilot in case another airplane gets too close; it is also supposed to suggest a course of action. TCAS is a backup safety system; the eyes of pilots and air traffic controllers are supposed to serve this function as well.

Mode C transponders are on their way, too. Mode C transponders will enable air traffic controllers to transmit data—commands—directly to an airplane's digital flight control system. Bypassing those pesky pilots, one is tempted to add. Okay, I know that's extreme, but they do give the entire enterprise an air of controllers flying their model airplanes by remote control. Mode C transponders are a key component of the Advanced Automation System, the system that will integrate and automate air traffic control over the entire North American continent. Like it or not, the United States commercial air traffic system is due for lots more big changes—soon. It might be worth it to step back and look at the big picture.

Consider the system of airports and airlines and air traffic control and airplanes and pilots and mechanics and fuel suppliers and baggage handlers and reservation systems and ticket agents and travel agents and even passengers as one big system. What functions does it serve? Which are best to digitize? Where does integration serve us best? Which physical interfaces are inevitable? What is the proper role of the pilot? Of the air traffic controller? Where, in this whole system, can computers serve us best?

Now is also a good time to start asking these questions about our system of automobiles and roads. The automobile has been rapidly colonized by more and more software. It started in the mid-1980s, when the Audi 5000 became one of the first commercially available automobiles to incorporate a microprocessor. This represented a significant social and technological experiment, although manufacturers and the public alike seemed unaware of it at the time. It has since taken off in a big way. Sensors of various kinds are springing up in and around roads, and traffic control for automobiles seems to be headed in the digital direction, too. Do we want to do this? If so, how?

Taking a whole-systems approach requires us to analyze the role that digital technology is asked to play. It leads us to consider designs we might not otherwise have considered.

### 5. What Will It Require of Its Users and Operators?

People are part of any system—what role will they play in the one being proposed? Are they monitors, operators, or users? What is the best way to enhance that role?

People and computers have complementary strengths. People are good at recognizing patterns, understanding human language, taking into account circumstances external to the system, taking initiative. Computers are bad at these things.

Computers are good at attentively monitoring large numbers of unchanging details for *one* new datum. They are good at cranking flawlessly through large numbers of computations. People are bad at these things.

One other important difference exists. People have a stake in the outcome of the situation. They are motivated, and motivation is often useful. Computers, on the other hand, do not care about the outcome of the situation. They can be counted on to be dispassionate, or unflustered by high stakes. This can also be useful.

Systems can be designed to maximize the strengths of both people and computers. This principle sounds obvious, but it continues to be flouted. As McDonald's should now know, the most fault-tolerant and robust components of a system are usually the operators. It is expensive to withhold from them the authority to correct any errors they may perceive.

And it is inhumane to use people as passive monitors, and then require them to intervene suddenly when things go astray. We don't improve the situation when we turn airline pilots or nuclear power plant operators into scapegoats for bad system design.

### 6. Will It Require Extensive Security?

An expert in spreading information by computer is called a data communications expert. An expert in restricting that information is called a computer security expert. Who do you think is paid more?

Digital data flows like water, ever outward, to ever further memory banks. This general proclivity makes digital systems useful for communication. But requirements on communication systems can vary. The telephone system requires that nearly *all* information be passed, and with nearly complete fidelity. This is a tough requirement. Industrial and political security systems require that information be passed—up to a point. *No* information must escape beyond that point—it's the system's Hoover Dam. This is a tougher requirement. Fulfilling it is liable to cost nearly as much as the Hoover Dam.

Hordes of smart, marginally socialized young men[8] view industrial and governmental security measures as merely opportunities to test their skills. Ways to break into UNIX or DOS or other commonly used operating systems are widely known and discussed in the computer science community. Even supposedly secure systems such as military computers have been broken into.[9] Indeed, for $10 you could (maybe you still can) buy a videotape purporting to show the activities of some not-quite-grown-up young men in the Netherlands breaking into a U. S. Army computer that allegedly contained sensitive information.[10] (They hastened to point out that they stole or altered nothing. This is quite plausible, actually—these folks frequently do what they do "just for fun.") Break-ins are so common that increased penalties for such computer crimes have been proposed in the United States.[11] The truth is that picking electronic locks is just not as difficult as fashioning credible ones. Access is so much easier and cheaper than security that some people in the field have coined the phrase, "data wants to be free."

Take e-mail, for example. Electronic mail systems exist purely for the purpose of spreading information. E-mail is an easy, disinhibiting medium. Organizations that introduce e-mail soon discover that people use it freely and copiously.

Colonel Oliver North and National Security Advisor John Poindexter learned the hard way about the disinhibiting effects of e-mail. They used e-mail messages to authorize weapons sales to Iran and to use the profits to fund an undeclared and illegal war in Central America. These messages were copied along with the rest of their files when their computer system was backed up onto tape, a precaution all good system administrators regularly take to prevent loss of information in case the computer fails catastrophically. The Bush administration fought for the right to erase e-mail, contending that it amounts to no more than a lot of telephone messages.[12] Historians see it as more akin to memos; they, librarians, and public interest groups are fighting to preserve the e-mail under the Federal Records Act, which preserves such documents for historical study.

The truth is that some of those e-mail messages probably *are* telephone messages, while others are memos. Still others are letters, policy statements, scurrilous gossip, luncheon appointments, flirtations, meeting agenda, or announcements of office renovations. People say anything and everything over e-mail. It is as easy as typing, as intimate as talking, and handier than paper mail. The person you are talking to is absent—you see no smiles or grimaces, hear no sighs or chuckles or snorts of disdain. Your message is delivered as swiftly as a phone call, but unlike a phone call, the recipient is not required to read the message until it is convenient. Given the option, people will use e-mail.

If anyone ought to be able to restrict access to its information, it's the White House. And for the most part, they seem to—someone may have cracked into the White House e-mail system, but it doesn't seem to be a common occurrence. Yet the system administrator makes backups, just like everyone else. And the backup tapes are suddenly out there, over the dam, archived in the real world, exposed to the Federal Records Act. Oops. Whatever the courts decide, if the White House really wishes to prevent public access to its backup tapes, it will have an upstream swim.

Access, on the other hand, is cheap and easy. Useful information access systems can be built with merely the funding available to a university research project. For example, there's SeniorNet, a computer network in the United States allowing people fifty-five and over to join electronic discussion groups or send each other e-mail.[13] Now a nonprofit organization, the project has been an enormous success, attracting over 15,000 members in six years.

The attractions of on-line communication took the London Stock Exchange by surprise. Officials, bent on a major modernization, inaugurated an electronic trading system in 1986. They spent a fortune outfitting the trading floor with computer displays. Incidentally, they included modem lines, allowing traders with computers and modems to access the system from their offices.[14] Within a week, the expensive new trading floor was empty as traders discovered the sudden irrelevance of geography. Brokers became dispensable as traders conducted their business over the phone lines—over the computer network. The former London Stock Exchange trading floor now looks like a warehouse for expensive equipment.

The existence of computer networks changes politics irrevocably. For one thing, propaganda can really spread. At least one corporate employee has flooded a local network with thousands of copies of an evangelical Christmas message, and partisan causes have been espoused over international networks, too.[15]

The easy flow of information across international boundaries can support a resistance movement handily. During the death throes of the Soviet Union—the attempted coup against Gorbachev in August 1991—e-mail messages reached throughout the Soviet Union, describing the situation in Moscow as seen by Vadim Antonov, Polina Antonova, and their fellow programmers at the Demos Cooperative.[16] Through Helsinki, their messages reached the West. The coup plotters moved swiftly to control traditional mass media, but messages describing tanks in the streets and resistance demonstrations reached from Leningrad to Vladivostok, and from Menlo Park to Brisbane. In turn, the coup resistors received messages of Western news coverage, world support, and practical information about tank movements. They gained the emotional strength that springs from knowing that millions are watching and listening.

Television and radio broadcasts can be quelled by an attack on a central location. Computer networks are decentralized—distributed. Ultrareliable communication can be difficult, but political resistance has different requirements, and computer networks are perfect for it. One attack on a network does not knock out communication. A network is naturally robust; it can withstand many attacks and still function. Some information can always get through, and even a trickle will grow, in the end, to a river. On these terms, nothing is more fault-tolerant than a computer network. Having them, the world will never be the same.

## 7. Will There Be a Backup?

The first thing you learn when you start to use a computer is: how to make a backup copy of your work. It's not that the computer is going to crash any second. *But it might.* After all, the system is unreliable, so you protect yourself from its worst consequences.

In the same vein, database developers spend an enormous proportion of their energies creating a database that can flawlessly revert to a previous view of the world, just in case something goes wrong in the middle of modifying some data, in that twilight time between starting a transaction and finishing it. A corporation simply can't afford to let the system get muddled. It cannot afford to lose all that data.

The same principle applies to deploying new systems. It's foolish to rely completely on a brand new system. When Maritime Tel & Tel assured the Liberal Party of Nova Scotia that nothing could possibly go wrong with their vote-by-phone scheme, why did the party believe them? What possessed the telephone company to make such an assurance, anyway? Why not keep the usual voting system around as a backup, at least the first time?

We would do well to back up new systems—at least at first. How can a corporation know a new management information system is reporting accurately? Have they instituted any form of reality check? Are the answers they are getting even close to the truth? The system has no common sense, but the managers had better. Inaccurate information risks bankruptcy.[17]

We can approach the application of digital technology like mountain climbers—never making a move without considering what might go wrong and what we could do about it. When we introduce a new system, we should keep a copy of the old, tried-and-true system around for a while, even if it requires ancient hardware or makes inefficient use of people. If a system is critical, another system should be available to back it up when it fails. We don't always have to learn the hard way.

## TWO MODEST PROPOSALS

Given the number and variety of digital systems people are proposing, it seems superfluous to suggest any others. But you knew it was bound to happen. It seems to me that we have neglected two areas that are ideal for the application of digital technology. In both education and legislation, the peculiar characteristics of digital systems would help, not hinder.

### The Educational Software Foundation

Certain characteristics of software make it excellent for instruction: it is patient, consistent, and can be programmed to be flexible and responsive. It is blind to gender, race, and other irrelevancies. And children love playing with computers—at least, those children lucky enough to have the chance.

Industry knows the advantages of computerized instruction. "Two decades of research show that computer-based instruction produces at least 30 percent more learning in 40 percent less time at 30 percent less cost than traditional classroom teaching," says a *Wall Street Journal* article on the subject.[18] An accurate but frustrating analysis can be found in a book entitled *Software Shock*.[19] "Today's use of computers in education barely scratches the surface of their potential," rightly say the authors, who could be doing something about it. Yet they unquestioningly accept the *status quo:* that education will continue to glean what crumbs it can from industry.

It's a shame. Think what use education could make of virtual reality, for example. Walk children through a molecule and watch a catalyst at work. Float down the bloodstream on a raft. Watch tectonic movement create underwater volcanoes, stitching the Hawaiian islands across the Pacific. See the phases of the moon change from a vantage point beyond Earth's orbit. Fingerpaint on air. Even the difficult abstractions of arithmetic and mathematics could be made more concrete. Educational software has amazing potential, yet there has been no wild rush to develop any. I can only conclude it's because few see any opportunity to make money with such applications. That's too bad. The resources we dedicate to children are paltry.

The market is a good mechanism, but nothing's perfect. Perhaps we need a foundation to develop educational software. Software designers and developers could work with educators and students, creating applications to supplement the teacher's efforts and enrich education in ways we cannot yet envision. I know many talented and creative software professionals who have wrestled with their roles developing wasteful or destructive systems. I know many who would be overjoyed to sign up for such creative, constructive, and socially useful work. Teachers need help with overflowing classrooms. Students need patient, creative instruction. Let's provide them.

### Congress On-line

During the 1980s, U. S. lawmakers proved willing to give away future tax money—lots of it—in return for the campaign contributions of lob-

byists.[20] This is a fundamentally political, human problem whose ultimate solution lies beyond technology's reach. Technology can, however,
make a contribution.

Lawmakers are all concentrated in Washington, D. C., where it is easy
for lobbyists to reach them. They do not live among their constituents.
A capital city used to be necessary for the seat of government, but no
longer: no less an authority than Senator Robert Byrd has said so himself. He has quite a record locating lucrative federal complexes in his
home state of West Virginia. The *New York Times News Service* describes
his argument: "Modern-day communications and transportation systems,
Byrd contends, make it feasible to put federal complexes anywhere."[21] I
agree. So let's move him. Washington, D. C., has outlived its usefulness
in American political life. Congress can conduct its business nearly as
easily and much more efficiently using a computerized bulletin board.

If our representatives lived among us, lobbyists would find their jobs
not impossible, but more arduous. They would have to make fifty trips
or more to visit all Congressional representatives; even a subcommittee
might require at least half a dozen. It might slow lobbyists down. It
would certainly make the lobbying process more visible to the representatives' neighbors—us. Congressional representatives would find living at home more economical, too. They would no longer need to be
paid to maintain two households.

It is time for our legislators to become citizens of this country again,
instead of denizens of some remote, privileged land where they never
have to pay the bills. Let them forsake the fern bar for the local diner.
Let them send their children to local schools. Let them park at downtown parking meters and walk on local streets just like everybody else.

Yes, it's hard to restrict access to on-line information. But how much
security is really necessary for an on-line system to transact the business
of Congress? Yes, clever and undisciplined souls could break into the system. The knowledge that no communication was really, truly confiden-
tial might act as a brake on some of the more larcenous or unethical
Congressional instincts. Rambunctious adolescents could be doing us a
favor. Why shouldn't we, the people, be privileged to read the transactions of our lawmakers, anyway?

For those items on the Congressional agenda that are genuine national
security issues, taxpayers could buy airline tickets. The representatives
concerned could meet in person just as securely as they do now. If they
flew economy class and stayed at modest motels, they might not be
eager to do so any more than necessary.

Implementing this proposal would change the entire experience of
serving in Congress. It might also change the kind of people who seek

the job. More of them might be people who see public life as an opportunity for service instead of plunder.

## ONE FINAL HOPE

Digital technology is a useful tool, but the hammer doesn't build the house by itself. It must be wielded with purpose and judgment. Digital technology is a fascinating tool, but fascination is not an end in itself. We can fall prey to foolish fascinations.

It takes a clever question to turn data into information, but it takes intelligence to use the result. Intelligence can create systems of enormous complexity, but it takes wisdom to determine which ones are worth the trouble.

I'm sitting at my desk now, thinking about sitting in an airplane, looking out the window at the tops of fluffy white clouds. Commercial air travel has changed a lot about life in the twentieth century. I expect computers and software will change even more about life in the twenty-first. Digital technology can enhance our lives enormously, or it can make them living hell. We should be choosing our systems with our eyes open.

## AND ONLY TWENTY-ONE NOTES

1 "Lotus—new program spurs fears privacy could be undermined." *The Wall Street Journal,* Nov. 13, 1990, p. B1, and follow-up article on Jan. 23, 1991. Also see *comp.risks,* 10:61–63, 68, 74, 79–81, covering the period from Nov. 16, 1990 to Jan. 28, 1991; 11:86, June 11, 1991; and 12:12, Aug. 12, 1991. The participation of folks on Internet was crucial to defeating the release of Lotus marketplace. This worked out well, but we run another risk when we conduct business this way—that of disenfranchising people without access to Internet.

2 For a thought-provoking discussion of a joint GM-Japanese venture that invested heavily in workers with excellent results, see "Return of the stopwatch." *The Economist,* Jan. 23, 1993, p. 69.

3 Weizenbaum, Joseph. *Computer Power and Human Reason: From Judgment to Calculation.* San Francisco: W. H. Freeman & Co. 1976, pp. 6–7.

4 Gleick, James E. "Chasing Bugs in the Electronic Village." *New York Times Magazine,* June 14, 1992, pp. 38–42.

5 Twice a day. Now you know.

6 Adam, John A., and Paul Wallich. "SDI: The Grand Experiment. Mind-Boggling Complexity." IEEE *Spectrum,* Sept. 1985, pp. 36–46. The calculations are from a sidebar on p. 45 entitled "A Strategist's Back-of-the-Envelope," from Stephen Rockwood, "Technical Issues for Strategic Defense Initiative," *International Peace Research Institute Conference,* Stockholm, Sweden, July 5–7, 1985. The entire September, 1985 issue of the IEEE *Spectrum* is devoted to the Strategic Defense Initiative. It is fascinating reading for those interested in the topic.

7 Begley, Sharon, and Daniel Glick. "A Safety Net Full of Holes." *Newsweek,* March 23, 1992, pp. 56–9.

8 No, this is not sexist. Few women have ever engaged in these activities. Why? Who knows?

9 For example, see Stoll, Clifford. *The Cuckoo's Egg: Tracking a Spy Through the Maze of Computer Espionage.* New York: Doubleday, 1989.

10 "The Hacker Video." *2600: The Hacker Quarterly,* 8:3, Autumn 1991, pp. 14–17.

11 *comp.risks,* 14:32, Feb. 5, 1993.

12 Miller, Michael W. "Historians Crusade to Preserve 'E-Mail.'" *The Wall Street Journal,* March 31, 1992, p. B1.

13 Beck, Melinda, and Nadine Joseph. "Never Too Old to Go On Line." *Newsweek,* June 15, 1992, p. 64.

14 "Magnetic Attractions," pp. 5–9, and "Capitals of capital?," pp. 25–26, of the "Survey on Financial Centres" in *The Economist,* June 27, 1992. The story is also mentioned in "The World at Your Fingertips," Episode 5 of *The Machine That Changed the World,* aired on PBS on May 4, 1992.

15 For a view of the darker side of this phenomenon, see Goodman, S.E. "Inside Risks: Political Activity and International Computer Networks." *Communications of the ACM,* 35:2, Feb. 1992, p. 174.

16 Press, Larry. "Wide-Area Collaboration" and "Relcom During the Coup." *Communications of the ACM,* 34:12, Dec. 1991, pp. 21–24. This shows the most hopeful side of this phenomenon.

17 Govindan, Marshall, and John Picard. *Manifesto on Information Systems Control and Management: A New World Order.* New York: McGraw-Hill, 1990.

18 Perelman, Lewis J. "Luddite Schools Wage a Wasteful War." *The Wall Street Journal,* Sept. 10, 1990, p. A14.

19 Pressman, Roger S., and S. Russell Herron. *Software Shock: The Danger and the Opportunity.* New York: Dorset House, 1991. See pp. 43–50. The quote is from p. 44.

20 Greider, William. *Who Will Tell the People.* New York: Simon and Schuster, 1992.

21 Ayres, B. Drummond, Jr. "West Virginia's Byrd: king of 'pork.'" *Oregonian,* Sept. 8, 1991, p. A12.

# GLOSSARY

**accident**
An event that causes harm, injury, or damage. Compare *failure, hazard, risk.*

**application**
A specific use of software to solve a problem or meet a need, such as a word-processing application or a financial report-generating application. Application software is usually contrasted with system software, the software that comprises the operating system and makes the computer minimally usable. See *operating system, processor.*

**arithmetic logic unit**
The part of the processor that manipulates binary values (zeroes and ones) according to the rules of arithmetic and Boolean logic. The den of the beast itself. See *processor.*

**ASCII**
An acronym (pronounced "ask'-ee") for the American Standard Code for Information Interchange. ASCII assigns a numeric code to each key on a computer keyboard. These codes are the way most computers interpret keyboard characters.

**batch**
A mode of computer operation. The user types a command to start the execution of a program and then awaits results, which may come in seconds, minutes, hours, or even days. Until the program has finished execution, the user cannot intervene nor modify anything. Second thoughts are useless. Batch programs can be useful, but they can also be frustrating and wasteful of paper. Compare *interactive, real time.*

**beta site**
An organization used to test software that is deemed almost ready to release to real users. Beta sites are supposed to consist of people whose use of the software is either typical, or more rigorous than usual. These people use the beta software and find bugs that the quality assurance team has so far missed. The bugs are then supposed to be fixed before the software is released to customers. See *beta software, bug, testing.*

**211**

**beta software**   Software that is fully functional (or nearly so) and has been tested, but is suspected of still harboring unexpected and undesirable behavior. See *beta site, testing*.

**boot**   To turn on a computer or start a processor. This is seldom done for the first time, but often done repeatedly, as a last resort to clear an error out of the system—hence the more common term *reboot*. The term *boot* comes from the expression "to lift oneself by one's bootstraps," an apt picture of a processor that must start executing its instructions to start executing.

**bug**   Behavior on the part of a computer program that is contrary to what a user reasonably requires or expects. Yes, this definition is vague. The situation can be vague, too. Well-intentioned people can argue whether a specific behavior is a bug or not. Hence the humorous definition of *feature:* a bug redefined by Marketing. See *maintenance*.

**comment**   A remark (in a human language) added to the source code of a program to help the programmer remember why she or he wrote this piece of the program, or to help another programmer figure out later how it works. The remark is prefaced by special characters that tell the compiler to ignore it. See *compiler, source code*.

**compiler**   A special program that takes as input the source code that the programmer writes, and produces as output an executable file that the processor can execute. See *executable file, processor, source code*.

**computer**   A multipurpose machine including a processor (or more than one) and usually a keyboard or other device for accepting input from people, and a display or other device for producing output. See *input device, output device, processor*.

**concurrency**   A characteristic of a system in which more than one thread can be executing at the same time. See *parallel processing, thread of execution*.

**continuity**   A property of a system such that small changes to inputs produce correspondingly small changes to outputs. Transforming inputs into outputs is a mathematical function. A graph of the function performed by a continuous system can be represented by an unbroken line.

data
Records of items, events, or transactions stored in a computer, especially in a database. See *database.* Compare *information.*

database
A repository of data, usually a great deal of data on many unique but similar subjects, such as hospital patients or securities transactions. The database is structured in a specific manner so that one can obtain information from it. For example, all hospital patient records will include places for such specific data as the patient's name, diagnosis, treatment, cost of treatment, name of insurer and insurance policy number. One can therefore ask a question about all patients with a specific diagnosis, for instance. See *information.*

debugging
An attempt by programmers to remove undesired and unexpected behavior from a program. Debugging consists of discovering the undesirable behavior during testing or use, finding the cause of the behavior, modifying the source code so that the undesirable behavior is eliminated, and then retesting to ascertain that the undesirable behavior is really gone, and that no new undesirable behavior has appeared in its place. It is not easy.

design
The stage of developing software in which (ideally) experienced and talented programmers determine the most pertinent model of the world, the appropriate structure of the software and, incidentally, the best way to divide up the work of writing it.

determinism
A characteristic of a system such that the same inputs and initial state always results in the same outputs. A deterministic system is predictable.

digital system
A system that uses some scheme to represent binary values: on and off, ones and zeroes, high and low voltages, and manipulates them with Boolean logic. In practice, this usually means a system that uses software and a processor. See *software, processor.*

| | |
|---|---|
| distributed system | A system whose components are not all within one physical box or at one physical location. |
| e-mail | Electronic mail, a communication mechanism in which the sender types a message at a computer keyboard, the message is sent to the receiver (usually as fast as a phone call would be), and the receiver reads the message at leisure on a computer display. |
| embedded system | A system that contains a processor embedded within a machine. A program is written for the system and downloaded into the processor during manufacture. It is pretty much inaccessible thereafter. The software that runs a microwave oven or antilock brakes is embedded. |
| environment | The world outside the system, in which the system resides. Aspects of the environment such as temperature, humidity, or vibration must be considered when designing the system. |
| execute | To perform instructions, as by a computer processor. See *processor*. |
| executable file | The output of a compiler. The executable file is binary, consisting of ones and zeroes incomprehensible to humans, but that the processor can execute. See *compiler, processor*. |
| expert system | A system that attempts to incorporate the knowledge of an expert in a particular field, in order to help another person make a decision or otherwise function knowledgeably in that field. The term comes from artificial intelligence work. |
| failure | An inability of some part of the system to perform its intended function. Compare *accident, hazard, risk*. |
| fault-tolerant | A characteristic of a system that can accept unexpected input, or the failure of one of its components, without itself failing. |
| formal methods | Methods that use mathematics and formal logic to determine whether a program functions correctly. See *quality assurance, testing*. |
| hazard | A condition that can cause an accident, if other events also occur. See *accident*. Compare *failure, risk*. |

| | |
|---|---|
| hexadecimal number | A number in the base 16 numbering system. The digits 0 through 9 represent the same numbers as in the familiar base 10 system. Ten is represented with the letter 'A,' 11 with 'B,' and so on through 15 ('F'). The digits 10 represent the number 16: a zero in the ones column and a one in the sixteens column. |
| implementation | The stage of developing software in which programmers write the source code. See *source code.* |
| information | The result of performing some operation on data. For example, a hospital may use its database of patient records to determine the incidence of specific cancer diagnoses this year, the previous year, and the year before that. The list of these diagnoses is data. It can then compare these numbers to each other to determine if the incidence of the condition is increasing or decreasing, thus obtaining information. Compare *data.* See *database.* |
| input | Something, such as a series of keystrokes, that is accepted by a program and upon which some operation is performed. Compare *output.* |
| input device | A physical device used to create input, such as a keyboard or a mouse. Specialized systems may include such devices as a microphone or a magnetic card reader. See *input, mouse.* Compare *output device.* |
| integrated circuit | A small miracle. The integrated circuit (chip) replaces miles of wires hooked together in an intricate, messy, error-prone tangle with precise patterns of conductive paths etched into a layer of nonconductive material. They can be printed in newspaper quantities before you could reproduce your tangle correctly even once. The chip makes It all possible. |
| integrated system | A system that incorporates more than one digital device or system and attempts to tie them together in such a way that the integrated system is more useful than each device or system would be individually. For example, a house controller could integrate a thermostat, alarm clock, and coffeemaker to turn up the heat and start the coffee just before it woke you. |

| | |
|---|---|
| interactive | A system that responds to a user or operator either in real time or with such small delays that the user or operator feels that the system is responding in real time. Examples of interactive programs include most software for personal computers, as well as such applications as the software that runs on automated teller machines. See *real time.* Compare *batch.* |
| interface | A piece of a system that connects two different components, or that connects a component with the environment or a user. An interface often passes the output of one side of the connection to become the input of the other side. See *input, output, system.* |
| maintenance | That stage of developing software that occurs after it has been released to its users. Users invariably find bugs and sometimes request new features. Maintenance involves fixing the bugs, or trying to, and adding the features, when possible. See *bug.* |
| memory | The part of the processor that stores data or instructions. Think of it as many tiny cells, each cupping its allotted one or zero. Thus, the processor holds strings of characters—the words you type as you write your letter—cradling each ASCII code in the mold poured by your word processing application. See *application, ASCII, processor.* |
| microprocessor | A variant of the term "processor" that emphasizes how small it is. We are still breathless about this, I guess. See *processor.* |
| microsecond | One-millionth of a second, a unit of time meaningful to those who work with process-control software. See *process-control software.* |
| mission-critical | Software whose failure can cause the failure of the mission. Telephone-switching software is critical to the mission of a telephone company, funds-transfer software is critical to the mission of a bank, corporate information systems software is critical to the mission of making a profit. Compare *safety-critical.* |
| model | An abstraction of certain aspects of the world deemed pertinent to a specific application. See *simulation.* |

modem

A device that allows one computer to communicate with another using a telephone line. With a modem, a person with a personal computer at home can connect to the computer at the office, participate in professional discourse, make lunch dates, be part of an office culture (sort of), and burn no gasoline to do so. Also with a modem, a frisky teenager can trespass.

monitor

A person whose function is to watch over a system, intervening only when something goes wrong. Compare *operator, user*. (This term is sometimes also used to mean "computer display," but, to avoid confusion, not in this book.)

mouse

An input device for a computer that allows a user to point to an item of interest. It doesn't look much like a mouse, but it does have a tail. It squeaks if it needs oiling. Italians call it a "mole," for some reason. See *input device*.

nanosecond

One-billionth of a second, a unit of time meaningful to processors and those who work with them. See *processor*.

natural language

What those in the technical community call languages such as English or Chinese or sign language, which children learn to use naturally, without years of schooling. Instead of restricted codes such as programming languages, natural languages are open systems that constantly produce novel forms according to rules understood by native speakers. These rules, which children can internalize, are subtle, complex, and fiendishly difficult to verbalize to others, much less completely describe to a computer. Children can master the creative outpouring of natural language, but we have not yet been able to tell a computer how. It is hard to avoid the conclusion that children have special wiring. By comparison, a programming language is a dry, unsubtle stick. Compare *programming language*.

operating system

Software that mediates between the processor, the input and output devices, and the application programs. It is the underlying foundation required for the computer to wake up, find its disk, deal with files, obey the keyboard, and run application programs. See *application, processor.*

**operator**
A person who uses a system and has some responsibility to ensure that it functions correctly. Operators have more actions available to them than users, and are often employed to function in that role; for example, subway operators, telephone operators, bank employees as operators of automated teller machines. Compare *monitor, user.*

**output**
The product of a program or a system, the result of performing some operation on the input—words on the display, for example. Compare *input.*

**output device**
A physical device used to display the output of software, such as a printer or a computer display. Specialized systems may include such devices as a film recorder or a machine that encodes information on magnetic card strips. See *output.* Compare *input device.*

**parallel processing**
Using more than one processor at a time in order to accomplish a computationally intensive task faster than one processor could accomplish it.

**patch**
An awkward attempt to fix a bug; a hasty, makeshift accommodation allowing users to avoid the bug. Patches are sometimes temporary fixes that allow users access to the system until the problem can be solved properly. They are sometimes more permanent arrangements by someone who does not understand the system or its misbehavior. Sometimes the patch perpetrator has no clue *why* the patch works; he or she got the system into a state in which the unwanted behavior does not occur, but has no idea how. Patches feel as tentative as they sound. See *bug.*

**pixel**
A word formed from the phrase *picture element*—the dots that make up a computer display or printout. A pixel is the smallest piece of the display or printout that a programmer can manipulate.

**port**
The process of adapting a program written for one computer or processor so that it can execute on another computer or processor. See *execute, processor.*

| | |
|---|---|
| **problem domain** | The world of the user or the customer, the universe of entities and processes that will concern the program. |
| **process-control software** | Software to control a physical process, such as a chemical reaction in a refinery or the combustion occurring within an automobile engine. Physical processes occur at rates dictated by the laws of physics—they cannot be slowed or hastened. Process-control software must therefore respond within a guaranteed minimum time period, no matter what; it usually cannot afford even small delays. The phrase "real time" captures the inference that this is a tough requirement. See *real time*. Compare *batch, interactive*. |
| **processor** | The most complex part of a computer, a hardware component that performs the computations we mean when we say that software executes an instruction. Memory stores both data and instructions. When they are needed, they are fetched and placed in registers. The arithmetic logic unit (ALU) performs computations on the values in the registers and replaces them with the results. The results are then returned to memory. |
| | If you are running an application, the application is providing the next instruction, determining what computations are performed and what values are stored. If no application is running, the operating system plays this role. See *application, operating system*. |
| **programming language** | Any of many different systems for specifying what a program is to do. *Programming language* is, unfortunately, a misnomer—they are codes, not languages. A programming language consists of a finite set of key words and syntax rules that the compiler knows how to translate into something the processor can execute. This finite set of commands includes ways to build other commands. |
| | There are many different programming languages. In theory, they are all functionally equivalent; in practice, programmers have strong preferences for some over others. Programming languages can be custom- |

ized for particular kinds of tasks, such as robotics or business applications or delighting the programmer. Compare *natural language*.

**prototype**  A fully or partly functional model of the final system implemented to teach the developers more about the problem and the users more about the solution. A prototype is not a product. It may not be testable or maintainable, it may perform too slowly, or it may not be sufficiently robust.

**quality assurance**  The stage of software development in which an organization tests the software to verify that it functions as required, or to determine how it departs from its requirements so that it can be corrected. Depending upon the organization and the software, quality assurance may include activities in addition to testing, such as formal methods for verifying program correctness. See *testing, formal methods*.

**query language**  A code that allows users to ask for information from a database. See *data, database, information*.

**read-only**  A property, usually said of memory, in which values can be accessed (read) but not modified (written). Read-only memory (ROM) is useful for embedded processors running programs that must not be altered, such as the software running on an automotive engine controller. See *embedded system, memory, processor*.

**real time**  A mode of computer operation in which the software responds to events within a guaranteed minimum time period, no matter what. This is not easy. See *interactive, process control software*. Compare *batch*.

**reboot**  See *boot*.

**redundancy**  A strategy to achieve fault-tolerance and guard against system failure by including spare components. Then, if a component fails, the redundant component—the spare—can take over, thus ensuring that the system as a whole does not fail. See *fault-tolerant*.

**register**  The part of the processor that stores a binary number required for the present computation. See *processor*.

| | |
|---|---|
| **requirements** | How the system is expected to behave, under what circumstances and constraints, and with what resources, according to the users or customers. |
| **risk** | The probability of a failure, combined with its consequences. See *failure*. Compare *accident, hazard*. |
| **safety-critical** | Software whose failure can cause injuries or deaths, or damage the life-sustaining qualities of the earth. Compare *mission-critical*. |
| **script** | Common sense and background knowledge that enable you to behave appropriately in a specific situation. A script allows you to make assumptions, unfazed by missing or unclear information. The term comes from the artificial intelligence field. |
| **simulation** | An attempt to solve a problem using a model, taking into account what you hope are all relevant parameters and applying what you hope are rules approximating the way the world behaves. The results are accurate to the extent that you have modeled the world accurately. See *model*. |
| **software** | The result of applying human intelligence and ingenuity, using programming languages and other tools, to induce a computer or processor to behave in a manner that is useful to someone. See *programming language, processor*. |
| **source code** | Lines of computer instructions in a programming language, written by a programmer. It can be read and understood (with some difficulty) by those with programming skills. The compiler transforms it into a file the processor can execute, which cannot be read by anyone. See *compiler, executable file, programming language*. |
| **specification (spec)** | A document (usually quite long) that specifies the required behavior of a system, and the circumstances under which it is required to behave in that manner. A custom more honored in the breach, the spec captures the requirements specified by the customers. It can be used as a guide during system design, implementation, and testing. |

**spiral model**   An idealized model of the software development process in which it is assumed that the developers will revisit previous stages as they gain new understanding from later stages. Compare *waterfall model.*

**spreadsheet**   A computer file that represents an executable model of an accountant's spreadsheet.

**system**   A set of systems that interact to provide a function or service. This definition is recursive because systems are infinitely hierarchical—all systems are made up of components which, when viewed closely, are systems in their own right. It is a characteristic of the real world that the series never ends. Everything is complex when you look closely enough; no fundamental building blocks exist. The paradox of digital systems is simply this: such fractal wealth of detail can never be faithfully represented in a system that requires a finite number of ones and zeroes, a finite resolution below which all detail ends. A system is a system of systems. See *system.*

**testing**   A method of determining whether a program functions correctly by running it with particular inputs to see whether it produces the correct outputs in each case. The inputs may be representative of real use, or they may be borderline cases to ensure that the program does not fail if something unexpected occurs.

**thread of execution**   The specific sequence of instructions that a program executes in response to specific inputs. For the same program, different inputs may produce different threads of execution.

**user**   A person who uses a system, with or without any special responsibilities for ensuring its correct functioning. Users are often customers; for example, subway users, telephone users, bank customers as users of automated teller machines. Compare *monitor, operator.*

**user interface**   The portion of the system that presents information to the user and accepts input from the user—the console, the buttons, or what you see on the display. Not the machinery clanking in the basement.

**voting**       A method by which redundant processors in a system determine whether any has experienced a failure, and if so, which. See *redundancy*.

**waterfall model**  An idealized model of the software development process that assumes that the developers progress in order from defining the requirements, to writing the specification, to designing the system, to implementing it, to testing it, and finally to maintaining it. Compare *spiral model*.

# BIBLIOGRAPHY

## ADVENTURE STORIES

Carroll, Paul B. "Painful Birth: Creating New Software Was Agonizing Task for Mitch Kapor Firm." *The Wall Street Journal*, May 11, 1990, pp. A1, A5.

Ceruzzi, Paul. *Beyond the Limits: Flight Enters the Computer Age*. Cambridge, MA: MIT Press, 1989.

Green, Michael. *Zen & the Art of the Macintosh*. Philadelphia, PA: Running Press, 1986.

Kidder, Tracy. *The Soul of a New Machine*. New York: Avon, 1981.

Murray, Charles, and Catherine Bly Cox. *Apollo: The Race to the Moon*. New York: Simon and Schuster, 1989.

PBS. *The Machine That Changed the World*, Public television series:
- "Giant Brains" (Original U.S. broadcast April 6, 1992)
- "Inventing the Future" (Original U.S. broadcast April 13, 1992)
- "The Paperback Computer" (Original U.S. broadcast April 20, 1992)
- "The Thinking Machine" (Original U.S. broadcast April 27, 1992)
- "The World at Your Fingertips" (Original U.S. broadcast May 4, 1992)

Stoll, Clifford. *The Cuckoo's Egg: Tracking a Spy Through the Maze of Computer Espionage*. New York: Doubleday, 1989.

## DESIGN AND PUBLIC POLICY

Caplan, Ralph. *By Design*. New York: St. Martin's Press, 1982.

Dugger, Ronnie. "Annals of Democracy: Counting Votes." *New Yorker*, Nov. 7, 1988, pp. 40ff.

Ferrell, J. E. "The Big Fix." *Los Angeles Times Magazine*, April 14, 1991, pp. 14, 16, 18, 38–40.

Gleick, James. "Chasing Bugs in the Electronic Village." *New York Times Magazine*, June 14, 1992, pp. 38–42.

Govindan, Marshall, and John Picard. *Manifesto on Information Systems Control and Management: A New World Order*. New York: McGraw-Hill, 1990.

Jacky, Jonathan. "Programmed for Disaster: Software Errors That Imperil Lives." *The Sciences*, Sept./Oct. 1989, pp. 22ff.

Jacky, Jonathan. "The Star Wars Defense Won't Compute." *Atlantic Monthly*, June 1985, pp. 18–30.

Leveson, Nancy G., and Clark S. Turner. "An Investigation of the Therac-25 Accidents." Univ. of Washington Technical Report #92-11-05 (also UCI TR #92-108), Nov., 1992.

Mander, Jerry. *Four Arguments for the Elimination of Television*. New York: Morrow, 1978.

Norman, Donald. *The Design of Everyday Things* (a previous edition was titled *The Psychology of Everyday Things*). New York: Doubleday, 1988.

Norman, Donald. *Turn Signals Are the Facial Expressions of Automobiles*. Reading, MA: Addison-Wesley, 1992.

Parnas, David L. "SDI: A Violation of Professional Responsibility." *Abacus*, 4:2, Winter 1987, pp. 46–52.

Paté-Cornell, M. Elisabeth. "Organizational Aspects of Engineering System Safety: The Case of Offshore Platforms." *Science*, Nov. 30, 1991, pp. 1210–1217.

Perrow, Charles. *Normal Accidents: Living With High-risk Technologies*. New York: Basic Books, 1984.

Petroski, Henry. *To Engineer is Human: The Role of Failure in Successful Design*. New York: St. Martin's Press, 1985.

Postman, Neil. *Technopoly: The Surrender of Culture to Technology*. New York: Alfred A. Knopf, 1992.

Taylor, Ronald B. "Street Smart: Testing High Tech on the Santa Monica Freeway." *Los Angeles Times Magazine*, April 14, 1991, pp. 16, 38.

Tuttle, Jim. *All About You*, television broadcast by Oregon Public Broadcasting on Oct. 2, 1991.

## HUMOR

Augustine, Norman R. *Augustine's Laws*. New York: Penguin Books, 1986.

Jennings, Karla. *The Devouring Fungus: Tales of the Computer Age*. New York: W. W. Norton and Co., 1990.

Raymond, Eric. *The New Hacker's Dictionary*. Cambridge, MA: MIT Press, 1991.

Sheldon, Kenneth M. "Moby Dick 2.1." *Byte*, July 1989, p. 344.

## TECHNICAL BACKGROUND FOR NONTECHNICAL READERS

Bylinsky, Gene. "Help Wanted: 50,000 Programmers." *Fortune*, March 1967, pp. 141ff.

Huff, Darrell. *How to Lie With Statistics*. New York: W. W. Norton and Co., 1954.

Penzias, Arno. *Ideas and Information: Managing in a High Tech World*. New York: W. W. Norton and Co., 1989.

Shore, John. *The Sachertorte Algorithm and Other Antidotes to Computer Anxiety.* New York: Penguin, 1985.

Weizenbaum, Joseph. *Computer Power and Human Reason: From Judgment to Calculation.* San Francisco: W. H. Freeman & Co., 1976.

## IMPORTANT AND ACCESSIBLE TECHNICAL MATERIAL

Borning, Alan. "Computer System Reliability and Nuclear War." *Communications of the ACM,* 30:2, Feb. 1987, pp. 112–131.

Brooks, Frederick P. *The Mythical Man-Month.* Reading, MA: Addison-Wesley, 1978.

Brooks, Frederick P. "No Silver Bullet: Essence and Accidents of Software Engineering." IEEE *Computer,* April 1987, pp. 10–19.

IEEE *Computer,* February 1987, on the Advanced Automation System.

DeMillo, Lipton, and Perlis, "Proof as a Social Process." *Communications of the ACM,* 22:5, May 1979, pp. 271–79.

Denning, Peter J., ed. *Computers Under Attack: Intruders, Worms, and Viruses.* Reading, MA: Addison-Wesley, 1990.

Dijkstra, Edsger W. "On the Cruelty of Really Teaching Computer Science" (and the ensuing discussion among seven leading computer science professionals), *Communications of the ACM,* 32:12, Dec., 1989, pp. 1398–1414.

Dunlop, Charles, and Robert Kling, eds. *Computerization and Controversy.* Boston, MA: Academic Press, 1991.

Forester, Tom, and Perry Morrison. *Computer Ethics: Cautionary Tales and Ethical Dilemmas in Computing.* Cambridge, MA: MIT Press, 1990.

Garman, John R. "The 'Bug' Heard 'Round the World." ACM SIGSOFT *Software Engineering Notes,* 6:5, October, 1981, pp. 3–10.

Leveson, Nancy G. "Software Safety: What, Why, and How." *Computing Surveys,* 18:2, June 1986, pp. 125–163.

Littlewood, Bev, and Lorenzo Strigini. "The Risks of Software." *Scientific American,* Nov. 1992, pp. 62–75.

Neumann, Peter G. "Inside Risks." A regular column featured at the back of *Communications of the ACM.*

Neumann, Peter G., moderator: *Forum on Risks to the Public in Computers and Related Systems.* Available through Internet as the *comp.risks* newsgroup.

Parnas, David L. "Software Aspects of Strategic Defense Systems." *American Scientist,* 73:5, Sept./Oct. 1985, pp. 432–40. Reprinted by permission in *Communications of the ACM,* 28:12, Dec. 1985, pp. 1326–35.

Peterson, Ivars. "Finding Fault: The formidable task of eradicating software bugs." *Science News,* vol. 139, Feb. 16, 1991, pp. 104–106.

Samuelson, Pamela. "Digital Media and the Law." *Communications of the ACM,* 34:10, Oct., 1991, pp. 23–28.

IEEE *Spectrum,* June 1989, on engineering large, complex systems.

IEEE *Spectrum,* Sept. 1985, on SDI.

Stix, Gary. "Along for the Ride?" *Scientific American,* July 1991, pp. 94–106.

Weinberg, Gerald. *The Psychology of Computer Programming.* New York: Van Nostrand Reinhold, 1971.

Wiener, Lauren. "A Trip Report on SIGSOFT '91." ACM SIGSOFT *Software Engineering Notes,* 17:2, April 1992, pp. 23–38.

Yourdon, Edward, ed. *Classics in Software Engineering.* New York: Yourdon Press, 1979. See especially Dijkstra, Edsger W. "Programming Considered as a Human Activity."

# Epilogue to the Paperback Edition

This book has tried to explain why it would be wise to expect less from software. I sent the manuscript off about a year and a half ago, but the story has continued without me.

Some users are growing more skeptical about software—my accountant, for example. He sends his clients a newsletter every couple of months. Usually it's full of tax tips, but once he warned us to avoid the .0 version of any software application. Wait for the .1 version that includes bug fixes, he advised. Well, okay, it's not a bad rule of thumb, I guess.

But versioning isn't everything. My accountant seems unaware of the perils faced by his colleagues who used (a presumably mature version of) TurboTax for the 1993 tax season. The software had a bug that prevented them from processing refund-anticipation loans promptly, and people got pretty steamed about it. A mob threw a bottle through one accountant's office window; another was faced with a .357 Magnum; a third received bomb threats.[1] Tax preparation is less boring with software.

### A Single Line of Code

Even when you're careful about it, designing and deploying a new version can cause its measure of mayhem. Chemical Bank, for example, wanted to upgrade the software for its ATMs. It chose to do so in stages, which sounds as if it might be a sensible, carefully chosen strategy. At one stage, engineers placed some code into the system that was not supposed to execute until other code was modified at a later stage.

The single line of code was supposed, according to a senior vice president of the bank, to remain "dormant" for the time being. And the engineers were seemingly confident that, in the present state of the system, the thread of execution would never snake its way over to that code. But they were only guessing, and they guessed wrong; on the night of Tuesday, February 15, 1994, that line of code executed about 150,000 times, and any Chemical Bank customer who used a Chemical Bank or affili-

**228**

ated ATM machine to withdraw money from a checking or savings account was debited twice for a single transaction. Over 100,000 New York-area customers were mistakenly debited about $15 million. The dormant code awoke with an ursine stretch and bit off all that money.

On the morning of Wednesday, February 16, 1994, Chemical Bank apologized to its customers and set things to rights, while Stuart R. Bloom, a banking consultant in Ridgewood, New Jersey, was explaining to *The New York Times* that "similar episodes take place all the time, but we never hear about them because the bank is able to get the accounts straight before it opens its doors in the morning. The problem in this case is [that] the ATM system . . . runs 24 hours a day, seven days a week."[2]

### An Incorrect Spec

Even if the lines of code are right, the effect can be wrong anyway. On February 3, 1994, two commercial airplanes carrying 113 people near Portland International Airport each obeyed alerts given by their onboard Traffic Collision Avoidance Systems (TCAS) and narrowly avoided colliding with each other as a result.[3] An Alaska Airlines jet that was taking off was told to climb, and a Horizon Air jet that was landing was told to descend. Both pilots did as the system told them and got less than a mile away from each other, which, at the speed of a jet, is *darned* close.

If they had ignored TCAS and obeyed the air traffic controller, who has an overview that includes them both, they would have remained farther apart. The problem is that each TCAS box is suggesting a course of action independent of the other, but Horizon Air Flight 2155 and Alaska Airlines Flight 548 were not, at that moment, two independent systems. They were two complex components of the greater system that is the busy airspace under the control of Portland International Airport, and because the TCAS box is a local patch to a system problem, it can make matters worse just as easily as better.

### Behind Schedule, Over Budget, and Buggy

So what's been behind schedule, over budget, and not quite as functional as hoped for lately? We turn again to the United States government, just as we did the last time we asked this question. The Internal Revenue Service has recently decided to scrap part of the Automated Examination System, whose projected costs had nearly doubled. The U.S Navy is about twelve years late (and counting) on a project that was supposed to improve its payroll and accounting system by 1982. The National Institutes of Health spent $800 million on an IBM mainframe that

idles while the scientists use the desktop Macintoshes or Sun workstations they favor.[4] The Pentagon continues its tradition of overpaying and
undermanaging software development projects with the Air Force's C-17
cargo aircraft (two years behind and $1.5 billion over) and the Navy's
F-14D fighter jet (serious defects evidenced during flight tests).[5] The
head of the Federal Aviation Administration has threatened to cancel the
Advanced Automation System, designed to modernize commercial air
traffic control, because it is $2.7 billion over budget already and so far
behind schedule (it was originally supposed to be deployed in the late
1980s) that no one commits to *any* completion date.[6]

In 1988, the California Department of Motor Vehicles decided to upgrade its 1960s-era database to a more modern and robust form. Six
years later, it informed the state legislature that it had spent $44.3 mil-
lion on a modernization effort that would never work and asked for $7.5
million to start over again on a new design. "The department's position
is that the software maker isn't responsible, the hardware maker isn't responsible, and the taxpayers are just going to eat the cost," said Richard
Katz, the bemused chairman of the Transportation Committee.[7] Yum,
yum.

Closer to home, my local county tax assessor's office is in the same
morass as it attempts to develop software to account for changes in local
tax laws. So far the project is two years behind schedule and expected to
cost twice as much as originally planned.[8] We've had problems with Portland's new 911 emergency response system, too. The $5.6 million system
suffers from several problems, not all computer-related, but it has its
share of technical glitches—lost or misrouted calls, display terminals
blanking in mid-call, and poor user interface design frustrating the 911
dispatchers.[9]

Most frightening of all, the new London ambulance dispatching system cost £1.1 million and proved completely incapable of handling peak
call rates. Calls were lost or delayed for minutes, even hours, forcing
staff on at least one occasion to revert to paper and pencil. The delays
proved fatal to at least ten, and possibly as many as forty-eight, people
whose ambulances did not arrive soon enough. "It seems insufficient attention has been paid to the need for thorough testing," says one critical
systems expert, exemplifying the fine British tradition of under-
statement.[10]

### Development Hell

Meanwhile, the troops at the front aren't exactly having a ball.

Once upon a time in the crazy 1980s, a soft-drink executive somehow
wound up running a large computer company. As the 1990s dawned, he

outlined an ambitious vision for a palm-sized computer that would un-derstand your handwriting and anticipate your needs like a human secre-tary.[11] He promised the product by early 1992 and I imagine the experience taught him, however belatedly, something of the difference be-tween engineering and mixing sugar water.

It's too bad that John Sculley's education had to come at such high cost to the engineers who, lashed to an unfulfillable promise, worked eighteen-hour days on projects with goals they could not hope to reach. At the end of 1993, a morbidly fascinating account in *The New York Times* described the development of the Newton as follows: "some engi-neers went home and cried. Some quit. One had a breakdown and ended up in jail. One took a pistol and killed himself."[12] Admittedly, the engineer who committed suicide also suffered from personal problems. Still, work is a large and important part of life, certainly for engineers. If we are worrying about cigarette smoke in the workplace, as we should be, is it not appropriate also to consider the effects of more serious stressors?

As it worked out, Apple's Newton finally shipped over a year late, and its initial functionality was disappointing to nearly everyone except those who enjoyed writing their own versions of *Jabberwocky,* several of which circulated on Internet, chiefly to the amusement of those who had not spent $700 on the thing.

### Systems of Systems, Remember?

Meanwhile, the baggage-handling system for the new Denver Interna-tional Airport has been developing into a full-blown systems fiasco. Here was the initial problem: increasingly many commercial flights cross the country, stopping at Stapleton, a hub airport. Some or all of its runways are closed sometimes in the snowy Rockies, making it a wintertime bot-tleneck. So the city of Denver chose to build a new airport.[13]

An airport is a complex system whose many components are them-selves complex systems—baggage-handling, and also ticketing, aircraft fu-eling and maintenance, people maintenance (restaurants, restrooms, gift shops, janitorial services, employee lounges), air traffic control, cargo transport, vehicle parking for passengers, employees, rental cars, service vehicles, and more.

Meanwhile, the baggage-handling system for the new Denver airport is an ambitious leap upwards in scale. It's supposed to be able to handle 1400 bags a minute—14 times the capacity of San Francisco Interna-tional Airport. Four thousand automated baggage carts travel 17–22 miles per hour on 21 miles of track, guided by 100 computers and 400 radio monitors, accepting digital input from 56 laser scanners and getting baggage from, or supplying it to, 5.6 miles of conveyor belts. It is a significantly larger and more complex system than any ever built before by its developers, BAE Automated Systems, Inc., and as such confronts them with many new problems to solve. They haven't solved them all.

I don't imagine that BAE has had an easy time of it. According to some reports, they expected to be able to rely on a clean, uninterrupted power supply which has not been forthcoming.[14] They also maintain that the city of Denver altered the system repeatedly while the project was underway, an assertion I find easy to believe. In a project this big and complex, an extremely fluid design stage is both probable and desirable, but as usual, short-term financial pressures dictate pretending otherwise. So you get the situation enshrined in that beloved old cartoon: "You guys start coding—I'll go up and find out what they want."

Whatever they want, they can't do it without software, and the software is bound to be complex, embedded as it is in a system with:

• many components of many kinds in many locations

• a high need for security

• distributed processing

• lots of mission-critical data.

Sure enough, as BAE fixes bugs seven days a week, the company sales manager admits that "even the electrical engineers don't understand completely what's going on."

The airport's designers, however, have made the most dubious decision of all: to tightly couple the design of the entire airport to the design of the baggage-handling system. Baggage tunnels assume automated vehicles running on tracks. They are too narrow and poorly ventilated to accommodate motorized vehicles run by human beings. And the airport itself is too sprawling for such stopgap measures as hiring armies of people to transport baggage manually.

One of the first airports to have an automated baggage-handling system was the Frankfurt/Main airport in Germany, which installed the system in the early 1970s. It was reportedly six months late, but at least they already had a functioning airport.[15] The new Denver airport has no backup: without *this* baggage-handling system, the whole costly airport is useless.

Development often takes longer than expected, eating into the time allotted for testing. Delaying shipment is often unthinkable, so, ordinarily, the testing schedule is truncated instead. But now we get a new movie:

## The Revenge of QA!

*A superhero stands, cape waving in the breeze, the letters QA
emblazoned in red across his muscular chest.
He holds aloft a scroll, unfurls it, and we see:*

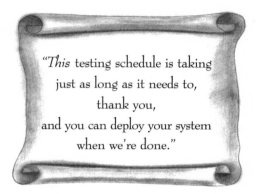

*"This* testing schedule is taking
just as long as it needs to,
thank you,
and you can deploy your system
when we're done."

*Behind him, a grateful and giddy QA department throws confetti
and toasts each other with* Jolt *Cola.*

Airlines that financed the project have been losing a million dollars a
day on an airport that was supposed to open in October 1993.

### Accidents Waiting to Happen

Other than my accountant, though, few seem to be learning caution.

Smart houses, for example, are starting to be aggressively hyped. Your
house computer will integrate control of the lights, heating and cooling
system, humidifier, kitchen appliances, entertainment system, telephone
and answering machine, garage door, digital locking, and security alarm
system. The smoke alarm can call the fire department. The stereo can
dim the lights. And, at least in some implementations, you can repro-
gram such security features as lighting schedule and door lock combina-
tions—*by telephone.* With just a PIN. Really.

The PINs on ATM cards have not prevented millions of dollars' worth
of ATM fraud. Do we really want teenage boys hacking into the house
computer while we're away? Don't these people have any imagination?

Other bizarre new developments spring from digitizing the automobile: consider the grey market in engine-management ROMs. "The clas-
sified ads in certain esoteric automotive magazines offer for sale various

alternative chips for various cars, which are claimed to do astounding things . . ." for the car's performance, points out a magazine for computer professionals.[16] Somehow, I doubt that these chips have been carefully tested to ensure that they do not compromise system safety.

Even if the chips vanished tomorrow, though, we'd still have folks like the garage owner described in a BBC program who accesses the engine management ROM with his PC and soups it up by trial and error, blindly poking binary values into what he hopes are tables of engine parameters.[17]

### Updates

Since I first wrote about them, a couple of the original tales have developed interestingly. In December, 1992, *The Wall Street Journal* reported that, while TRW admitted no wrongdoing in its treatment of the residents of Norwich, Vermont, it nevertheless fired National Data Retrieval, deleted tax information for four states that had been collected by NDR, and agreed to pay up to $1000 to any 1991 Vermont resident who can show that he or she "suffered damages due to the errors" in its credit reports.[18] (No, I am not missing any zeroes in that number. Generous, aren't they?)

And an agency I applauded for its good sense proved me wrong. Oh, well—I tried. In 1992 the Washington State Ferry *Elwha* underwent a $24 million overhaul that included installing a computer-aided propulsion system. (By the way, the project cost twice the money budgeted.) In January 1994, about a hundred passengers took the early morning run from Friday Harbor to Anacortes. About a half hour before docking at Anacortes, a minor electrical problem caused one of the ferry's two motors to shut down. As the ferry approached the dock, the other engine suffered a software glitch and mysteriously lost power. Unable to reverse propulsion, the ferry rammed the dock. The ferry was not damaged and no one was injured, but the impact damaged the dock, and it will cost about $500,000 to repair.

Ferry officials instituted new operating procedures and placed the ferry back in service about a week later, apparently before fixing the software. Officials are optimistic that "once adjustments are made to the software, there is *little chance* a similar shutdown of *Elwha*'s motors will occur."[19] The italics are mine; I claim them; and I have a question for Washington State Ferries:

For heaven's sake, guys, why?

## Notes

1 Gluck, Andrew. "Unhappy Returns." *Worth,* Nov. 1993, p. 29.

2 Hansell, Saul. "Glitch Makes Teller Machines Take Twice What They Give." *The New York Times,* Feb. 18, 1994, pp. A1, D16.

3 Snell, John. "Near collision at PDX prompts investigation." *Oregonian,* Feb. 5, 1994, pp. B1, B3. Also an Associated Press follow-up: "FAA wants to know why system sent 2 jets toward each other." *Oregonian,* March 14, 1994, p. B3.

4 Deagon, Brian. "Military Programs Provide Painful Lessons in Designing Software Mega-Projects." *Investor's Business Daily,* June 17, 1992, p. 3.

5 *Ibid.*

6 Tolchin, Martin. "F.A.A. Is Threatening to Cancel New Air Traffic System." *The New York Times,* April 14, 1994, p. B11.

7 Webb, Gary. "DMV careens into $44 million dead end." *San Diego Union,* April 27, 1994, p. A3.

8 Mayes, Steve. "County's software overdue, over cost." *Oregonian,* March 27, 1994, pp. B1, B8.

9 Tomlinson, Stuart. "Serious problems beset new 911 system." *Oregonian,* May 14, 1994, pp. A1, A13.

10 Hayward, Douglas. "London Ambulance System on sick list before collapse." *Computing,* Nov. 5, 1992.

11 The "vision," such as it was, was not even his own. The Newton clearly resembles the DynaBook, long the dream of genuine visionary and Apple Fellow Alan Kay, but, as might be expected, it has a long way yet to go.

12 Markoff, John. "Marketer's Dream, Engineer's Nightmare." *The New York Times,* Dec. 12, 1993, Business pp. 1*ff*.

13 Numerous reports about Denver's new airport and its ill-fated baggage-handling system have appeared in the media, as well as being discussed in *comp.risks.* Two references are:
Meyerson, Allen R. "Baggage system woes plague Denver." *Oregonian,* March 20, 1994, p. F2.
Shore, Sandy. "New Denver airport can't just bag it." *Oregonian,* May 7, 1994, p. A16.

14 *comp.risks* Vol. 15 Issue 69, March 25, 1994. Item contributed by Colorado resident Bear Giles.

15 *comp.risks* Vol. 15 Issue 70, March 28, 1994. Item contributed by Jan Vorbrueggen.

16 O'Brien, Michael. "On the Failure of Protocols." *SunExpert Magazine,* May 1994, pp. 18–22.

17 "File on Four" BBC Radio 4 program on safety-critical software, broadcast Tuesday, Oct. 19, 1993, and discussed in *comp.risks* Vol. 15 Issue 19, Oct. 28, 1993.

18 "TRW Will Pay Vermont Residents Hurt By Firm's Credit-Report Errors in 1991." *The Wall Street Journal,* Dec. 23, 1992.

19 Higgins, Mark. "*Elwha* back in service." *Seattle Post-Intelligencer,* Jan. 29, 1994.

# INDEX